Displacement, Identity and Belonging

TEACHING RACE AND ETHNICITY

Volume 2

Series Editor

Scope

The *Teaching Race and Ethnicity series* publishes monographs, anthologies and reference books that deal centrally with race and/or ethnicity. The books are intended to be used in undergraduate and graduate classes across the disciplines. The series aims to promote social justice with an emphasis on multicultural, indigenous, intersectionality and critical race perspectives.

Please email queries to the series editor at pleavy7@aol.com

Displacement, Identity and Belonging

An Arts-Based, Auto/Biographical Portrayal of Ethnicity and Experience

Alexandra J. Cutcher

SENSE PUBLISHERS
ROTTERDAM/BOSTON/TAIPEI

A C.I.P. record for this book is available from the Library of Congress.

ISBN: 978-94-6300-068-0 (paperback)
ISBN: 978-94-6300-069-7 (hardback)
ISBN: 978-94-6300-070-3 (e-book)

Published by: Sense Publishers,
P.O. Box 21858,
3001 AW Rotterdam,
The Netherlands
https://www.sensepublishers.com/

Printed on acid-free paper

ADVANCE PRAISE FOR
DISPLACEMENT, IDENTITY AND BELONGING

Displacement, Identity and Belonging offers an excellent example of the use of novel approaches to social research that are designed to raise important questions and provide unique insights into complex issues in various fields of the humanities. The inquiry and representational strategies employed here, as the subtitle suggests, arise from within what is known as arts-based research. This is a form of inquiry that honors the premises, principles, and procedures employed in the creation of works of art. And indeed the text itself resembles a talented work of artistry in both form and substance. Here, the particular form of arts-based research and scholarship is that of auto/biographical portraiture. So the text evidences various discursive modalities — some gloriously poetic; others decidedly prosaic — in the presentation and discussion of findings. The more aesthetic, storied forms of representation enable the reader to relive empathically the life experiences of the characters portrayed in the book. This arts-based dimension serves as ballast for the more lofty, scholarly discourse that, in turn, allows the text to escape what one might call the tyranny of the local and specific. Moreover, the complex discursive format of the book is in a mutual relationship with the important and timely content (or aesthetic substance) of the book: the immigrant experiences that are present in various parts of the world today. The multigenerational perspective of Hungarian migrants to, and immigrants in, Australia, disclosed and examined herein, is not merely a fascinating and urgent topic in itself. It also encourages and enables the reader to imagine analogous social phenomena in other places and times. This fact, in conjunction with an extraordinarily effective format, is what makes this, for readers of all sorts, an important and empowering book — one that I heartily recommend.
Tom Barone, Professor Emeritus, Arizona State University (USA)

Alexandra Cutcher is an empowered Gypsy metaphorically weaving together fiction, art, poetry, and narrative to create a rich tapestry of memories and stories as she examines some of the most important issues of our time: displacement, identity and belonging. This compelling auto/biography grips the reader in a seductive way, reminding us that many nation states of today welcome displaced persons, immigrants, asylum seekers, refugees and transnational persons, and yet, much work needs to happen if we are to truly understand what these transitions mean to individuals and their families. Arts based research offers a distinctive array of aesthetic engagements that help us grapple with these stories in powerfully revealing and instructive ways. Cutcher does a remarkable job of bringing her auto/biography to life and ultimately provides an exceptional example for others.
Rita L. Irwin, Professor, Art Education and Curriculum Studies, The University of British Columbia (Canada)

This rich and layered book explores Alexandra Cutcher's transformative search for a sense of belonging and identity through rediscovering her Hungarian heritage. Originally a ground-breaking and highly visual arts based doctoral portfolio, the research journey has fared well in its translation to a book. Through the well-crafted and warm personal stories and images we as readers are able to consider our own search for meaning and purpose and the resonances with our own lived experiences. At the same time and on another level Australia's search for identity and struggle with difference and diversity, with inclusion and exclusion, can be explored. An important, highly readable contribution to this burgeoning field.

Robyn Ewing, AM, Professor of Education and the Arts, The University of Sydney (Australia)

Displacement, Identity and Belonging is an evocative, beautifully-written love letter to arts based research. Written in the first person, present tense, it compellingly urges readers forward in this blend of Hungarian legend, contemporary researcher, and feminist perspectives. We experience, first-hand, how these narratives are interwoven in the experience and voice of the author. Blending part history of Hungary after the war and Australia after post-war migration, the author importantly points out that this is "a particular story," but a universal one. It is universal in the migrant experience, the leaving, the arriving, the suffering.

The structure of the text is itself an unfolding, modelling the journey that the author narrates so that we readers can experience it for ourselves. Travelling, in this way, is also a central experience alongside displacement – that is, travelling or movement is itself a kind of *emplacement*, one that co-exists with the notion and experience of *dis*placement. Indeed, as the author says, "I have felt forever in transit," and this text takes the reader on her lifelong journey right along with her, sharing the gypsy consciousness that pervades this wonderful book. Cutcher argues (as all good arts based researchers do) that telling is just not as good as doing, and this book is a first-hand 'doing' that every reader, every migrant, every parent, child, artist and scholar should experience for themselves. Go buy a copy now! You won't be sorry.

Anne Harris, PhD, Monash University, (Australia)

This work has qualities which rank it on par with the very best research texts with which I have engaged. It is at once, thought provoking, polyvocal, narratively and visually coherent and, most of all, there is a strong and purposeful relationship between the various two-dimensional art forms and the written text, between the purpose of the scholarship and the bound work itself. It is a courageously successful piece of scholartistry, which combines the very best qualities of traditional, intellectually strong, vigorous scholarship with qualities which make for fine artistry.

The power of narrative stories and the compelling nature of personal arresting, artful experience is very evident in this work; it is a sweeping manuscript. Cutcher has represented complex human experiences in a manner that is largely seamless. The polyvocal forms of the work are powerfully evocative and one can hardly not be moved by the textual narratives, the photographic narratives and the conceptual artwork and, together, these work to induce high levels of resonance; I was alternatively moved, face tear-streaked, inspired, informed, challenged and impressed. This work is accessible to many readers and the writing is gloriously strong.

J. Gary Knowles, Professor Emeritus, University of Toronto (Canada)

This work is dedicated to my noble parents Zita and Lászlo,
to my valiant grandparents Juliánna and Gábor
and to the extraordinary women
who are our children:
Bronte and Remy.

This book is for you.

TABLE OF CONTENTS

TABLE OF CONTENTS

ACKNOWLEDGEMENTS

In the first instance, I am and will always be grateful to Patricia Leavy for her faith in this work and the inspirational example she continues to set to all of us, but especially to those of us who dwell in the margins of the research world. Indeed her efforts are instrumental to bringing us all with her to the fore. Thank you also to Peter de Leifde for the chance he has taken in agreeing to publish this very personal story; Sense continues to be a gracious leader in the publishing world for practice-based educational research.

In the original doctoral inquiry that this booked is based upon, Professor Robyn Ewing as my research supervisor gave me my first suite of permissions; she has always believed in my work. Robyn is the earliest and most influential proponent of arts-informed inquiry in Australia and has argued energetically on my behalf on more than one occasion. Robyn's support, advice and contributions cannot be underestimated. For all of this and more, I am so very grateful.

Professor Elliot Eisner has had a profound influence on my work, as he has indeed upon many others' in Arts education and Arts-based research. In so many ways, Eisner is arguably ground zero of the form. His thinking has been an anchor for me with respect to research, but also with respect to my own objective of improving the education and Arts experiences of children in schools. This research would not have happened in the form that it has, were it not for Eisner's leadership, intellect and influence.

Finally and perhaps most importantly, as with the original research that gives this book its breath, I acknowledge the absolute and constant support my husband Stu has enthusiastically, yet calmly offers me in both thought and deed. Stu is my champion, my best friend and my most constant ally. He has continued to encourage me for almost 35 years, gently urging me onwards and inspiring me to see the world anew. In countless ways, Stu continues to support me, in making all of this possible.

"…everything I say, therefore, is incomplete"
(Elliot Eisner, 2011).

PROLOGUE

It is 1966 and I'm sitting on his knee. To me he is my Nagyapa, my Grandpapa. I feel his solid and loving presence curved around my little back like a pillowy buttress, monumental and safe. He smells of tobacco, Old Spice and brandy. The bouquet is distinctively Nagyapa and is a scent that will stay with me always, despite the fact that he has only months to live.

It is Saturday afternoon, and together we watch the cartoons, as is our habit. Our favorite is Bugs Bunny, and today the reel is "Rhapsody Rabbit". We watch Bugs' antics with a magic piano and a pesky mouse as he attempts Hungarian Rhapsody No. 2.

Nagyapa chuckles during the *lassan*; I can feel him shaking with mirth, and looking up at him I giggle too through the *friska*, because he is. The particular Hungarian Rhapsody in this cartoon is perhaps the most popular of Liszt's compositions. It is my father's favorite.

But I don't know any of this now; I am only three. Together we doze, and ever so gently we float into sleep, me in his lap, safe and warm and unaware and loved, Nagyapa relaxed and snoring softly. This is our habit; it is our Saturday afternoon routine.

*

As the cadence of our breathing synchronizes, we become conscious together, in another place.

I am grown and with Nagyapa still, but this can't be so because I know he will die soon. Nevertheless we are here together, he is still 55 and I am almost 40, yet it is strangely ordinary.

He is holding my hand and walking with me along a lingering sweep of sand and ocean. I look up at him; we are alone on the beach. It is a cool, sunny day and the azure canopy stretches above us for miles. The reflections of the clouds are mirrored on the wet sand as we walk close to the edge of the water. Its lacy patterns and deep green texture are punctuated with white froth here and there. I half expect to see Aphrodite rise from its foam, though it's not a Greek goddess I'm about to encounter, but something else entirely.

"*Édesem* [sweet one]," Nagyapa says gently as he turns to me, "there are things you need to know". I look up at him curiously as he continues, "You need to know you are *Magyar*. You need to know who you are!"

He is emphatic, and almost distressed. I'm bewildered at this, because in my three-year-old mind I know that of course I am Lexi and I am Hungarian. We speak Hungarian, we eat Hungarian food, and we go to Hungarian gatherings. Everyone I know is Hungarian. I mean, what else is there?

"Lexi, listen to me," he says, sensing my confusion. "You need to know this. I need to show you, so that you know, so that you'll always know."

And with this last, he stops and I look into his grey-green eyes as the sky darkens. The night drops suddenly around us like an opera curtain. Nagyapa takes my hand and holds it tightly and together we walk into the gloom.

*

I rise.

I rise and I lift. With every breath I feel myself floating upwards into the ether, up into the air. I become weightless, insubstantial, ephemeral. I am of the earth no longer, almost dissolved. I am conscious of my tiny, wispy, gossamer self as I float and flutter, drift and dash. I am aware of Nagyapa's presence with me, but I cannot see him.

The dark sky parts ahead of me as the light rises to greet my almost-nothing self. I find myself in movement, surging ahead at speed. I soar over the landscape, close to the earth beneath us and at one with the sky; it is glorious, it is liberating, I feel complete.

Suddenly and without warning, I halt and hover as a tableau opens below. I am curious and I look; the scene holds my gaze.

I see the giant Nimrod, the mighty hunter, son of Kush, great-grandson of Noah, King in the land of Shinar. I can see that it is between two generous rivers.

I sense Nimrod's strength and his individuality and know that this warrior is a man of extravagant power. He sits calmly by a magnificent yet docile panther and beside his beautiful wife, Eneth. Subconsciously I know her name means 'deer'. They are both richly robed and glorious and lounging at their feet are their virile twin sons, Hunor and Magor. I come to realize that this is a place of abundance, of wisdom, of science and culture and civilization. I know that this is an ancient place and instinctively, that this family is my kin.

Unaware of my presence Eneth and Nimrod rise and move to retire to their tents. I notice movement beyond the court and see that a hunting party is readying itself, horses and tribesmen are gathering. Almost immediately I see Hunor and Magor mount their horses and depart suddenly and at great speed, warriors themselves and mighty hunters too, their father's pleasure and delight is obvious as he watches them take their leave.

Instantly I am with the brothers, galloping forwards. I can smell the horses underneath and hear their heavy blowing. I feel the cooling wind whip my hair and the unmistakable thrill of the hunt. We travel on and on and ever onwards without sighting worthy prey for hours as the twins grow weary and malcontent. In time, we dismount and we rest; I hear the susurrus of displeasure amongst the tribal hunters.

Ever so gradually, in a clearing beyond our campsite, I become aware of a majestic and serene presence. Hunor and Magor turn as one to see, as the *Fehér Szarvas* is revealed; I feel Nagyapa quiver with barely contained excitement at my side. It is the White Stag who stands just out of reach, an enormously powerful, glorious creature, silvery and silent in the fading light. He stands on the rise just beyond us, his head and mighty antlers proudly raised to our scent.

In this second of stillness, I feel the legend begin.

A flurry of movement and the camp instantly collapses. We are off. I feel the exhilaration of the tribe, the anticipation of the brothers and the vitality of their purpose.

At once I realize I have left them but am moving still, as I see the landscape clearing before me. I feel the strength in my breath, in my four legs and in my hindquarters, the weight on my head, the thrill and fear of the escape, the strength of my resolve, the integrity of my purpose. I glide tirelessly ahead. The twins get close enough to release their arrows, but they never find me for I am too quick, too temporary. Hunor and Magor stop to rest the horses, then again they thunder on. They chase and stop, chase and stop for days, yet neither will surrender. They shoot and I fly away. They feverishly pursue as I lead them ever westwards through familiar terrain, out into the marshlands and beyond. Onwards we thunder, through alien territory, on and on. Out into the open spaces of Scythia, into the sun and the verdant green.

For only a moment I am fully revealed in this exposed space. As abruptly I am gone, disappearing once more into the ether, concealed for all time. Surprised and disheartened, Hunor and Magor hold each other's gaze, blowing hard from the effort, perplexed, frustrated and disbelieving.

I can feel their frustration as Nagyapa and I regard them from above. With my mind, I entice them to look beyond themselves and their impossible prey to the opportunities that present themselves beyond the hunt. In the pursuit of the majestic White Stag, Hunor and Magor have found a new land.

The brothers have indeed been displaced; they have unwittingly journeyed to another place far beyond the borders of their own. It is unfamiliar and strange, yet beautiful and bountiful. There are game aplenty, ample and varied sources of water, plants in abundance. There are timber for tents, fish in the waters and birds in the air. Silently, the twins become aware of their surroundings and begin to see the prospects that present themselves in a new life. They make plans for their newfound futures as they rapidly return and report to Nimrod, begging his indulgence to migrate permanently to this new land. With excitement and great energy, the brothers tell him of the magnificence of Scythia, of the opportunities and of their schemes.

I feel Nimrod's pride and also his sadness; I feel Eneth's despondency and her acceptance. The parents release their sons with blessings and wealth; they take their parting sorrowfully. They know it is the last time.

Full of ideas and enthusiasm and vigor, Hunor and Magor leave their homeland never to return. They ride out of their father's camp without so much as a backward glance, moving ever westwards towards their destiny.

As I stand beside a desolate Eneth, I watch them go and Nagyapa whispers close to my ear, "*Édesem*, it is your destiny too".

I follow Hunor and Magor on their final migration westwards, watching from above, and at times below as camp follower. Life is in constant movement, in constant flux.

In this quest, this journey, I am a gypsy, a wanderer, a nomad, a migrant. As I follow these beginnings, this land-taking, Nagyapa is a stable and constant guide, ensuring that I notice, that I see, that I know.

I watch as Hunor snatches Ilona and Magor kidnaps Temese, the Alan princesses from King Dula's untended camp.

I watch, as they are married.

I watch, as they begin new lives; from their unions will spring all Huns from Hunor and all Magyars from Magor. And I witness the sweep of history unfolding before me.

I see Hunor's descendant Attila and his pastoral, rebellious Huns, who generate a vast empire from China to Siberia to Persia to Western Europe. I watch Attila, a short yet powerful warrior with dark skin, a massive head, flattened face and the same beady eyes, high cheekbones and sparsely bearded face as my father. He is fierce and unrelenting, a consummate horseman and an aggressive prince.

I join him as he obliterates Pannonia and the Holy Roman Empire there; he is the scourge of Europe, striking fear into all peoples. I watch him with the *Isten Kardja*, the fiery Sword of God, and know that whomever possesses it is indestructible, destined to rule the world.

He does.

I see the *Turul Madár*, the turul falcon, bearing the Isten Kardja to Emese, wife of Ügyek, descendant of Attila. I lay with her as she sleeps and bear witness to her dreamings, her vision of a pure and luminous stream moving westward into an expansive river, flowing directly from her womb. The symbolism of this prophecy is not lost on me; I watch as Emese and Ügyek animate a dynasty of noble and heroic Magyar leaders who continue to migrate westwards.

It begins with the birth of their son Álmos, who in his time sires the gallant and courageous Árpád. I watch this Árpád, with his expert military skills and his generous wisdom become the founder of the Hungarian state, conquering the Carpathian basin and Danube plain, the land that is Magyarország: Hungary.

I am in Etelköz when the Covenant of Blood is settled between the Magyars and the other Hun tribes.

Nagyapa whispers close by, "*Édesem*, this is important, a great moment for the Magyars".

I am with Árpád as he occupies the Carpathian Basin in a series of carefully planned diplomatic and military manoeuvres. I observe him as he and the other Magyar leaders hold their first assembly at Pusztaszer, establishing the Hungarian state on the foundations of a solid constitution. I see that Hungary is a sophisticated culture, internally stable and externally secure.

I bear witness to the settling of the Magyars in their land as pastoral peoples, free and faithful to only one God. I see their broadmindedness, their tolerance of different religions, other races, foreign languages, new cultures; all are welcomed. It soothes me to know this.

Hungary is an unusual place, I see. She has a strong identity, her language is unique and her ethnic character intact. I notice the myriad advancements in craftsmanship, horsemanship and military concerns, personal hygiene and medical knowledge. I cast my gaze around the rest of the terrain and I see it isn't so elsewhere in medieval Europe.

As Nagyapa continually shows me, I understand that Hungarian nationality is not exclusive, but rather open to all peoples regardless of their ethnic origin. People are invited, rather than forced to assimilate.

Nagyapa holds me close and tells me quietly, "All citizens enjoy equal rights under a democratic tribal system Lexi. This society is peaceful. People are well behaved, personal honor and strong moral standards are important".

I soar over the landscape, light in being, secure in my growing understandings and enriched by my experiences, and I observe Hungary as she changes. Nagyapa and I are thrust forward through the ages. It is at once unpredictable and enchanting.

Christianity comes to Hungary; the church becomes all-powerful. As the year 1000 approaches and the world does not end, I watch as the beloved King István, applies to Rome to recognize his status as monarch. I observe Rome's response in the shape of the distinctive crown and apostolic cross, gifted to the King; as I peek down through the corridor of history, I see them become symbols not only of István's rule but also of Hungary's nationhood.

On a wintry Christmas Day I bear witness to a celebrated coronation and see that István is majestic. I am soothed to notice how his people adore him, and delighted that he is regarded as a sincere, moral, ethnically tolerant and merciful monarch. Afterwards, I sit by István's shoulder as he drafts a letter of advice to his son, Imre.

"Guests and strangers", he writes in faultless script on the vellum page, "must occupy a place of their own in your kingdom. Make them welcome and let them keep their languages and customs, for weak and fragile is the realm where a unique language and a unique set of customs hold sway".

I ponder this as he reloads the quill and continues, "Do not ever fail to be equitable and kind to those who have come to settle here; treat them with benevolence so that they may feel more at home with you than anywhere else".

This notion of a tolerant monarchy is beguiling to me as I admire the King's restrained insight as well as his perfect penmanship.

It comes as no surprise to witness István's beatification in 1083.

Time rushes by again and Nagyapa and I are in the wind once more. We witness János Hunyadi as he stops the Ottoman invasion at Nándorfehérvár in a triumphant victory.

Nagyapa whispers close to my ear, "This conquest is still celebrated in Hungary today Lexi. At midday everyday, the bells of every church in the country ring in honor of this achievement. This was ordered by the Pope, and has continued for five centuries".

As the temporal becomes reality, we witness Hunyadi's son Mátyás Corvinus assume a thirty-year reign and put his energies into a short-lived flowering of Renaissance culture. I find this moment particularly captivating as I sit in his extensive library, reveling in the beauty of the books. I observe, as it becomes celebrated throughout Europe. It is with regret that I take my leave; Nagyapa is urging me onwards.

Centuries pass like pages in those manuscripts and I watch from a distance, the Turks, as they persist in their yearning for Hungary's lands. I see them as they try again and again to occupy her and eventually, succeed.

And as always, time marches ever forwards.

I see the Hapsburgs triumphing and Ferenc Rákoczi II leading a failed war of independence.

I see the manipulation of the monarchy, a joint kingdom giving birth to itself, the Austro-Hungarian Empire.

I see the remarkable resilience of the people as Hungary continues to develop culturally and economically. The Hungarians persist, and the land flourishes. We soar over the landscape as I watch and learn.

And then it all comes to an ignominious, inglorious end.

I sense rather than see Nagyapa by my side, quaking with impotent fury, "Hungary is about to enter the Great War Lexi," he tells me with controlled gentleness, "And lose."

At the same time as the fatal shots are fired in Sarajevo, I see my grandparents as small children. I see my grandmother growing up in a two-roomed, thatched house in the small village of Györszemere in northwestern Hungary. I see Nagyapa as a young boy, living in the nation's capital of Budapest.

I ponder this; I know that it is my family, yet it is so strangely unfamiliar. I wonder and I pause. Unable to shake this disquiet, we move onwards.

I am there at Versailles when The Treaty of Trianon is signed. I see firsthand that it is achieved under duress, as Hungary's historic lands are demolished.

It is the end of the war and it is also the end of Hungary. I hear the timeless echoes of the multitudes exclaiming through the years, "A dismemberment!"

"A vivisection!"

"A monstrous dissection!"

"A mutilation!"

I see that despite Hungary's remarkable powers of recovery and vitality, the people are left feeling oppressed, deeply disheartened and determined to fight for their freedom, whatever the cost.

In the next moment, I watch as my father grows up poor, his own father dying so young. I see my mother being birthed in a wine barrel bath under an arbor of summer grape vines. Nagyapa looks across at me, and for a quiet moment, he beams. It is all too brief.

Again, I feel this disquiet, this unsettledness. It is peculiar...

I cast my gaze below again and notice that in these years of the Second World War, Hungary struggles to remain neutral. I see too much bloodshed, untold evil and extreme domination; people are stolen and tormented. As I watch the ruthlessness and persecution, I see Hungary ignored and used in equal measure. I see pacts signed and trampled and land given and withdrawn; Hungary bullied, abandoned, used and overlooked. And then she joins in.

As this is happening, Nagyapa holds me close. He senses my fear and my dismay. I see below as he and my grandmother grasp my six-year old mother and flee their homeland forever, making it to the relative safety of Germany.

I see my seventeen-year-old father begin his peripatetic existence all over Europe.

I come to understand that back home in Hungary, things are becoming frightening. I watch as the Russians advance through the country. I watch as my father and his friends listen to Admiral Horthy on the radio, announcing that negotiations with the Russians are taking place.

I observe the Russian armies occupying two-thirds of Hungary as conscription is introduced, even for the middle-aged. I see that the threat of physical and mental abuse is very real. Refugees, women and children are fired upon and old people are slain.

As the army starts retreating and the English and American bombers raze Budapest, I bear witness to trainloads of refugees escaping the Russians who are advancing without delay. I see fourteen-year-old boys being taken from their families under threat of execution.

Budapest falls to the Russians; it is a wasteland. The Soviet Army plunders, loots and rapes; they imprison, inter and torture. Armistices and treaties are signed and ignored, a farcical election is held.

A new constitution is described, which mimics the Russian's. The People's Republic of Hungary is born.

I can see unambiguously, that the glorious days of Nimrod, Attila, Árpád and István are gone forever.

I watch as my parents leave their beloved Magyarország behind, tormented, traumatized and in shock. I watch as my grandparents and my father make plans for newfound futures as displaced persons and refugees.

I watch as my family departs and I see that they, like Hunor and Magor before them, have indeed been dislocated; they will journey to a new land far beyond the borders of their own. It will be unfamiliar and strange, yet full of possibility.

*

In this moment of realization, I find myself spinning in Nagyapa's arms, falling, floating down and down, wafting downwards. As I glide gently towards the beach where we started our journey, I see the port of Naples in the distance, the ships, the people, the heartbreak and the hope.

I pirouette from this view to watch my grandfather fading, vanishing. I reach for him and I miss.

"No!" I scream.

In my anguish, I race through my memories, our time together and the lessons Nagyapa wanted me to heed. In this moment and in my distress, I can feel his calming presence and his warmth. Yet, in my confusion I am still anxious about his earlier warning.

The disquiet lingers and my sense of panic blooms. I wonder at its meaning, I wonder at his message.

"Don't leave me!" I shriek, my distress is absolute, "You can't leave me! Nagyapa!"

He is disappearing. I can still smell him around me, the scent of tobacco, Old Spice and brandy linger, like a cloak. I continue to sense him, but it doesn't comfort me.

"Lexi!" he cries into the ether, locking eyes with me as he fades. His next words are said deliberately and slowly, "Don't forget *édesem*. You are Magyar!"

And with this last sentence echoing into the void he is gone, forever.

For the first time in my life I feel utterly alone.

Art is among the few occupations where it is not an initial disadvantage to be a foreigner – indeed, to have come from certain countries is almost an advantage, and Hungary may be counted among these. (Kunz, 1985, p. 109)

CHAPTER 1

ORIENTATION

This is a story of trauma, loss and gain, of place and displacement, of identity, alienation and belonging. It is a story of survival.

This is a particular story, but it is not a peculiar one. It takes as its central premise one small Hungarian immigrant family to Australia, who are not particularly special or extraordinary. We are a small family, relatively isolated, devoid of a large ethnic community with which to connect and thus we have always been somewhat self-contained. Our experience may appear, at least on first blush, to be paralleled by the post-war diasporic experience for a range of nations and peoples. However in many ways as you will come to know, this is not necessarily so. It is this crucial aspect, of the idiosyncrasies of difference that is at the core of this work.

Many families do indeed share the superficial aspects of the experience of diaspora and some may be of the view that since the surface details of this 'other' are quite similar, then the experiences of each cultural group must therefore be the same. Such homogenizing of difference fails to acknowledge and represent the encounters of the smaller collectives and the individuals within them; not all of us have had the same experience nor are we left with the same constructions of ethnicity and identity. The experience of difference can differ greatly within the larger collectives, and it is within the details of the specific that we are able to (and should) expose the particular. Silence and assumption are fertile spaces for ignorance and misunderstandings to propagate, with sometimes-dire consequences.

The experiences shared within this book are to be viewed through the primary conceptual framework of displacement, belonging and alienation, supported by the concepts of transformation and the constructions of identity. This is a somewhat grand assertion, given that this is also a deeply personal story and one that was pursued for profoundly private reasons. These tensions are both purposeful and self-conscious in the text, as will become obvious in the reading.

As may have already been presumed from the tenor of the prologue, although this is a book about ethnicity and constructions of the self, it is also a work of arts-based, auto/biographical research. As such, it is a book that confronts what an academic text can be. History, culture, experience, memory, theory and the spiritual have been creatively entwined in this account in order to be both provocative and informative, whilst as importantly, be engaging for the audience, who is invited into the story through both their feeling and thinking.

Thus, expressiveness in the context of this story and for arts-based research (ABR) in general, is a primary vehicle for learning (Eisner, 2011). Attention is given

3

to the qualities of the representation, as well as to meaning. Form and content in this work are inextricably entwined; meanings are revealed rather than reported and it is the aesthetic qualities of the work that will determine the type of reading experience that transpires.

In many ways this is a true story, full of lies, deceptions and inventions intentionally designed to generate understandings of difference, of ethnicity and of migrant experience. There are also many ghosts in this story, both discursive and real, to be encountered on the journey who will appear, disappear and reappear in the reading. As you will come to know in this work, the very form of the ruptured narrative is indeed a fundamental metaphor for the shifting constructions of multiple identities and moments of belonging in which I find my self.

THE RESEARCH

This inquiry revolves around several components. Essentially it is about an auto/biographical expression of the Hungarian migrant experience in Australia and is underpinned by notions of belonging and identity. These aspects are wrapped in a cloak of stories, constructed in language and in imagery. It is a *creating-through* of the self, using words and images (Trezise, 2011); a self-portrait.

Story is the central motif in this work; this portrayal is what Battiste calls a *langscape* (2011). The languages in this langscape are both verbal and visual. Thus, contained within this text are a myriad of creative representations including: the contextualizing legend in the prologue; artworks arranged in strategic places throughout; photographs; fictionalized memoir that interrupts and illuminates; metaphor that is deliberately provocative; poetry embedded in places; historical passages that give context; cultural material that informs; and academic theory that intrudes. These voices purposefully compete with and complement each other.

Although the chapters, imagery and stories are designed to build upon and disrupt each other for an in/complete view of the langscape, it should be noted that a linear reading is not necessary, although the book has indeed been designed this way. However, some readers may find it equally enlightening to view just the images or the narratives or the theoretical chapters or the fictionalized memoir or any combination of these in any sequence, in order to get a glimpse of the langscape within. Such incomplete readings may indeed be sufficiently satisfying and instructive.

Further, a minimum of academic jargon is utilized so that the texts are ergonomic: 'readable', available and comprehensible for a range of readers. This is also a purposeful device and one that speaks to my deep philosophy regarding the accessibility of research to a wider audience than the merely academic. As someone from a non-English speaking background, notions of language are profoundly recognized. Further discussion regarding democratic access to the language of research is explored in Chapter Three.

Issues of self and authorship within this text may be confounding. The stories are representative of the multiple and varied expressions of the self and identity, and it this multivocality that is a metaphor for the contemporary self, amongst many other things. The polyvocal nature of this research speaks directly to the complex issues of identity and belonging that this inquiry reveals.

In this story, there is duality and contradiction with respect to notions of the self, other and the necessary entwinement of self and other that is inevitable when one writes about their own experience. Although I claim that the work is polyphonic, in the sense of many voices and visual and verbal texts, it is also acknowledged that by virtue of the monologic nature of writing, it is my voice that is ultimately in control of framing the story. Such contradictions are self-conscious and intentionally employed, which is one reason I privilege the term auto/biography.

Thus, in much the same way as we can express differing constructions of identity, there are many voices in this work that the reader will recognize as the author/artist. Beginning with the voice of the *granddaughter* introduced in the prologue, we are provided with a glimpse into the character of the protagonist.

Later, we encounter her as another identity when the *gypsy* passages disrupt the reading. The gypsy is a provocative character whose very identification as 'gypsy' may be challenging for some; this gypsy is a nomad, forever travelling and rarely still. She is utilized as a deliberately confrontational device and speaks to unresolved identity issues. She positions herself as the commentator who interrupts the other readings, as well as providing a narration, or back-story. Her tale is both integral and transcendent of the research.

Later still, the reader will encounter *Lexi* in her account of experience and memory, in which she expands the accounts of her parents into the second-generation. This voice and this story moor all of the other identities.

Further, scattered throughout the text are several artworks created as yet another layer of reading, of identity, narrative and meaning. As in many auto/biographical accounts, photographs and other documents are also included by way of illustration, embellishment and description. In this work, this type of imagery in embedded into the narratives to both interrupt and enhance.

It is envisioned that all of these expressions be read both separately and together, as they are both transcendent of and embedded in the work.

Although the layers of meaning throughout and within all of the texts both visual and verbal, are analyzed in the theoretical passages, these particular discussions are not privileged over the other stories; they get equal exposure. Indeed the use of artistic devices in the presentation, creation and analysis of the evidence is a central feature of this work. A more fully articulated discussion of the specifics of the methodology is explored in Chapter Three.

Originals and Reproductions

This inquiry was initially undertaken as a doctoral dissertation. It was a work that was highly visual, with coloured folios that signified the separate sections, full colour pages of paintings and hand-coloured prints, works of digital imagery and visually embellished narratives (or *illuminated manuscripts*). It also employed literary devices, on equal par with the highly visual representations of the story. Such are the creative freedoms of contemporary doctoral dissertations.

I delayed publishing it as a book because I know of no publisher (or reader for that matter) who would be willing to shoulder the cost of producing more than two hundred full-color pages, along with the more traditional written text. Representation continues to be an issue for works of ABR. Meanwhile, the years rolled on and the field of ABR evolved and grew, most significantly (for this work) the literary iterations of the form. Concurrently, I began my second career as an academic, after having spent almost three decades as a high school Visual Arts teacher.

It was within this scholarly environment that my attention turned more vigorously to writing and to grappling with notions of the complexities of representations of ABR works in traditional text-based formats (see Cutcher, 2013; Cutcher, 2014). Then, wondrously, a combination of attendance at international conferences and the explosion of social media gave me the gift of confidence and contact with the leaders in my field. My live encounters with these leaders and continuing dialogue with their work (e.g. Elliot Eisner, Tom Barone, Gary Knowles, Rita Irwin, Kit Grauer, Donald Blumenfeld-Jones, Carl Leggo, Richard Siegesmund, Graeme Sullivan to name but a few, with Patricia Leavy being especially significant) motivated me to think again about how this work might be translated into a further iteration of the original text, one which might privilege words in a black and white format. More importantly these giants of the field, and Patricia most notably, gave me the permissions to explore the possibilities of writing, to explore another experience of crafting research-as-artwork, of translation, of interpretation. I was inspired anew.

Thus, this book differs somewhat from the original reportage of the research, which gave it life. As the book form of the doctoral dissertation upon which this is based, it operates within literary, color and formatting constraints, in much the same way that the original, highly visual thesis worked within the extant academic constraints of the time it was written. As such, it takes its creative liberties with words and only black and white imagery, a somewhat foreign territory for someone who has always identified themselves as a maker of colorful images and objects, and quite confronting for someone whose first language is the visual. Rather than seeing this as restrictive, I have chosen to view it as a challenge, one that has been both stimulating and remarkable. With the enthusiastic support of the relatively small but ever expanding ABR community, who are generous, impressive and encouraging and who continue to energize and inspire me, I no longer feel alone on this journey.

My hope is that the reader does not simply read and disregard this work after the demands of whatever the purpose in reading is over. My hope is that these stories touch you, enhance your knowing, resonate with you and expand your understandings. My hope is that you return to the stories again and again, if only in your memory.

During a recent conversation about this book, an old friend asked what my ethnicity meant to me. The question surprised me, since we've known each other for almost twenty years. I began by saying that ethnicity could be many things – mask, weapon, consolation, sentimentality, gesture, even a kind of inner voyage. On a roll, I gave examples of these, some historical, others anecdotal. But I didn't speak of myself.

My friend listened patiently and then persisted: "What do you feel about being Hungarian?"

Finally it occurred to me that I should tell a story. (Teleky, 1997, p. 165)

CHAPTER 2

GYPSY

The last time I saw my grandmother she bit me.

It was only a small bite and a loving one. It was lucky that I quickly withdrew my hand from her mouth, otherwise, who knows what would have happened? How would I explain a wound to my anxious Mama, fussing around behind me making sure my grandmother's things were in order, her laundry folded and put away, the bed tidy? It was lucky that I acted quickly, but I fear that the sudden removal of my fingers from her mouth may have dislodged her false teeth.

I didn't want to upset Mama any more than necessary. She had been my grandmother's primary carer for the past eighteen months, and it had been especially stressful. Her responsibilities and obligations are so many − a mother who was virtually dependent on her for everything, an elderly husband who was as challenging as he was adorable; and a middle aged daughter, strong willed and spirited.

I didn't want to upset her. Mama had spent the last year and a half watching her mother slide into dementia. It started with a few falls, in the bathroom once breaking a rib, and once on the path outside her little home. It was the beginning of the Alzheimer's. Mama had sensed it you see, the decline, but the rest of us told her not to be silly, that she was being overly dramatic. Drama is an enduring motif in our family.

In this case, however, Mama was quite correct. Her feeling of impending doom was exactly right, and it is her, after all, who has had to deal with all of the challenges that caring for a demented, geriatric parent entails. Mama is an only child; her difficult mother has always been demanding, often unkind and constantly calculating. In her time, my grandmother was strong, dominating, charming and cruel, but always, always the ultimate survivor. After sixty-six years with such a prevailing presence in Mama's life, it's a wonder that she has endured it with such grace. But then Mama is used to hardships; they are old friends really.

As I watched Mama buzz around, I wondered why my Nonya had decided to sink her teeth into me. Was it because she was trying to kiss my hand but had forgotten how? Was it that she was trying to eat me? She had forgotten how to feed herself, but also how to eat, as the result of the last stroke. The carers at the transitional care facility had just told Mama that they had found Nonya's wedding ring in her mouth yesterday. Was she trying to kiss that too, and slipped? Or was she trying to swallow the ring in some attempt to absorb the love of her darling Gábor, dead now for thirty-

9

six years? Perhaps she was returning to her infant self, mouthing everything by way of sensory exploration.

These questions will of course go unanswered, as will all my questions of Nonya now. She is living inside a still physically healthy yet decimated body, with a shrinking mind and the likelihood of more of what the doctors call 'cerebral episodes' happening to her.

As I looked at my Nonya, her small shrunken body still and unmoving in the bed, her eyes locked into mine, none of these thoughts were in my head. I was simply thinking that although the animation of her body language, her mobility and most of her speech were now gone, she spoke volumes to me with her dark, ebony eyes. She looked at me, and she looked into me, and at that moment her eyes said more loving things to me than I think I had ever heard from that once beautifully shaped mouth. The fierceness and the bitterness were gone. The hostility and discontent had moved to another place. There were a few things left, however. Her fighting spirit and her tenacity were obvious in her struggle to stay connected to me. Occasionally her eyes would glaze over and I could tell that she didn't recognize me. At other times, her mind simply went somewhere else, but through sheer effort of will, she'd struggle to the surface to talk to me again, without words. My Nonya is a fighter.

She brought my hand to her mouth again, and kissed it. Once, twice, four times. I told her, with my mouth and my own dark eyes that I loved her dearly, and she smiled. High, unmistakable cheekbones, face rosy with health, lined by experience and time. White hair against the white pillow, white sheets, white blankets, white bed.

And a dark swarthy countenance that gave lie to the fact that she had not been outside in months. Her black velvet eyes, her spirit and her strength. She's denied it forever, but deep down I know. My grandmother is a gypsy.

*

I am a second-generation-Hungarian-Australian woman.

Notice all those hyphens? I'm neither one thing nor the other, neither one identity or both. This is the way I have felt my whole life, nothing singular defines me. I find myself now actively defying any sort of definition. I resist being classified. No, not even resist it – I despize it. Such definitions have had such an enduring effect, enduring since my childhood of loneliness and isolation.

The consequences of this traumatic childhood linger with me still, more than thirty years later. This is both a blessing and a curse.

"Oh, come on", some of my friends say to me, "That was so long ago."

They are well meaning really, these friends, just impatient with me.

If only it were that easy. Most of my current friends didn't know me as a child, so they cannot possibly understand. Some of them don't remember what it was like back then; most of them have forgotten.

The biggest insult I have ever had when I was young, and one I didn't really understand at the time, was, I think, intended to be a compliment.

"Don't be silly Lexi; you don't look like a wog..."

In 1960s Australia when I was a child, the wogs were the migrants, the refugees, the Displaced Persons. People from Europe were "greasy, dirty wogs". We were the untouchables, the social pariahs; responsible for all that was wrong with Australia at that time.

These heartfelt platitudes were sincere and said so generously, as if I could hide my difference, as if that was a good thing. I was OK to them because I didn't stand out too much, I didn't look too different. You know, with the correct lighting and a little bit of makeup, I could look just like them.

Until of course, they came to my house, or met my parents, or saw the contents of my lunch box. Or smelt it.

Really? This was meant to be a compliment?

Some of my friends don't understand my perspective and they don't want to, impatient in a culture that now proclaims its tolerance. But some of them know; they know what I mean, without having to say it. They understand, because they empathize, because to an extent we have a shared history. We know what it's like to feel alienated, in the most vivid sense of the word; like aliens from another universe, speaking an entirely different language, eating different foods, having different habits, different rituals. So incredibly foreign, so incomprehensible.

That's a funny word, 'wog'. A reclaimed word in the Australian vernacular these days, an empowerment. It has become shorthand for something entirely different, something to be admired. A badge of honour, and at times, a weapon.

Life is funny don't you think? That same word had so much power to wound us, to make us feel small, insignificant, like a nothing, as if we had no right to breathe the same air. How quickly we forget what it was like to be a wog in the sixties in Australia, especially if you didn't live in Sydney or Melbourne.

But perhaps not. What we are doing to our newest Australians these days makes me think we haven't learnt anything from the flowering of multiculturalism. The 'One Nation' political party has a lot to answer for; a lid was lifted in the '90s and the xenophobes, contained for so long, flew back out. Pandora had nothing on Pauline Hanson. And the way asylum seekers and refugees have been so utterly demonized, driven by politics and swept into a fury by the media, makes me feel like I'm still living in the sixties. All of a sudden it's OK to be racist and small-minded again.

Have we learnt nothing?

Anyway, I digress. Those women, my friends who know what I mean, in a sense know the real me, without having to ask questions, spend girly time or bond. They know the me deep inside myself. The me that had to live two lives, but fit into neither. The me that knew what it was like to suffer the torment of a salami sandwich on black bread when all around me were the culinary triumphs of vegemite sandwiches, and devon and tomato sauce on 'white boy' bread. The all-pervasive smell of mutton cooking; the variations of steak and egg, steak and chips, a mixed grill as your choices at a 'restaurant', or a 'café'. Milky, cold tea or a sherry. People have forgotten.

11

Those women, my friends who know are wogs too of course. They are like me and yet they are not. Almost all of the ethnic women of my acquaintance hail from one of the majority minorities in Australia. Their vigor and their ability to maintain their cultural strength comes from their large numbers, their political clout, their (it's ironic really) cultural omnipotence, their credibility. It's cool to be Greek, Italian, French, Spanish.

The Anglos now envy us! We were all once so despised, and now, over a dinner party table, or a dark, noisy corner in a smoky party haze, I get, "I wish I was Italian" or "I wish I had a heritage that was exotic, historical, interesting".

Can you imagine? Once told, pressured, forced to assimilate, we are now being urged to embrace our ethnicity, to flaunt it, to be proud of it. It leaves me scratching my head. From where does this mass acceptance come? Surely it cannot be all about the food?

Anyway, for me, it's a little different. I belong to one of the minority minorities; there aren't many of us in Australia. Even today, when people realize that my heritage is Hungarian, one of two things will happen. They will say, "Do you ever get hungry? Are you hungry? Ha, ha, ha!"

I couldn't possibly calculate the amount of times I have heard that one. Not very original. The other reaction is one of awe. Mind you, I had to wait until I developed breasts to earn this one. It's, "Wow. You're Hungarian, you're a gypsy. That's so sexy."

I have two issues with this. Firstly, it's usually lascivious, ignorant Australian males that react this way, and secondly, any Hungarian would take this as an insult. Racist? Yes, but you need to understand the history. Being a gypsy in Hungary has no cultural (or any other) capital. And although I find this apalling, that's the way it is.

*

Beggars, thieves and troublemakers. This is the image of the gypsy in the Hungarian consciousness.

"It's like calling her a bag lady!" Mama gasps, livid when I say that this is how I see Nonya.

"I don't like it. I don't like it at all. Hungarians will think that you're serious. It's insulting."

I try to explain to Mama that in the Australian consciousness, the connotations of 'gypsy' are far more favourable. Australians see gypsies as exotic, artistic, clever, passionate.

"I don't care", she says, "I don't like it at all. And your grandmother would have a fit!"

This last comment I think, is amusing under the circumstances. The purposes of this latest phone call between my mother and me, is to tell me that Nonya has had yet another stroke. She has now lost her vision, her hearing and therefore her ability to communicate and understand.

This is heartbreaking. I feel that she is now lost to us forever.

The good news, however, is that Mama has found a permanent nursing home place for her at pretty Fingal Bay, north of Newcastle. A beautiful facility I am told, four star. A long way for Mama to travel to see her, but Nonya will have good care. Will she even be aware of it at all, I wonder?

I ponder this question over the next days, and in my despair, I find myself going back through the photo albums to see her as I remember her at that last, difficult Christmas. Still in possession of most of her faculties, still herself, slightly disconnected from us all, but aware and happy.

For all intents and purposes now, however, she has slipped away. Even though the last time I saw her I thought she had quite an engaging internal life, a dialogue that she would sometimes participate in, evidenced by random and (to us) disconnected mutterings and half sentences, she was not herself. She had softened, and all of the harsh edges and prickliness were gone. Strong she most certainly is, still. She is fighting this newest challenge, unwilling to give up, unable to let go.

It is largely because of her that my grandparents and my mother established themselves so quickly and efficiently firstly in Germany during the war, and then six years later, in Australia. She has been a wanderer, a dark-eyed beauty; shrewd and ingenious. She constantly used to say, "I always know what to do", and that is an absolute truth. Nonya has always been enduring, hardworking, inventive, steadfast. She is, quite simply, a survivor.

She inspires me to look further backwards in time. I want to see her face when she was my age, and younger. I want to see if I had inherited anything from her. Mama always says that I have her eyes and her mouth, and as I look through the photographs, I see that this is true. She was beautiful in an archetypal European sense, more elegant than pretty, more stylish than fashionable.

I am not satisfied. I look at photos of her as a girl, a young woman, a mother, a grandmother and an old woman and I realize that the only sense I have of her was within these documents and the relationship I have had with her. Neither is very satisfying, and both are intangible to me.

In that moment I understand that my direct and physical connection to my history and that of my daughters, is also slipping away. Soon it would be gone forever.

Who is this woman? This woman that I see in the pictures, born thousands of miles away in the early years of last century, in a small land-locked country at the heart of Europe? I know Nonya, but only as her granddaughter. She is a formidable woman of great courage and verve, her presence and personality has permeated the lives of all the people in my family, over four generations.

This realization leads me to some big questions.

As I think about them, I look at her reflected gaze in my favourite photo of her, taken by my grandfather with the small box brownie camera that now sits on the shelf in my lounge room. Nonya is dressed in black and is smoking a cigarette –a real femme fatale. The room is harshly lit, and large shadows are cast on the walls and floor in angular shapes. She is posing, as all the women in my family do when a camera is pointed at them, and her expression tells me that she is powerful and confident in her belief of both her own beauty and her formidable strength.

Over the next few hours and days, the questions in my head will not be silenced. We are losing her. She is not the beloved old granny, innocent, doting, involved in our lives. She never has been. My feelings towards her have always been complex. But somehow, I feel a large open wound blossoming inside of me, and a rising sense of panic. I have work to do.

*

Focusing, I begin to tease out my idea, and pondering Nonya's beginnings and her journey, I also begin to think of my father. He too had been a nomadic youth. For many years he was a man without a country. Hungary was always home, but its situation after the war had become unbearable for him.

It also occurred to me that over the years I had let their often-repeated stories wash over me. I have stopped listening to them decades ago; through boredom and repetition, I have switched off.

Now I was ashamed.

I have to write these stories, I have to document them somehow – they are my history, the history of my people. Gypsies we may not be, wanderers we have definitely been and Australians we now are. But just how did we get here?

*

And in my reverie, it begins, this journey of mine into unchartered territories. Nonya, because she is our oldest living relative in this country, is our matriarch. From her and my Nagyapa, now gone from our lives for 36 years, came my mother and myself. Similarly, Dad came to Australia, but this was a journey he made alone. He met and married Mama in that working class bastion of Newcastle, that had a tiny and now almost extinct Hungarian community.

I start the journey backwards, in time and experience; mine and those who came before me, as well as those who paralleled my life in a different country, my unknown, huge, extended Hungarian family.

This family had not existed for me as a child, except as thin blue letters that came about once a month, with foreign stamps and untranslatable pages. These people belonged to another place; caught forever it seemed, in time and my parent's memories, half a world away in a tiny but proud country, somewhere in the middle of Europe.

My search begins with Mama. She is the essential link between my grandmother and me. Ironically, she is the lynch pin of our family. I say 'ironically', because her relationships with all the family members this side of the equator are somewhat complex.

Mama is far from the indulgent mother or the traditional subservient, dependent wife, although she loves us all dearly. She is however, a dutiful daughter, wife and mother, and always has been, often at the expense of her own fulfilment. Mama is the epicentre of our family, and she is directly connected to all of us – her mother, me and of course to her husband. Much like the centre of a flower, my mother anchors all the parts together. This is why I went to her first.

*

Over the bones of yet another family feast at my parents' house, my children watching television in the next room, the menfolk snoozing, Mama and I sit, as is our tradition, sharing the last of the fizzy wine, chatting over the catastrophe that was our lunch.

"So this is what I want to do," I say to her as I explain my deep need to connect myself to a past that exists for me only as a ghost. "I want to find out all I can about you and Dad, and Nonya and Nagyapa, and our Hungarian family that I've never known, and about the journeys you all made to get here. I want to know who we are and where we belong. I need to know who I am. I need your help…What do you think?"

Art is among the few occupations where it is not an initial disadvantage to be a foreigner – indeed, to have come from certain countries is almost an advantage, and Hungary may be counted among these. (Kunz, 1985, p. 109)

CHAPTER 3

JOURNEYS AND INVESTIGATIONS

THE JOURNEY BEGINS

This research journey has been an expedition into unknown places. Since this book focuses upon migrations, displacements and transitions, the metaphor of *journey* is an appropriate allegory (Jasman, 2002). Border crossings and border guards have confronted me along the way and threatened my progress. I have had to acquire my 'passport' and 'visas' for travel to enable me to leave my 'country' for territories unknown. I have often languished in (literal) 'no-man's-lands' where I thought I would never be permitted to continue, yet could never go back. I have carried much baggage with me along the way, some of it practical, some playful, all necessary. I have been both conqueror and conquered, both colonizer and colonized. However, I have never lost my spirit of adventure in this bountiful enterprise; it has been captivating, gratifying and well worth the cost.

I style myself as a traveller rather than as a tourist, pioneering challenging and difficult lands. I am an adventurer and eyewitness – resourceful, flexible and motivated. This is an identity I know well; during my life I have made many journeys, both metaphorical and real. All of my real adventures have genuinely changed me and each time I have been lucky enough to return to the safety of my home. I have had to call upon these experiences in this most testing of journeys, this foray into unchartered territories. These territories are places I have come to know well.

ORIENTATION TO THE HOWS AND WHYS OF THIS WORK

With respect to the *investigations* of this inquiry, the methods, processes and aesthetic devices utilized reflect an emergent trend within the academy to aestheticize traditional forms of academic writing (Barone & Eisner, 2012; Leavy, 2009; Osei-Kofi, 2013). Within such aesthetically crafted texts, multiple subjectivities such as emotion, creativity, story, intuition, resonance and sensation are compelled into increasingly synergistic relationships with cognition, logic and research traditions (Barone & Eisner, 2012). These notions are privileged within the representations of this work.

My lived experiences as artist, researcher and teacher are entwined in my ways of knowing and of being, developed through all of my artist, researcher and teaching actions (Sinner, Leggo, Irwin, Gouzouasis & Grauer, 2006). These actions fold back upon themselves, informing my research, teaching and arts approaches, in order to communicate knowledge, understandings and intent in ways that are ergonomically effective. In this inquiry, the form of the work is both expressively and artfully represented in order to be accessible and educative to diverse audiences.

Over the past two decades the field of educational research has witnessed increasingly available research representations (Barone, 2008; Barone & Eisner, 2012; Cole, Neilsen, Knowles & Luciani, 2004; Eisner, 2011; Leavy, 2009), which appeal to wider audiences than the merely academic, particularly with respect to 'languages'. As a researcher, I have focused broadly upon the way inquiry can be communicated and represented (Cutcher, 2014, 2013, 2004). The languages of form and expression are intimately entangled and inform (and feed off) each other in my work. As a teacher of more than thirty years' experience in some of Australia's most challenging educational settings, I am well versed in using multiple ways of communicating complex content to students from a range of backgrounds, abilities, ages and learning styles. These experiences have ensured that I have developed innovative approaches to accommodating diversity and need through a multiplicity of experiential perspectives. One way I do this is through accessible research representations, through modalities that generate understandings through empathy and resonance (Eisner, 2011). Further, if the purpose of research is to expose, scrutinize, investigate and disseminate, it follows that as a good teacher I must ensure the reception of such inquiry be available to different ways of learning, perceiving and being. In order to ensure that research furnishes teachable moments (O'Donoghue, 2009), it must not be opaque and exclusive, rather, as educators we must strive for transparency and inclusivity. This is simply good teaching practice and ultimately attends to social justice imperatives.

Therefore, with respect to the mode of 'transport' on the collective journeys of lived experience shared in this inquiry, content is embodied in and through accessible, multiple languages. This has been a conscious choice, largely because opaque academic language has traditionally prevented egalitarian access to knowledge, particularly in higher education. Such self-perpetuating institutionalization is entirely limiting and quite at odds with the imperative to disseminate research to a wide audience, particularly to a professional audience. In the case of education, this means that research and its reception should travel beyond the borders of the academy and into the profession and out into the world where, arguably, it is of most (applied) use. Surely the imperative of educational research is to edify, and in myriad ways and to a multitude of audiences.

A further issue with respect to educational texts is a tendency to use semantics, sequestered language and somewhat clandestine jargon. The academy's insistence on the exclusivity of language in discourse and theory means that it is complicit in participating in the same tactics it vows to abolish through research, discussion and argument, especially for those for who English is a second language. As in any foreign territory, if you are not able to speak the language, you are denied access to understanding. You are rendered mute, being somewhat lost in any translation since an interpretation can only give you so much. As a woman from a non-English speaking background, I am hyperaware of the restrictions and gifts of language.

This research text therefore, is the open story itself, relatively free of academic jargon and opaque theoretical terminology. The stories are of equal value with the analyses, enabling a multiplicity of readings and interpretations beyond my own. Stories are the privileged medium and the central motif in this research for several reasons. This study is concerned with the richness of human experience. Hence, since this research is concerned with the description of culture and experience, a storied approach is the most appropriate medium as it is linked to the customs of the people of Europe, of oral history and the sharing of family chronicles through narrative performance. Through storytelling, cultural integrity remains intact and the individual is able to make sense of her experiences, constructing order and meaning (Carter, 1993; Clandinin & Connelly, 2000). Indeed, as individuals and communities, we all live storied lives (Craig & Huber, 2006; Britton & Pellegrini, 1990; Bruner, 1990); it is a fundamental human activity, translating knowing and doing into telling.

The truths (and lies) of this story are exposed when the audience are my proactive and self-conscious accomplices, as we harmonize within the reading; collectively we bring the tales to life, ambiguously and expressively (O'Donoghue, 2009). In the forms of writing used in this work, whether it be story, poetry, fictionalized memoir or narrative account, the portrayals are deliberately evocative, in order to gently decelerate the reading experience and allow for reflection through empathy (Eisner, 2008). It is upon auto/biographical candour that the writing is performed in this work, in order to generate such resonances. In this way, the reader accesses the experiences of my family in a candid transaction that renders both parties somewhat exposed. Such 'uncovering' seeks to compel insights and understandings, which are dialogic, demonstrative and affecting. The next sections explore the forms of auto/biography and arts-based research utilized to accomplish these goals, by way of a foundation for the methodological frameworks for this inquiry.

THE WHYS OF THIS WORK

For this inquiry, because it explores both biographical and autobiographical perspectives, I use the term auto/biography as a kind of shorthand descriptive of the method. However, the following discussion focuses on the form of autobiography in order to simplify the discussion and as both context and rationale for this inquiry.

Auto/biography: History, Contexts, Research Method

Autobiography has existed in various structures and disguises for the past fifteen hundred years. From the fifth century *Confessions* of St Augustine, it has been a genre largely dominated by male authorship. In recent decades the centrality of the masculine experience has been challenged and indeed exploded. In its place have come the multiple subject positions of the postmodern age and the shifting ontologies of post structuralism. In the latter part of the twentieth century an acceptance of the significance of the lives of hitherto insignificant individuals and their contributions to history at the micro level were celebrated. Such individuals, previously ignored, gained credibility and found a voice within a social fabric that celebrates individual achievements, regardless of material status or success.

Many attribute Rousseau to be the founder of the modern genre of autobiography (e.g. Horowitz, 1987; LeJeune, 1989). Considered to be a theorist of utopias, a political philosopher, a theorist of drama, an innovator in educational philosophy, an anthropologist and a believer in deism, Rousseau has much to offer the scholar of the autobiographical form, even though his controversial work has been much criticized and commented upon (e.g. Gay, in Horowitz, 1987). The French, however, consider his work as archetypal to autobiography's modern form (LeJeune, 1989).

Critics agree on the importance at the beginning of the eighteenth century of the first person autobiographical novel or memoir-novel (Marcus, 1994). This is no doubt due to Enlightenment philosophies such as the celebration of the individual, tolerance of difference, and the belief in the ability of the individual to change the world (Brians, 2000). Since this time the memoir novel, the heroic autobiography (e.g. Benjamin Franklin, Henry Ford, David Livingston, and James D. Watson), and the romantic heroine (e.g. Margaret Fuller and George Sand), have given way to feminist representations and accounts documenting the ethnic experience. During the twentieth century, many of the archetypes of the male hero persisted, and it was during the 1960s that the female archetype of the supportive woman behind the great and glorious hero was to be shattered forever. Even though the feminist period of the 1840s produced accounts of women who sought to achieve on their own, they were criticized thoroughly by their male contemporaries (Conway, 1998). Empowered by the wave of feminism during the 1960s and 1970s, women were inspired by the writings of Betty Friedan (*The Feminine Mystique*, 1963), Shulamith Firestone (*Dialectic of Sex*, 1970) and an example that changed world views, Gloria Steinem's moving description (*Ruth's Song (Because she could not Sing It)*), 1983. Since this period of time, the character, style, subject and reception of autobiography have undergone transformations of huge proportions and it was postmodern theory that heralded an acceptance of multiple perspectives and subject positions in all areas of culture, theory and discourse.

There have been myriad theorists who have hypothesized about the nature of autobiography, and the justifications for it being utilized as a literary form (Benstock, 1988; Blackburn, 1980; Blaise, 1996; Codrescu, 1994; Fischer, 1994; Haaken, 1998; Iles, 1992; Jelinek, 1980; Johnson, 1996; Kuhn, 1995; Pirani, 1992; Rhiel & Suchoff, 1996; Rose, 1996; Sasaki, 1996).There has also been a growing interest on its usage as a research method for the past twenty five years (Brettell, 1997; Lionnet, 1989; Nilson, 1992). Autobiography relies upon the narrative form, in order to construct a personal, individual, oral history of a life lived and experienced, understood through the impulses of existence (Samuel, 2003). The narrative form is a medium that is as old as civilization itself. Many cultures embrace storytelling as the medium by which history is passed from generation to generation, with or without the support of a written language. In some cultures, such as those of the Australian Aborigine (who indeed do not utilize a written form of communication), it takes on ritualistic and spiritual proportions, and is an essential and significant ingredient of cultural practices. Through storytelling, cultural integrity remains intact and the individual is able to make sense of her experiences, constructing order and meaning (Carter, 1993). In fact, as individuals and communities, we all live storied lives (Britton & Pellegrini, 1990; Bruner, 1990; Sarbin, 1986), and it is a fundamental human activity, translating knowing and doing into telling. We rely upon the medium of storytelling to dream, plan lives, gossip, share experiences, express ourselves creatively, reflect and think (Hardy, 1968). The social conventions upon which stories rest, such as stereotypes, symbols, beliefs, assumptions and typicalities, all evoke responses in audiences who receive them in an immediate and relative manner (Carter, 1993; Carr, 1986; Heilbrun, 1988; MacIntyre, 1981; Mitchell, 1981).

The earliest proponents of the form include George Gusdorf, James Olney and Emile Benveniste. According to Marcus (1994), Olney has done the most to promote autobiographical studies. His work, she asserts, is strongly affiliated to phenomenological criticism, and to the work of Gusdorf who, according to Conway (1998), was the first to focus attention on autobiography as something more than a maverick type of fiction in his famous essay *Conditions and Limits of Autobiography* (1956). Gusdorf later asserted that autobiography was "the knowing of knowing, where subject and object overlap each other" (in Conway, 1998, p. 193).

According to Olney, autobiography is about individual history and narrative, understood through the impulses of life (Marcus, 1994). Autobiography is both a record of an event, situation or a person, and a furtherance of its continuance (Steele, 1989). The passion to know, is but one of an ensemble of passions, which drives the autobiographer in the act of self-appropriation (Steele, 1989). Stanley supports this notion, and further asserted that,

> [a]utobiography is typically a chronological narrative which tells the story of a life. Its defining concern is with being, with the nature of ontological existence as seen within the exemplar of the life investigated and discussed…biography is not only a narrative; it is also and self-evidently based on *investigation* [and] *inquiry* and on the process of selection in and out of not only the facts but the *salient* facts. It is to express it in the rhetoric of epistemology, a theory: a theory of character or a person, but a theory nonetheless. (1992, p. 120–121, emphasis in original)

Or, put more succinctly as Roland Barthes said, "I am the story which happens to me" (1994, p. 56). Anne Sexton made an incisive argument when she argued that by sharing our life experiences, we open a dialogue not only with ourselves, but also with others. She said,

> I can invade my own privacy. That's my right. It's embarrassing for someone to expose their body to you. You don't learn anything from it. But if they expose their soul, you learn something. That's true of great writers. They

expose their soul: then suddenly I am moved and I understand my life better. (in Middlebrook 1996, p. 7)

Contemporary interest in autobiography has to do with its function as a locus for the junction between theory and experience, and that this site allows for an interplay of different voices and their readings. Bergland (1994) asserted that despite postmodern challenges to traditional notions of the self, autobiographical narratives continue to multiply and scholarship and debate continues to surround the form. This is probably because autobiography serves important philosophical functions within the culture, and creates an awareness of difference, thereby producing more equitable social relationships.

In this study consciousness-raising is certainly an aim. This is made possible through the form of autobiographical research, through which the lives and experiences previously ignored like those of my family, can be examined in an intimate and direct manner. To paraphrase Tom Barone, I attempt to reveal questions that have been hidden by answers (2001).

By utilizing the medium to focus attention upon individuals who dwell in the margins of society, we not only celebrate and recognize social and cultural difference, but also force an examination of historical reality, thereby encouraging governments to consider contextual circumstances, particularity and diversity. The individualizing that autobiography permits is a powerful and persuasive argument for social change, since, "many things only make sense as exemplified in the life of one person" (Stuart, 1992, p. 59). An "*n* of 1 can help you understand situations" (Eisner, 2006, p. 15), an "N of 1 is a provocateur" (Siegesmund, 2014, p. 12).

Through such a reconsideration of history at the micro and humanistic level, we avoid compartmentalizing diversity, and the composition of individual difference into one category labelled 'other'. Therefore such a research method as autobiography enables the exploration of uniqueness, giving recognition for distinction and individuality. However, when does the opening up of the cultural marketplace by portraying distinction and difference become the mass marketing of difference (Rhiel & Suchoff, 1996)? And is this a bad thing? By destabilizing traditional culture in the telling of stories that deal with individual difference, do we abandon generic conventions completely? And if the answers to these questions are in the affirmative, how do policy makers then cater for the myriad of identities within their communities? These are the difficult questions that governments must address, since we now exist in polyethnic societies that aim to embrace, celebrate, cultivate and encourage individual identity and experience.

There is no secret key that will unlock the mystery of experience and its meanings. It is labyrinthine, and it has no fixed origins, structure, set of recurring meanings, or stable nucleus. As Denzin asserted,

Experiences constitute the flux and flow of consciousness. Experiences are constantly out of reach of language and discourse and on the borderlines of consciousness and awareness... it is possible to represent a life (or its meanings)

as it is told as a proverb, a story, a slice of a conversation, a folktale. Spoken, performed, told and retold in narrative form, this is the realm of live experience that is recoverable. (1997, p. 61)

Autobiographical narratives are a unique source that provides information not only about individuals, but also by those same individuals about their experiences. Such individuals create and utilize myths as a way to contextualize the past. This is achieved by the displacement, omitting and reinterpretation of past events. As educators we must emphasize and focus on experience as credentials for educators and their students – personal knowledge is valid and usable knowledge (Connelly & Clandinin, 1985). In the words of Waterhouse,

Learning and coming to know is as much in the gut as it is in the head; [the] gifts of ideas come cling-wrapped in emotions. Experiences come to us as a whole; messy, complicated and sometimes contradictory, with affect and intellect intermingled. Ordinary, everyday experiences may trigger profound learning, yet experiences intended to be instructive may leave us unaffected. (2000, p. 23)

Dewey stated that experience is vital and situated, and occurs with continuous and dynamic interactions between people, events, situations and objects (1934). It occurs and changes through time. Experience is constituted in and of language, but language will never replace the experience. By representing experience, through the interpretation of voice, both individual and shared and by learning from the voices of others (writers, participants, students, artists), learning occurs reflexively, which is crucial to representing an insider's view of a culture, as well as drawing out the responses of others (Diamond & Mullen, 2000).

Nietzsche asserted that the self is a construction, not a unified psychological condition and that it is a historically and traditionally constructed ideology, one uses language to bring the 'self' into existence. In this he is aligned with Lacan (1981; 1975). Nietzsche doesn't deny that the self exists, just that it must be acknowledged that we have created it as a fictive and discursive form (Jay, 1984). It is clear that the self is a construction of language and further, through the act of producing either a narrative or a discourse about the self, one realizes one's identity. Since the autobiographer is the person most intimately acquainted with the self being examined, she is also the privileged interpreter of her own representation. The subject is central to autobiography – it must provide the 'I' and the 'eye' of its telling (Benstock, 1988).

By studying minority individuals, the larger culture is able to reflect upon such individuality in ways that have ramifications for social policy and governance. My ethnic auto/biography, because it examines a minority group within a minority group, compels society to look more closely at what it perceives difference to be, and therefore become more sensitive and culturally aware. Such awareness-raising is critical if social policy is to meet the needs of all peoples.

25

The field of knowledge acquisition has been a contested zone for quite some time, never more so than in the postmodern moment. Research contributes to the body of knowledge that a society has about itself and others; knowledge is a human, constrained construction. Knowing is an experience; knowledge and the use of that knowledge are united in the individual. If research is to represent oneself, and embody one's own learning, it needs not only to recognize, but also to exemplify the relationship between learning and experience (Waterhouse, 2000). There is a very personal character, an individuality, to knowing and the ways of coming to know. Learning is a social process, and is embedded in contexts, historical and cultural. It is socially situated and shaped, and these contexts must be acknowledged and appreciated.

There is a vast amount of wisdom and knowledge in the lives of ordinary people, and this lies largely underutilized and under acknowledged, as well as devalued since it does not conform to the power discourses within the academy. By legitimating individual and personal voice, the voices of other individuals are also legitimated, empowering them to also speak, and thus exalting the viewpoint that there are many ways to learn and to know. These individual voices in their diversity, serve to strengthen our capacities as teachers, so that we may live and encourage compassionate and productive lives. The individual voices inherent to this auto/biography are represented through the methodology of Arts-based research (ABR). In countless ways, this auto/biography is also a self/portrait (Cutcher, 2004; 2001).

Arts-Based Research

The journey towards the expression of difference in this work privileges artistic, imaginative, intuitive and creative forms and representations. This is largely because aesthetics and Art allow, powerfully, for the cultivation of one's sensibilities, engendering empathy, provoking evocative responses, opening discourse, and celebrating humanity (Eisner, 2011; Piantanida, Garman & McMahon, 2000). The Arts are able to integrate feeling with cognitive awareness, and express knowledge about feeling (Grumet, 1995).

Poetry, images and literature all transcend the limits of literal language. Yet we usually limit ourselves to such literal language when we make a statement, or validate a position. Educational research must examine and exploit other forms of representation, thereby utilizing other capacities of the mind in order to further understandings as,

> [n]o other kind of relic or text from the past can offer such a direct testimony about the world which surrounded other people at other times. In this respect images are more precise and richer than literature. (Berger, 1972, p. 10)

The Art experience has a unique character. Both intellect and intuition are cognitive processes, the former being able to be taught, the latter being a perceptive skill, which Plato considered to be the highest level of wisdom that humans could possess.

Both are of equal value and both are indispensable. Unfortunately these subjective epistemologies are undervalued in our educational institutions. It is indeed unfortunate that, "there is little emphasis within our educational systems on the education of the *imagination* (Greene, 2000) which requires sustained encounters with uncertainty [and] embrac[ing]the unknown" (McNiff, 1998, p. 23, emphasis in the original).

Aesthetics and art allow, powerfully, for the cultivation of one's sensibilities, engendering empathy, to provoke evocative responses, to open discourse, and to celebrate humanity (Piantanida et al., 2000). It can be a cathartic process. It can transcend language barriers and give voice to the marginalized. The therapeutic benefits are a positive by-product. In arts-based research, the representation and generation of knowledge are sometimes inseparable. Making meaning of one's own life through aesthetic modalities can be powerfully revealing and productive. It is impossible to know the world in its pristine state through an 'immaculate perception' (Eisner, 1991), since perception is framework dependent. World viewpoints and their perception are influenced by skill, focus, language, and frameworks. An empty mind sees little or nothing, and the mind mediates the world. Because it does, perception is a cognitive event (ibid).

The correlation between Art and research is not only the similarity of goals, but also the processes one goes through in order to create each (Grumet, 1995). Both demand rigor, skill, insight and persistence. Coherence in an artwork is critical for its credibility, as well as for its aesthetic clout, through the relationships and qualities of the work. Art makes the ambiguous lucid and makes empathy a possibility (Eisner, 2011). It draws our attention to the individual, as well as locating in this individuality what is universal. It also possesses a sense of wholeness and a natural harmony that therefore makes the aesthetic experience and coherence possible. These are important characteristics of educational research.

It is generally acknowledged that Elliot Eisner and Tom Barone are the pioneers of arts-based research (Diamond & Mullen, 1999; Greene, 2000; Piantanida et al., 2000; Willis, 2000). Artistically crafted research generally means the use of one or more of the forms of painting, sculpture, film, video, music, dance, literature, poetry or other aesthetic modalities in order to communicate findings (Eisner, 1995).

The form began with the telling of narratives, with some scholars since having completed their doctoral dissertations as fictional accounts, or novels (e.g. Sameshima, 2010). The literary text can act as a heuristic device, which represents the issues of the everyday, so that the reader may vicariously experience a credible virtual world. Thus, this vicarious experience may be enough for the reader to question established norms and ideologies about education and to challenge them. Further, "[j]ust as there is no single, simple definition of "artistic" (Eisner, 1981), so too there is no single, simple definition of arts-based inquiry and development" (Diamond & Mullen, 2000, p. 9).

There have been two traditions of arts-based genres that have been accepted by the academy, namely educational criticism and narrative storytelling (Barone &

Eisner, 1997). These are the direct ancestors of arts-based inquiry as we know it today. Arts-based research can be defined by the presence of aesthetic qualities or design elements that inculcate the research and its writing. Although these aesthetic qualities are present to some degree in all educational research, the more pronounced they are, the more the research may be categorized as arts-based (Barone & Eisner, 1997; 2012).

The fundamental difference between arts-based inquiries and scientific inquiries is that arts-based inquiries are self-consciously shaped (Diamond & Mullen, 1999). The medium through which the phenomena or experience is presented is foregrounded to a more prominent degree, and this mode is more faithful to the expression of the direct aspects of experience (Eisner, 2011). Working with imagination, the arts-based inquirer may use one or more of a range of devices such as poetry, allegory, fiction, performance, images or objects. The aesthetic and the personal are significant, and indeed central to arts-based research. Reflexivity, intuition and emotion are all exploited in this methodology. Diamond & Mullen emphasize several of these characteristics,

> [We consider] teacher educator researcher inquiry and development as arts-based in several ways: as forms of artistic expression with aesthetic qualities; as requiring imaginative and creative responses because of their spontaneous nature; as defying rules because of their unpredictable qualities; and as emerging in process and through improvization. Inquiry and development are incorrigibly artistic activities. Finding ways to articulate and represent them and to provoke new interpretations is a daunting but inescapable aesthetic challenge. (2000, p. 10)

The construction of a compelling narrative depends on the writer's ability to 'read the scene'. The writer therefore needs to ensure that the "scene is seen" (Barone & Eisner, 1997, p. 101). One must notice what counts. This cannot occur without the ability to appreciate the potential meanings of what has been seen, and indeed, "noticing what counts requires some sense of what counts in the first place" (ibid). To do this successfully, rigor and skill are necessary, as is sustained effort, insight and sensitivity. Storytelling is not only intuitive – it relies on the real experiences of a lifetime in the real world of the storyteller. Indeed the author of stories searches the world repeatedly in order to create a plausible text (Barone, 1995). Ambiguity, risk and uneven results are involved in the creation of an arts-based research 'text'. However, the outcomes are more creative, and more favorable to advancing the erudition of practice. Arts-based studies are individual, idiosyncratic and more likely to differ from other arts-based inquiries than be similar to them,

> [A]rtistically crafted research can inform practicing educators and scholars in ways that are both powerful and illuminating. Research with no coherent story, no vivid images, and no sense of the particular is unlikely to stick. Coherence, imagery, and particularity are the fruits of artistic thinking…the education of researchers, in a very deep sense, should be regarded as the education of artists.

Artists need skill, discipline, imagination, sensibility, and insight, and so do those doing social science research. (Eisner, 1995, p. 5)

Art can be a cathartic process; it can transcend language barriers, and give voice to the marginalized. The therapeutic benefits are a positive by-product. Making meaning of one's own life through aesthetic modalities can be powerfully revealing and productive. In such arts-based research portrayals as in this work, the representations and generation of knowledge are sometimes inseparable (Barone & Eisner, 1997; 2012). As Grumet asserted,

> Art, like research, like all knowledge is a construction, an interpretation…the role of artists as creators of meaning and interpretation [indicates that] artwork provides new gestalts and creates new knowledge. (1995, p. 64)

When I reveal private details, it heightens the emotive qualities of the text and challenges rational models of social science and of education. In Art, as in arts-based research, the work of the artist is to engender feeling, to provoke a response that resonates (Sullivan, 2006). Evocative language activates the reader's and writer's subjectivities, compelling an emotional response. In such a crafting of the text as is possible through the lens of arts-based research, presentations are intentionally expressive. It is this deliberate shaping of the form that seeks to engage the reader in a satisfying way, in a transformative way. As Eisner said,

> Transformation is of course, what writing is about. Somehow the writer must find a way within the affordances and constraints of a linguistic medium to try to create the structural equivalent of the experience. (2006, p. 13)

In such a way, the writer seeks an aesthetic, rather than an anaesthetic response (Cutcher, 2014; Eisner, 2011; Robinson, 2010). Scholarly writing in the context of arts-based research maintains its rigor by observing dichotomy closely, and aspects such as paradox, complementarity and ambivalence are acknowledged, a range of dualities applied (Knowles, Promislow & Cole 2008; Neville, 2000). Thus the language used in this inquiry utilizes metaphor, the evocative, figurative, connotative, poetic and playful (Diamond & Mullen, 1999; Neilsen, Cole & Knowles, 2001; Leggo, 2008; Heywood, 2000). Being responsive to nuance, to idiosyncrasy and to resonance is the task of the arts-based researcher (Eisner, 2011, Leavy 2009), and it in these spaces that teachable moments (O'Donoghue, 2009) are revealed.

Arts-based research 'texts' seek to enable the experience being studied to become real, in order for the audience to stand face-to-face with it as a lived experience (Springgay, Irwin & Kind, 2005). Such work tends to have an effect on the researcher, who can expect to be challenged and changed, both throughout and as a result of the process. This has certainly been the case for me.

In the case of this arts-based auto/biographical research, I am less interested in whether my story reflects the past as an absolute truth, than in the consequences that telling my story generates. I therefore seek an *authenticity of meaning* as my goal in maintaining fidelity to the stories being told and shared (Nilson, 1992, p. 106).

29

Silence causes ignorance and rather than dwell on the insistence to be faithful to absolutes, per se, it is far more productive to create a culture that encourages the telling of personal stories, honestly portrayed, authentic in meaning, and faithful to the individual from which the story springs. These are the 'truths' I seek, as I concur with Nietzche when he said that all truths that are kept silent become poisonous (in Jay, 1984).

With respect to the qualities of quality when one works through arts-based methodologies, Barone & Eisner (1997; 2012) posit several characteristics, which include expressive, contextualized, vernacular language and the presence of aesthetic form in order to evoke, illuminate and generate. Thus, the way arts-based research is 'written' matters; the mode of communication will determine the type of learning that occurs. Since the aim of education should be to cultivate individual differences rather than flatten them (Eisner, 2011), multiple expressions must be generated, heard, represented and considered.

As Barone & Eisner (2012) further assert, what is to be promoted through such research approaches is the enhancement of uncertainty. In this case, the uncertainty leads to arresting issues of ambiguity and of that which is almost out of reach, so that we may continue to reveal. Thus, the question of: Why do we stay with artworks that are troubling and unsettling? (Eisner, 2012), is a key motivator for the representations within this research. The next section explores the form of this inquiry in material terms, exploring the 'hows' of this study.

The Hows of This Work

In the polyphonic portrayal of this research, the reader will notice that poetry interrupts image, which disrupts narrative, which intrudes upon memoir and interferes with argument, critique and theory. The form of this work illustrates much of the theoretical frameworks embedded within it. This is purposefully designed to be unsettling, so that the reader gets a sense of an identity in flux, an unresolved state of being.

As previously asserted, the subjective qualities of expressiveness and resonance, empathy and feeling are the lens through which the audience engages with this inquiry. The literary and artistic devices operate as collage and bricolage as well as collections of fragments when read together embody an identity under construction. In this way, form and content are inextricably linked to the embedded theoretical structures.

In this vein, rather than describing the methods utilized in this work in academic prose, I have chosen to present them poetically. This poem is a portrayal, further acquainting the reader to the processes and the approaches within the research representations that follow. By animating an expressive rendering and providing a glimpse of what is to come, through the conceptual framework of doing, knowing and telling, I continue the portrayal of the journey[1].

Doing

I gather my
grandmother's songs, my
                    mother's tears, my
                            father's words, my
                                    own. Travelling stories of
                                    blood and not belonging. Tales of
                                    outrageous acts and everyday
                            rebellions; the family legacy: survival; the
                            fabric of my being. Making
                                    history at the kitchen table, these
                                    sons of Nimrod, these
                                            refugees.

I gather these things and I entwine, with
                    an art that is
                    mine, a
                    mine to field, a

                                    mindfield.
                    I puddle; I
make smudges; smears and cracks and inkstains; I
                    rub and layer and reduce; I
                            add and take away. I
                            manipulate, I punctuate;
                    respond, perceive and organize. I
play: stain, daub, wipe, draw; paint, print, sketch. I
                            stumble. I
                    stall. The work breathes. I
                                    intuit. I
                            imagine and I
stop.
                    Chance becomes
                            my friend, serendipity my
                    playmate. Epiphanies happen.
                                    I go on.
                                            My hands, my
                                            arms, my
                    feet get dirty. I
                            weave the fractured fragments together.
                            Gather, collect, arrange; snapshots
                                    positioned to tell.
                            The voices
        simmer forth from invisible places, become

                                        understood.
                                        The work
                    comes into being, I

                                        go into the process, trust
                                        the process, let
                                                    go.

From the doing comes
the knowing. The action, the
            art action is
                the key.

Knowing

                                    In constant motion, I
                        wait for the right pencil to
                        write, the write pencil to
                        draw. The write way to
                        right, the right way to
                                                say 'I know'.
                                    Each brushstroke a word, each
                            word an image fragment; reflecting a likeness,
instantly read.
                            Images are metaphors for the failures of language.

                The research as self-portrait, reflected;
            the research as
                            artwork, telling stories.
                            Knowing through
                    material; knowing through
doing. I do, and
my mind goes
            quiet. New spaces are
                        revealed, thinking becomes
                            juicy; not
                                            transformed:
                                                    created.

Doing inspires: it
                breathes the thinking in. The
                    doing is enchanted, the
                                        art is

                                    imagical.

Sight
and insight are
one. Memory and
experience give them
form; from
the deep places, subjective
selves are
virtuously exhumed. There is
no truth, only lies
and authenticity of
meaning. Revealed
and yielding in a
marriage of form, and of substance.
Images and text hold hands
and faithfully
represent experience, and memory.

From the knowing, comes
the telling. The knowing
through the doing is
the key.

Telling

The telling, like
the doing, like
the knowing, is
eclectic. It is
fragmented, it is unpredictable.

Voices perform together:
the stories and poems,
the images, illuminated manuscripts,
the literature reviews, commentary, analysis
and interpretation. Metaphors
visual and poetic.
Multilayered, rich and
complex, the
absent presence of
the reader is
considered through
the layering of
images, of stories, of selves.
Strata, seams, levels of reading; ways

to view and ways to know. Ambiguities, disruptions, gaps

and spaces

there to construct meaning.
The telling flows, evolves, builds
upon; each
contextualizes the other.

The reading is not linear, but
it can be.

The self, revealed,
concealed, revealed.

The text, like
my Hungarian self
is busy, is
spirited, confronting; is
overdone: effusive, loquacious.
Montage, collage, bricolage, pastiche.

The Art is the Art
as well as the research.
It is self-referential, its
integrity maintained, it
transcends and surpasses.

The Art, like
the research is

imagical.

It tells
of selves, tells of
processes, creates a
portrait of the making as
biography of the self:
bricoleuse.

From the telling comes
research as
self-portrait, self-portrait
as research.

This is the key.

NOTE

¹ A version of this poem was originally performed at the Narrative, Arts-Based and "Post" Approaches to Social Research (NAPAR) Conference in Arizona, in January, 2011 before a backdrop of images and interruptions (see Cutcher & Ewing, 2011; Cutcher, 2014).

My name has always been a problem…as a child I often felt it a badge of foreignness; now it makes me impatient with the carelessness…it is regularly misspelled [and] far more fanciful versions are also common…it seems people refuse to believe the letters they see on the page, as if they spotted an error and want to correct it. (Teleky, 1997, p. 170)

CHAPTER 4

GYPSY

And so I begin this journey of discovery.

I realize that at times it will be an arduous voyage, but one that I am more than willing to take. No, it is far more than that, far more than the luxury that choice affords. I am compelled but a force I don't really understand, and my sense of panic is rising. I can't help but wonder at its meaning, or its message. I am profoundly conscious of the small window of time that is open to me.

Nonya's health is deteriorating slowly, and I know that she will not be with us for much longer. For a reason I cannot fully articulate, I feel that I have to quickly gather the information in order to preserve it before it is gone from me forever. It strikes me that Nonya is not alone in the impetus for this work; lately I have felt Nagyapa's presence around me like a mantle. I'm not sure why.

All I know is that I have a strong sense that the anchor is slipping off the chain.

*

Journeys are not new to me. I like adventures, and I have made many in my lifetime. These have included sustained forays through the developing worlds of Africa, the Subcontinent, Asia, and the Middle East, where I have been driven to rely upon my faculties when facing confronting challenges. I have sat with gorillas, witnessed the majesty of the world's hunters, climbed mountains, traversed deserts, dived deeply into oceans and been dreadfully ill, thirsty and hungry. I have had my passport lost, confiscated and sent halfway around the world without me, whilst I languished in a Central African village for thirty days, wondering if it would ever find its way back. I have dug trucks out of swampy roads in monsoonal North Africa; I have been arrested twice in Middle Eastern countries, narrowly avoided civil war twice and have survived without bathing or fresh food for weeks. I envisage that this latest journey may have elements of these hardships and adventures, but I reckon it will be worth the risks.

During one travelling adventure, we were stranded in the transit area between the borders of Iran and Pakistan for two days and two nights. We arrived at the small border town of Mirjawa, after having traversed the salt plains of eastern Iran for many endlessly glary and monotonous days. Iran in those days wasn't a very safe place for western women. We spoke to some Iranian girls coming home from a visit to Pakistan and they were incredulous, asking us why on earth we would come to such a godforsaken country as theirs. They couldn't understand our reasons, and it looked like they would have been happy to come with us all the way home.

We progressed into the transit area between the two countries and the gates to Iran closed behind us. We could not go backwards because we had cleared immigration. The customs officials had taken us apart, as we'd experienced on much of this trip through Africa and the Middle East, looking for contraband, emptying out our truck, packs and supplies. We'd become quite used to the mini despots unwrapping our feminine products and holding them aloft for each other to see and to laugh at. But these gatekeepers, the border guards in the immigration office for Pakistan, would not let us through.

We were being constantly watched and it was frustrating to know that beyond the gates to our right were Pakistan and a freer lifestyle. We couldn't go backwards because our Iranian visas had expired. We couldn't go forwards into the next country because we were at the mercy of the border guards. We had been on the road for nine months by this stage and we were used to the petty bureaucrats who relished and wielded whatever small powers they had to maximum benefit.

So we were stuck in no man's land, a veritable hellhole littered with human refuse and the pungently rotting carcasses of wild dogs whose cousins kept us awake at night. The compound was only about half an acre in size, so with all the mountains of rubbish, our truck, six border guards, and all twenty-five of us it was a cosy fit.

While we languished in this transit zone it became clear that we were really at the mercy of the gatekeepers. We were stuck, without access to consular assistance because of our location. Our passports were in the immigration office, so we couldn't even make a run for it. The borders were heavily protected, so this was probably not an option anyway. We could rot here forever, if those with the power to detain us saw fit. We were in neither one place nor another and our status as tourists did not exist. We were unprotected, vulnerable and incredibly discouraged.

Eventually, after the Pakistani border guards had dallied with us for as long as it takes to amuse and entertain, they let us through. We drove the long journey to the frontier town of Quetta, our next port of call.

As I reflected upon this difficulty, and one that I hadn't thought of in quite a while, it occurred to me that I have been a boundary hunter my whole life.

There have been many times I now see have created a pattern, where I have been in the margins, held back by a border I needed to cross before access was allowed. In my professional lives as teacher, researcher and artist, it has been necessary to fight for recognition within those respective communities, and to battle for time, resources and acknowledgement. Largely, the challenges at those borders have been about learning 'languages' and thereby gaining access.

And so with the first set of border crossings I was ever faced with, that of my birth and subsequent entry into Australian society, I never really felt like I belonged in either the Australian community or the Hungarian one. When I was growing up I always felt like an outsider even though, truthfully, I am Australian. Those first borders were about language and about culture; of longing and belonging.

And so I have felt forever in transit.

I am compelled to find out why this is so. I need to look more closely at my Nonya's life to try and understand the reasons for this; I need to understand Nagyapa and their motivations for coming here. I need to understand.

*

My Nonya was a fascinating woman. She was spellbinding to men, alluring and glamorous. She even managed to charm the Captain of the Fairsea, the ship that brought her little family to this country, so that they had smaller, more intimate living quarters and better food. And even when she became quite old, she still had the blokes at the bowls club after her.

She would never entertain the thought of another romance, let alone another husband. When my Nagyapa Gábor was gone that was it. She loved him passionately and I could clearly see this in the photos of the two of them together when they were very young. How sad it is that Nagyapa died so young, I miss him without understanding just what it is I miss. Despite this, I've always known he was with me, somehow.

Mama told me many times that my Nagyapa was considered quite a catch. Juliánna, my Nonya, was a peasant girl from a small village called Győrszemere. That she was able to seduce such a handsome man was a triumph of feminine charm and wiles. And unmistakably to me, as I looked back in time at their youthful selves, I saw it clearly. She adored him.

She had told me many things about the early days of this romance and how she 'captured' my grandfather. She was originally going out with his big brother, Joska, but as soon as she laid her eyes upon my grandfather's face, she was mesmerized. Poor old Joska, to be dumped so unceremoniously, but then I suppose it saved him from what happened next.

My Nagyapa, Gábor, and his then girlfriend (so the family mythology goes) were going off to the cinema. My Nonya, with her designs on Gábor firmly established (at least in her own mind), planned a subterfuge. She made the happy couple a gift of a wonderfully rich chocolate gateau for their trip to the cinema.

This cake, called Rigö Jancsi, is legendary in our family. The romance of Hungarian culture in the naming of this delicacy is evident in its own mythology. The enticing dessert is named for the virtuoso gypsy violinist who was involved in a scandalous affair in the late 19th century with the young American wife of a Belgian count.

Notwithstanding the somewhat wickedly romantic connotations of this treat, my Nonya is a master of her art – as an accomplished cook she is without equal. Her rich twelve-egg sponge, chocolate mousse filling and bittersweet chocolate glaze is a delicacy that is celebrated amongst our household and intimates. The menfolk, for example, can often be observed stuffing themselves with it before family dinners, and then jealously ensuring that nobody has more than his (or her) share as dessert.

Nonya always stood back watching on these occasions, with a mischievous beam. I can imagine her face as she gave Nagyapa and his girlfriend the 'gift'.

CHAPTER 4

"Thank you, thank you," the girlfriend said to Juliánna, my Nonya. "Isn't she sweet," she trilled to Gábor, "to think of us enjoying our evening?"

My grandfather just nodded in agreement, and looked over her head at Juliánna. Their eyes connected and, for the briefest of moments, both felt the frisson of a new love.

It was some time later, and after the intermission, that the girlfriend and her beau ran out of the cinema in search of the W.C. It was the cake, you see. Nonya had laced the chocolate cream with laxettes – lots and lots of laxettes!

Since that time she has made many batches of Rigö Jancsi, and it would seem with almost every one of those times, this story is shared and cherished. She is a character, my Nonya, and like her or not, she is always creative.

"I always know what to do," she said to me, as we made a batch of this heavenly cake together, some time ago.

She did know what to do, and that is so obvious to me that it could have gone unsaid. She has reminded me of this many times over the years, as if I could somehow assume her resourcefulness through the telling of this truth, that it could somehow transfer itself to me.

On that particular day, she was sharing the family secret. She had steadfastly refused to give any of us the recipe for Rigö Jancsi unless we came to her house and made it with her. So there I was, connecting myself to Nonya, her place and her past.

Years later I was frantically looking for the recipe, thinking that after such a long time I had lost it. When I found it I held it aloft triumphantly.

"What's that?" said Remy, my elder daughter.

"That my dear, is your inheritance!" I told her. And I meant it – it is one of the most precious things my grandmother has given me.

On another visit she gave me the family documents of her ancestors. When I asked her why she had these, she said in a matter of fact way, "I was going to open business in Hungary during the war. And we had to show it we had no Jews in the family."

Of course. How we forget with the passing of the years. When she said this, it gave me a mental jolt. Of course it was like that. What a frightful time. She wouldn't let me linger over this thought; she was insistent and demanding as she showed me the family photos.

Nonya said that her mother-in-law was not impressed with the union. Nagyapa was clearly captivated, since he had stopped sending all of his money home to his mother. Instead he spent it on his new love that made it her business to dress him in snappy suits, sharp looking fedoras and very good shoes.

"Yes I think so we was beautiful," she said to me, gazing into his photographed face. "We was nice couple. Fell in love with him straightaway, straightaway," she said, wistfully, inside her memory. "We was happy. I come every morning and I come here to my bedside, here, and I take it out that picture and say 'Good morning darling. I never forget you, never. Love you darling.' I say that every morning. Haven't got a morning that I don't do. And look he had such beautiful hair!"

40

At this last comment, I find that I am having difficulty focusing on the image she holds before me. I knew that Nagyapa was besotted early in their romance, but I had not really stopped to think about the depth of a love that survived his death by 37 years and was, according to my Nonya, still alive and strong. It was quite a legacy.

"And Lexi! He love you so much. You was always together. Always on Saturday afternoon," she pauses, thinking. "Do you remember?" she giggles, "He used dip your dummy in his brandy, and you like it." Her smile was huge, her eyes twinkling, "And then you both pass out! Sleep for hours! Every Saturday he was alive, you two do it."

I couldn't remember. I was only 3 when he died. I'd always felt so ripped off about that. All I have left of him are the stories Mama and Nonya share and the many photographs of him. And his smell, I can remember what he smelled like. I've always had a sense that he's near me, but it's not enough. Why can't I remember?

Nonya went on, ignoring my silence; she showed me another photo. We were eating pogácsa, a type of savoury scone (which my Dad never liked – he loves pogácsa, he just says that Nonya's tasted like door stoppers), and we were smoking (something I only ever indulged in with my grandmother; they were strong as coffin nails, but she liked the sisterhood of a shared smoke) and drinking brandy (of course).

She went on, "There's my mother. Her name was Mária. My father was Dániel. That is my Ida, Jolán, Dénes, Gyula, Piroska (everybody say we alike), Mariska, I on my mother's knee, Kálmán on my father's. Etel not yet born. She was a beautiful woman, my mother. But I loved my father! He liked to have a few drink," she laughs, "and he went out to the vineyard where our wine grow, he come home he always have a bag in his neck. And that two bottle of wine in it. What he grow. And then, who with he meet on the street 'Have a drink!' and everybody have a drink. When he come home from 3 kilometre away he was quite drunk Lexi, and everybody was drunk," she laughs again at this happy memory of her childhood. She goes on, "And when he come in the house he start to sing."

At this point, Nonya breaks into song. We are standing in her kitchen and she is checking on her pogácsa in the oven. She looks up at me, jet black eyes flashing, the ever-present tea towel over her shoulder and she sings, in full throaty and melodic Hungarian, the song that her father used to sing to his Mária. I am beside myself with emotion, and she looks so beautiful. Her 87-year-old face looks youthful again, and she remembers every word of that song. On and on she sings, and it is wonderful. What a gift she gave me that day; she opened a door to the past for me.

This is in my mind as I struggle to remember my beautiful Nagyapa. I know I have to remember. I have to remember and I have to search.

*

I'm so superstitious; my need to capture the information as quickly as I could was a compulsion, an obligation, a debt I had to pay. Not only did I want to find myself through my own journey, I also wanted to honour my parents and my grandparents and the profound sacrifices they had all made on my behalf. Many ethnic children feel this duty keenly I know, and some of us act upon it.

My desire is driven by my immense gratitude, but also by my sorrow. It is a sorrow borne of ignorance, the ignorance of many regarding the contributions that my parents and grandparents and people very much like them (but also unlike them), have made to the Australian cultural and economic landscape. And it is a sorrow that speaks of the vast distances from my extended family and from the country that is my heritage. It is also a sorrow of memory, of remembering and forgetting. This sorrow is captivating; it is driving me on.

My travelling companions on the other hand, may not be as passionate. Although Mama is committed and supportive and Dad is willing to help in any way he can, they are somewhat bewildered about my need to immediately ignite the journey. In a candid moment, Dad tells me that Nagyapa would have understood it. This warms my heart.

I gather myself and make some plans. I have a lot of work to do.

*

My first plan of action is to interview both my parents, with a view to getting the events of their lives into some sort of chronology, since most of their stories I've heard in the past have had atemporal qualities. If I had enough knowledge about the specific events of World War II, I probably could sort it out for myself, but I think that by revisiting these stories, I can perhaps capture more and of course record it all.

This last is an archival tactic as well, since I want the voices of my parents telling their humble stories to be preserved for future generations and indeed, as I listen to them speak the sensory qualities of my parents loom large. It was this sort of evocative material that I want to pass on to my children, as part of their grandparents' legacy.

After I spoke with Mama about my plans, I turn to my father because he is the correct and appropriate place to start the search. He 'frames' us in as many ways as you can imagine. Dad is the beginning of our little family here in Australia, he came here as an adult at the age of 24 with clear eyes, a willing work ethic and a flexible nature. Dad is my hero, the man to whom I matched all of my beaux – most of who were found wanting. He is the patriarch of our family and has been since Nagyapa, Mama's adored father, died in 1966.

Mama also tells me that Nagyapa and I were very close, and as she does I strive to remember. I find that yes; I can remember his presence, his solid presence, if not his face. Something is starting to come loose. I persevere with my memory.

Dad is a very willing conversational partner. He loves to talk, and will chew the ear off anyone who stands still long enough. His stories are famous among my friends, and some of them avidly look forward to spending time with him. His knowledge of Hungarian history is immense and he is extremely well read. One may say that he is a self-educated man. He loves the classics and is an avid fan of philosophers, especially Marcus Aurelius, his personal hero. He loves to perform dinner table monologues about whatever topic takes his fancy, but usually, it is about the great injustices that have been wrought on Hungary through the centuries, especially the travesty of Trianon. This is a common theme for many Hungarians.

Dad is animated and passionate and indeed he 'performs' his stories, and always has, complete with vocal elements, actions and changes in volume. My Dad is an actor and his narrative is a play of one part.

Mama's contribution has an entirely different texture. When I first prompt her with, "Tell me about your childhood", she says, "What childhood?" forcefully and with bitterness, "I didn't have a childhood". This is of course untrue, but it indicates Mama's pain.

We are in her kitchen and she is cooking paprikás csirke, my very favourite Hungarian dish. She has the wooden spoon raised like a weapon and uses it as a baton that punctuates her sentences. She is angry from the beginning of her narrative, and when this mask of anger slips, she cries. Clearly, the memories of these earlier times are both poignant and difficult to articulate. Many times I ask her if she wants to stop and she always shakes off this suggestion. My mother is used to pain, and to suffering. She has always lived up to her duties even if it cost her dearly. And it clearly has.

When I record this latest rendition of their stories, I am greatly relieved. I am excited that I have it all down, at last. It is these two narratives that are to frame my whole search, since they are my beloved parents and it is they who have separated me from my alternate life, what I've always thought of as my ghost life.

I started to think the 'what if' thoughts, which I know are an exercise in futility, but which I feel compelled to entertain, nevertheless. But I realize that before I can really indulge in this, I need to create a bed for these musings. I have to read about the history of my people in Hungary, their culture, their customs, their lifestyle.

The only connections I have to that place, are those mediated by Mama and Dad, the symbols of which are the weightless blue envelopes that come to our door every month or so, the missives from my unknown aunts and uncles, cousins and friends, the communications I can never read. These letters were mysterious to me, but mostly they are just a ritual in our lives. Dad would sometimes share their contents, but when he realized my interest level was zero or close to it, he stopped.

Now they interest me. Who is at the other end of these communiqués? The hands that created these messages are an unknown entity. I understand what I have to do next. I have to find out as much as I can about that land 'Hungary' as I can, independently of my parents, and then I have to revisit the ineffable blood ties, the familial connections. I need to get to know my family so I can get to know myself.

It is important to do a little background research. I need to discover the world into which my parents were born, and where they had spent their formative years. And I need to keep working on my memory; it's as if Nagyapa is calling me forward.

...the particular life of Budapest...is a world of gossip and innuendo, a world of cafes and intrigue, a city where long established social rituals and prejudices have survived changes of regime, a world where petty bureaucrats have always strutted in the confidence of their power, yet had, each of them, their particular price. A depressing world, certainly, but also one with a curious exhilaration...its inhabitants, who have always managed to spring back, cheeky, irreverent, wholly without illusions, no matter how brutally repressed or violently pushed down... Perhaps because Hungarians speak a language practically without affinities with any of the major European languages, Hungarians have always been obliged to be more outward looking than those of us unfortunate (or unlucky) enough to live in one of the great linguistic communities of the world... (Riemer, in Orkény, 1994, p. 11)

HUNGARY HUNGARIANS; AUSTRALIA HUNGARIANS

What is it to be Hungarian? What is it to be Hungarian in Hungary? What is it to be Hungarian in Australia? These are significant questions for me as they are such enigmatic and personal propositions.

Accordingly, this chapter is positioned as an illuminating travel guide, reflecting where I am in the journey. Since I have always existed in two worlds and feel like I belong to neither, this quandary of selves requires some consideration. Thus an exploration into these worlds is explored here as a prelude and as an exposé.

HUNGARIAN GEOGRAPHY, ETHNICITY AND CHARACTER

Hungary is a small country, located in the heart of Europe (or MittelEuropa) and has struggled with her own identity crisis for most of the twentieth century (Riemer, 1992). In fact, the region has been plagued with a crisis of identity since the end of World War I (Teleky, 1997), when after the Treaty of Trianon, she was diminished and reduced, with little thought for ethnicities and tribal borderlands (Hatoss, 2006).

It is Hungary's capital that is her most famous place and many domestic and foreign writers extol its beauties, nobleness and excitement (Curtis, 2001; Haywood et al., 2001; Magris, 1997). The city of Budapest, an amalgam of the ancient towns of Buda and Pest on either side of the Danube River, was once known as 'the Paris of the east'. It has been described as,

> the loveliest city on the Danube. [Budapest] has a crafty way of being its own stage-set, like Vienna, but also has a robust substance and a vitality unknown to its Austrian rival...It is no coincidence that at the beginning of the century Budapest was the cradle of an extraordinary culture...The splendour of Budapest is in part the compensation of a city which is losing its character, a mixture of giantism and exuberance, which corresponds to the hybrid alliance between the Hungarian capital and the Hapsburg eagle, and is also betrayed by the eclectic character of the architecture. (Magris, 1997, pp. 261–262)

Somewhat diminished by the vagaries of Communist rule that failed to maintain the public buildings, the city became somewhat shabby late in the twentieth century. However with foreign investment and interest as well as Hungary's membership to the European Economic Union, the country is rallying. Budapest is once again becoming a city to visit and to celebrate.

The character of the Hungarian people and their land is the result of wave after wave of invasion and the subsequent ethnic hybridity that is the inevitable result of such encounters. Hungary is a mosaic of different cultures, in which assorted dominions flourished and occasionally intersected. One Hungarian writer describes the people as having "a national pride that borders on paranoia" (Riemer 1993, p. 140) and they consider it a blessing to be a Hungarian, an honour (Teleky, 1997). The Hungarians are variously described as forthright, outspoken, original and courageous (De Daruvar, 1976) and they like to talk (Teleky, 1997). Such flowery and overdone descriptions are in character for the Hungarians; they are effusive, emotional and enthusiastic, with a lively sense of national identity.

Despite the highly emotional nature of the Hungarians, the national mood is one of melancholy. This is reflected in Hungarian poetry and music, which alternates "between sorrow and joy, melancholy and fierce self-assertion" (De Daruvar, 1976, p. 202). For decades, Hungary had the highest suicide rate in the world annually (Teleky, 1997). They are seen as being extreme in their behaviours with extreme mood swings and unpredictable behaviour (ibid).

Culture

Probably the most recognizable aspects of Hungarianeity are the unique language, the flavoursome cuisine, the stirring music, the enduring folk traditions and the grand literary customs.

The name of both the people and the language is *Magyar,* whilst the English word "Hungarian" is derived from the German, which has roots in the Medieval Latin "Hungarus". Speaking about the language, Teleky notes,

> [t]o my ear it has a rich, rough, primitive sound, in part caused by the stress pattern of pronouncing individual words with an emphasis on the first syllable, although this emphasis is modified if speaking a phrase. You can hear this distinctively Hungarian rhythm in the music of Bartok and Kodaly. (1997, p. 7)

There are a number of dialects of the language and it has agglutination and vowel harmony; postpositions and suffixes are extensively used and the first syllable of each word is emphasized. It is a notoriously difficult language to learn and to read and speak. Esterhazy states that the language that Hungarians speak,

> is alien and strange even after translation. Out of joint. Its reference system is different...its more lyrical, I'd say, masterly or masterless, but in any case, highly personal – verbal bouquets for facts, metaphors for theories. (1990, p. 424)

Indeed, Hungarian language has always been a core cultural value and an important way to maintain Hungarian identity (Hatoss, 2006). However, many famous Hungarians did not learn the language till far later in life, for example, the classical great Franz Liszt, although born in Hungary, is believed to never have learned the language. Also,

[t]he mother of Petofi, the Magyar national poet, could not speak Hungarian, while Count Szechenyi, a great patriot and father of the cultural conscience of the nation, learnt it when he was thirty four. (Magris, 1997, pp. 242–243)

Indeed, it is said that Hungary actually has two languages – its ancient spoken language and its ancient folk music. Neither of these languages is related to the peoples of Eastern Europe and both were bought from Asia many centuries ago (Hámori, 2003).

The folk music style is said to be at least 1500 years old, maintained through folk singing and performance. In fact, one musicologist argues that there is a striking resemblance between Chinese and Hungarian folk songs and the similarities are based upon the emphasis of the word accent in both the spoken languages (ibid). This is supported by the research of such Hungarian music greats as Béla Bártok and Zoltán Kodály and supports the finding that the Hungarians were originally of Asian stock. Hungarian music (particularly Bártok's) alternates between,

> brooding depression and rousing peasant dance...a description of manic depression, a term that has been used to characterize the Hungarian temperament. Hungarian Gypsy music was an ersatz creation by Hungarian composers often performed by Gypsies in small string ensembles. Genuine Gypsy music does exist, as does old Hungarian peasant music, but they are far removed from each other and unknown to most people outside Hungary except ethnomusicologists. The hybrid music had its origins in *verbunkos,* a style of Hungarian military dance music that developed in the 1700s and even influenced composers like Haydn and Beethoven. This music suited Hungary's growing national spirit and became associated with some legendary Gypsy performers. (Teleky, 1997, pp. 80–81)

In Hungary today, tourists are likely to find many of these ersatz Gypsy creations being performed in the grand hotel restaurants or if really fortunate at the local tavern, or *csarda* in the villages outside the city centres. This word, csarda (or czarda), is also given to a lively form of Hungarian dance, known as the *csardas.* It is a virile dance, compared slightly to the Highland fling (Curtis, 2001). Is a nineteenth century courtship dance, in double time, which alternates between slow and fast sections, and conveys an image of passionate dancers swinging to the music of cimbaloms and tambourines (Teleky, 1997).

Indeed if one were to venture into the csarda, one would be compelled to partake of the unique Hungarian cuisine available all over the country. Hungary's reputation as one of the culinary masters of Europe is largely based on one very simple recipe and indeed one unique ingredient. The dish is gulyás (goulash) and the spice is paprika, which seems to be synonymous with being Hungarian – its description as fiery, spicy and temperamental is suggestive of the national character as well as the spice (ibid). You won't find too many Hungarian dishes without it.

It has also been said that the feared Hungarian warriors of the early middle ages who rode through Europe on the backs of wild horses striking fear and terror into the hearts of the locals were fired up by paprika laden dishes (Gergely, 1999). Used with the onion, another important ingredient in Hungarian cuisine, this combination is the basic tone in gulyás (a type of meat and vegetable soup), paprikás (usually a chicken casserole type dish) and pörkölt (best made with pork fat). Gulyás has been said to be a plate of Hungarian history and in fact an entire epoch of Hungarian history is referred to as gulyás communism. The word gulyás originally meant herdsmen and *gulyás hus* is therefore herdsmen's meat. Gulyás is both the herdsmen and the soup, since it was the herdsmen who created it in the middle ages. It became a highly fashionable dish in the eighteenth century, but originally it was served in a shared kettle with wooden spoons over an open fire.

A fourteenth century Italian chronicler tells of the Magyars preserving meat for their nomadic lifestyle (ibid). It was boiled, salted and dried and then pounded into powder, and put into small linen bags. When the Magyar warriors went into battle they sprinkled the powder into boiling water, and made the very first instant soup. It helped the soldiers stay strong and undoubtedly contributed to their victories. This continued into the Alföld (The Great Plain) until very recently.

Much of the country's interior is taken up by the Alföld, where most crops are farmed and cattle raised. The soil is rich and the produce famous for its flavoursome character. Kálocsa is where most of the country's best paprika is grown, and salamis produced. It is also where the fruit for its pálinkas, or fruit brandies, is harvested.

Throughout the trials and tribulations that beset the Magyars over the centuries, they always could endure as long as, "the coffee [was] up to scratch and [they could] look forward with relish to the next meal" (Varga, 1994, p. 65). The cuisine is much more than simply nourishment for the body. It is a salve for the soul and an expression of profound emotions (Gergely, 1999). This belief continues today with Hungarians throughout the world, including my aunties, my grandmother, my mother and myself; we all believe that the food is not just about the food.

It is said that much of the true Hungarian folk culture can only be found in Transylvania, which now lies in the western part of modern Romania. Much of its population is still Hungarian speaking. This genuine folk culture,

> is to be found only there, in that world of farmers and shepherds where the authentic Hungarian folk music (not the phoney gypsy stuff) and traditions survive. (Riemer, 1993, p. 135)

Many Hungarians feel that the maintenance of the practice of embroidery is a link to the retention of the nation's identity. It is the most popular folk and craft activity in the country and for Hungarians beyond the borders. It is traditional to share patterns and skills with others and has been a continuous tradition since the needle was invented. Once embellishing the robes of the clergy and the wealthy, it became popular in the villages from about the 18th century (Gergely, 1999). During the communist epoch in Hungary, the craft flourished, probably due in part to the regime's persistent oppression of the Hungarian identity. This had the opposite effect and the craft continues to be a valuable and important tradition (ibid).

Another staple of Hungarian cultural life is the enjoyment of literature, particularly poetry, with Sándor Petöfi being considered to be Hungary's greatest poet (Magris, 1997). More than a cultural practice, Hungarian literature and its authors are often considered to be heroic in stature and sometimes influential in political life. As Teleky writes,

> [s]ince the revolution of 1848, Hungarian writers have been a major political force in national life, preserving Hungarian identity and speaking out against oppression. The Populists, who emerged in the early 1930s, were a loosely formed radical movement of peasant intelligentsia. Attempting to do for letters what Bartok had done for Hungarian Music, they studied the sociology of rural life and advocated partition of the great landed estates... They were, in effect, the progenitors of the revolution of 1956. (1997, p. 117)

The greatest examples of Hungarian literature are not those which glory in the valiant Hungary, but those which reveal the wretchedness and darkness of the Hungarian destiny (Magris, 1997). In his poetry, Petöfi roundly criticizes the immobile egocentricity of the aristocracy and the torpor of the nation. Endre Ady talks about the "gloomy Hungarian land", describes himself as "sadly Magyar" and declares that,

> the Magyar Messiahs are Messiahs a thousand times over because in their country tears are more salt, and they die having redeemed nothing. One born in Hungary already has a price on his head, because (as he says in another poem) the country is a stinking lake of death; the worn out Hungarians are "the buffoons of the world", and within himself, as he grieves, the poet bears the whole of that melancholy plain. (in Magris, 1997, pp. 256–257)

That is not to say that Hungary is a place entirely obsessed with melancholia. Many of the customs and traditions of the country are quite joyous and colourful. For example, during the Easter celebrations, eggs are beautifully and brightly painted with motifs similar to those found in the embroidery traditions. They are placed into the gardens for children to find on Easter morning and young girls are 'sprinkled' with either perfume or water by their prospective beaux in a modern interpretation of an ancient courtship ritual (Curtis, 2001).

On St Nicholas night (December 5th) it was customary for girls to receive midnight serenades from adoring young men. The romance continues when May trees (maypoles with ribbons and love messages written on little hearts) were planted on the night of May 1st and the lucky object of affection was again serenaded. Unfortunately many of these customs have disappeared, but some are still being practised in the country regions today, especially in Transylvania (ibid).

These cultural, geographical, ethnic and personality aspects are common to Hungarians in Hungary and exploring them has begun to give me a strong image of the Magyar identity. Whilst this is illuminating at this point in the journey, it is also important to explore the documented Hungarian appearance in Australia in order to further ease my ignorance. The next section explores the history of Hungarians in Australia, their experiences and their contributions. It also gives contextual gravitas to the narratives that follow.

HUNGARIANS IN AUSTRALIA

There has been an unbroken Hungarian presence in Australia for 150 years (Hatoss, 2006). The first to arrive was Isaac Friedman in 1833 with his wife and son and since that time the Hungarian presence has been continuous but not ample. Even at its highest point between 1945 and 1961, Hungarian immigration was only 2% of the migrant intake to Australia, being the seventh largest group behind, in order, the British, Italians, Dutch, Germans, Greeks and Yugoslavs (Hatoss, 2006; Kunz, 1969).

Australia was not the "promised land" of the downtrodden and the poor in the Hungarian consciousness that America became. This idea of Australia may have remained stable, had it not been for the 15000 strong wave of Hungarians (Andits, 2010) who came to Australia after the Second World War, and they (including my father) wrote home of a country that was developing rapidly, and was relatively friendly and accepting. When the revolution happened in 1956, many Hungarians made Australia their choice (Kunz, 1985).

Only a small proportion of Hungarian refugees chose Australia, but there were enough of them to be recognized as being noticeable in all states. In 1933, the census quoted only 272 Hungarian born people in Australia; by 1961 the figure had risen to 30553 (Australian Bureau of Statistics [ABS], n.d.). By 1981, with the aging Hungarian population resulting in either their return to their homeland or by their death, the number of first-generation Hungarians was reduced to 27987. In 2001, more Hungarian arrivals and the growth of the second-generation brought the number of those who identified that they were of Hungarian ancestry to being about twice that (ibid). The 2006 census data revealed there were 19 092 Hungarian born migrants living in Australia and 69160 people identified that they were of Hungarian ancestry (Australian Bureau of Statistics [ABS], 2011), suggesting second- third- and possibly fourth-generation Hungarian-Australians.

When the Displaced Persons started arriving in Australia in 1948, Hungary was permanently occupied by the Russian military. Passports were no longer being issued freely and the borders were closing. Thus,

> [a]lthough some chose fantastic ways of escaping, such as hi-jacking aircraft or hiding in specifically built railway 'coffins' resembling carriage toolboxes, most of the refugees came either alone, or in small groups through the border, choosing sectors where the fortifications were not yet completed. (Kunz, 1985, p. 80)

This description aptly describes both my father's exodus as well as that of my mother and her parents. Most of these refugees arrived in Australia without money, believing that they would not be here for long. There were only a few women amongst them, at a ratio of approximately 7:4. More than any other wave of Hungarian immigration, it was this vintage that were responsible for the high number of mixed marriages between Hungarian men and Australian women in the years that followed (ibid).

It was unfortunate that my father's family chose not to join us in Australia after the 1956 revolution, although Dad did coax them repeatedly. Hungarians were 'successful' immigrants as Kunz has described,

> Australia did benefit from the 150 years of Hungarian migrations: the small number of Hungarian immigrants contributed well beyond their numerical strength to the development of certain aspects of Australian life...they made visible contributions as Hungarians, as Europeans... (1985, p. 133)

The social composition of the Hungarian immigrants was quite complex. There were Jews, educated professionals, middle class, tradesmen (like my father and grandfather) and city workers (Kunz, 1985). Most Hungarian immigrants settled in the larger cities, such as Sydney and Melbourne, but my parents who settled in Newcastle were in the minority where there wasn't a large Hungarian community.

First Impressions, Culture Shock and Australian Reactions

The first weeks in Australia in the post-war period were traumatic for these immigrants, it was like a rebirth, without the luxury of a period of gestation (Varga, 1994). Knowledge had to be gained quickly and small mistakes often had huge consequences. But once these first months were over, life was good.

As my parents' narratives attest, carving out a new life was simple in its goals and each year tangible progress was made. It was safe in Australia, there was enough to eat and the children were being educated well and were making friends, but emigration was a cultural, emotional and intellectual shock. It was considered to be a worthwhile struggle because of the freedom that had been afforded. These people were already survivors, having been through so many traumas, and they endured it all with a combination of luck and determination (Andits, 2010).

The newly arrived Displaced Hungarian, by comparison with the cities he knew, often found Australian cities lifeless and their restaurants somewhat impersonal. The food was monotonous and unfamiliar (Curtis, 2001; Ferris, 1996; Kunz, 1985). As Varga writes,

> the Sydney of 1949; its colours were brown and drab, its buildings haphazard and unlovely, its people closed in, stiff. The men looked identical in shapeless grey suits, the women dowdy in floral dresses. Even the smells were alien; the rankness everywhere of mutton and dripping, the whiff of fish and chips.

The adults wandered the streets and ate in cheap cafes. The waitresses slopped milky tea at them without asking them how they drank it. Oh, Hungary where tea came amber coloured, served deliciously with rum or lemon or both! (1994, p. 181)

Some enterprising Hungarians took these problems on board and began new trades and services. These included manufactured food stuffs unknown to Australians at the time and the sale of these in delicatessens, friendly espresso bars to provide a familiar atmosphere and small eating establishments which provided "varied menus, excellent cooking and good service" (Kunz, 1985, p. 113). Curtis expresses the differences between the cultures as,

> we were grateful to Australia for giving us food and shelter when we had nothing. We had no great expectations when we arrived, only asking for the opportunity to work and to have a roof over our heads. We were not prepared however for the great cultural differences. Australia may have been the safest place to come in comparison with other countries but with the difference in our traditions and customs deep in my heart, it seemed irreconcilable. Many Australian people were unhappy about the arrival of so many foreign immigrants and they made sure we were aware of their feelings. (2001, p. 107)

As the narratives in the following chapters illustrate, these observations were certainly the case for my family. Australia at this time was a constricted, interior society, convinced of its unqualified pre-eminence, disdainful of anything alien or atypical (Riemer, 1992). The people were seen to be generally self-centred and acquisitive (Cassab, 1995) and foreigners were considered as 'nothing but bloody reffos here', noisy, with unpronounceable names, inedible food and strange behaviour (Altorjai-Albury, 1998; Trezise, 2011).

Assimilation and Multiculturalism

A study conducted in the early 1960s examined the effects of migration on a group of Hungarian intellectuals who had migrated to Australia between 1949-1951. It discovered that they had assimilated quite thoroughly, carving out new lives for themselves and their families, even though they had suffered losses in terms of occupational and social status (Ambrosy, 1984). There appeared to be a high degree of satisfaction with Australia and high degree of acculturalization and integration. Some Hungarians tended to regard themselves as superior in intellect and class (Kunz, 1985) and considered themselves to have sustained greater losses in occupational and social status than other ethnic groups – this led to some dissatisfaction (Ambrosy, 1984). There has not been a similar study conducted for the rest of the Hungarian population in Australia and indeed much of the literature regarding the Hungarians in Australia seems to focus on professionals, intellectuals and Holocaust survivors. My parents and grandparents do not fit into any of these groups.

Homesickness and Nostalgia

Many of the refugees who came to Australia between 1944 and 1956 believed that they would never see their home country or their relatives again. These feelings were reinforced when Communist propaganda in Hungary labelled the refugees "as fascist criminals, class enemies, and useless, work-shy rabble" (Kunz, 1985, p. 102). The Cold War did little to allay these feelings, and the Hungarian government reneged the citizenship of all Hungarians who had fled (Andits, 2010).

It is not surprising that under such circumstances, the Hungarians in Australia turned inwards to their communities for solace and support, whilst still following closely the political activities of their homeland (ibid). Many resisted the pressure to be integrated into Australian society, being largely rejected by the population taking, "refuge in a past which gets more and more glorious with the passing years" (Cassab, 1995, p. 142). Many Hungarians in Australia felt disenfranchised and deadened, expressing the sentiment that, "in Europe I feel alive and here I don't" (ibid). As Kunz comments more generally of immigrants,

> [h]omesickness is a universal affliction of people who live away from their original surroundings. The ageing process reinforces it, and as we grow older, we become more sentimental and more selective about our memories of childhood and youth. (1985, p. 101)

One writer acknowledges that much of the music played on the Hungarian radio broadcast in Australia on the weekends is "[s]entimental, pathetic and slightly ridiculous, but it still has the power to touch a deep, deep chord that can never be touched in quite the same way by anything else" (Cassab, 1995, p. 260). My parents would concur, often listening to these same broadcasts, becoming nostalgic and frequently homesick.

For a race of people so fiercely nationalistic and loyal to their culture, many Hungarians felt adrift in Australia, especially those without access to the cultural pursuits available in the larger cities. Later, in the 1960s, the Communists declared an amnesty for these refugees who wished to visit their homeland relaxing their hard-line attitude (Andits, 2010; Kunz, 1985). Some Hungarians went back to visit family for the first time in decades, others went back and stayed.

Settling in: Associations and Contributions

In light of the fact that most Hungarians arrived with no means, they managed to fulfil many constructive projects (Hatoss, 2006; Kunz, 1985). Hungarian newspapers in Australia have included association bulletins, church newsletters, journals and specialist newspapers. Special Broadcasting Service [SBS] television and radio stations each regularly broadcast Hungarian programs on the weekends from Melbourne and Sydney.

An expanding majority of Hungarians in Australia consider themselves to be Australian-Hungarians who are loyal to Australia, although there are many who would wish to return to the homeland (Andits, 2010). Many have made significant contributions to this country beyond their numerical strength as "whether self-employed or not, [they] are usually in pursuits where independence, integrity, imagination and initiative can be retained to a considerable degree" (Kunz, 1985, p. 103). Some significant contributors include many senior academics and scientists of note; the modernizers of the Australian flour milling industry; many significant contributors to the Arts, especially music and painting; successful businessmen; small goods manufacturers, restaurateurs and delicatessens; dress designers; corporate giants such as Westfield; engineers; sports people especially in the arenas of fencing, water polo and soccer; and television personalities (ibid).

The first associations created for fellowship for Hungarians in Australia were fairly ad hoc, small groups meeting regularly perhaps for a few hours a week in the larger Australian cities. As more Hungarians arrived, these associations grew in the major capital cities and were largely political in nature (Andits, 2010; Hatoss, 2006). Those who felt that the members were not actively participating in Australian life and were, in fact, creating enclaves often criticized these associations. A study during the 1970s found that such members actively involved in ethnic associations during their formative years, were more likely to 'fail' in their occupation of Australia (Kunz, 1985).

This orientation towards the past ended with the arrival of the fifty-sixers. Such associations then became lifelines to the disoriented and confused revolutionary refugees who sought democracy and a new life and did not want to dwell on past events. However, the associations also focused their political gaze on the homeland, with hope that things would improve (Andits, 2010). Concurrently, many of these associations were transformed into productive soccer clubs, fencing clubs, gentlemen's clubs and gymnastic associations, as well as scouting associations, Saturday schools and church associations in the major cities (Kunz, 1985).

Hungarians from all social backgrounds were welcome. Their aims were to enrich the lives of Hungarians on Australian soil in an atmosphere of entertainment, in a context of Hungarian language and companionship, rather than to separate themselves and complain about their lot. My own parents were part of a vigorous, albeit small, Hungarian community in their early years in Newcastle. However, after I started school, these events seemed to dwindle. I have little or no memory of these activities at all, as my narrative will elaborate.

Professional dance groups, Women's Auxiliaries and an Hungarian doctor's association were also founded. Many of these associations focused on charity work and companionship. Ultimately there were so many associations that The Federal Council of Hungarian Associations was established, but its "primary aim was to bring closer the day of the Russian army's departure and the holding of new elections in Hungary" (Kunz, 1985, p. 93). Politically conservative and right wing, it was these people who resented the integration of their children and grandchildren into Australian society (ibid).

Today, most Hungarians in Australia are not members of any Hungarian club and only a small percentage of such clubs are affiliated with the Council; therefore its political power is quite limited (Andits, 2010). Further, many of these events are held in the major cities, and there is a lack of Hungarian clubs and associations in regional areas because the population is too small to support them.

Hungarians see the Magyar language as being fundamental to their identity (Hatoss, 2006). The maintenance of the first language is also seen as a symbol of survival, which when lessened, weakens the chain of cultural transmission (Smolicz, 1999). Indeed the Australian policy of assimilation had a destructive effect on immigrant heritage languages (Hatoss, 2006). Thus, isolation and assimilation has meant that some Hungarians have lost much of their native tongue, largely due to acculturation and the raising of English-speaking children (Cassab, 1995). It could be considered inevitable that one would lose a first language if it were not being practised, especially if quite young. As Riemer asserts,

> even when fully integrated into the Australian context, the young will carry with them residual elements of Hungarian attitudes: idealism, binding self-pride, zest for living, generosity and respect for originality and excellence. No doubt their faults will also filtrate into the Australian texture, but all in all, Australians and a still emerging new Australia will be the beneficiaries. (1992, pp. 135–136)

As my narrative will assert, the above statement certainly describes my experience, even though my ties to the Hungarian culture were not repeatedly practised. In the larger cities, church-based Saturday schools were available for second-generation Hungarians, for those whose parents placed an importance upon the maintenance of the heritage language (Kunz, 1985). This was not available to me.

Most Australians would acknowledge that post-war immigrants have established a European lifestyle in this country. In any Australian capital city in the 1950s, the streets were deserted during weeknights and on weekends, a limited range of restaurants and other cultural pursuits were available (Kunz, 1985). By contrast,

> [t]he culinary and 'atmosphere' revolution which transformed Australian city life was accompanied almost exclusively by immigrants hailing from the area of the old Austro-Hungarian monarch, and Hungarians took a leading part in it. (ibid, p. 113)

Although, relatively speaking, the Hungarian community in Australia is small in number, they have been able to wield an impact analogous to immigrant societies several times their size. This is due to the fact that the middle and higher middle class elements were numerous. Ever-present, usually able to be independent thinkers and expressive of their feelings, as well as being used to insisting upon superior value in retail, culinary and cultural pursuits, their analysis and encouragement have added to the development of principles opposed to the practice of 'near-enough-good-enough' (ibid). In fact it has been themselves that frequently supplied these better services and this emphasizes their role as a significant group which brought about a tangible enhancement in "quality, service and standards in a wide variety of Australian enterprises" (ibid, p. 134).

Although I can recognize that the Hungarians have made an impact on Australian society beyond their numbers, it is clear that the cultural potency of this migrant group has been slight. Many sought to 'remain' Hungarian – *Megmaradásunk* (Hatoss, 2006). Despite the assertions of writers like Kunz (1985) and Andits (2010) who emphasize an almost mythic status to the Hungarian as the cognoscenti of Australia, this was certainly not the experience of my family. Nobody considered us to be superior, we were not admired, indeed in many cases our engagement with the locals was fraught; we were all reviled, discriminated against and alienated.

What unfolds next in this tale are the first suite of narratives of my parents, Laci and Zita, who reveal glimpses of their formative years in Hungary and their wartime experiences. Meanwhile, the world primed itself for the diaspora.

Jöjjön, aminek jönni kell
(Let it come, whatever must come)
Hungarian proverb

LACI (I)

I was about twelve years old. And it never used to be a habit I never used to sleep in the afternoon and this day nobody was at home. I was still a school kid, I must have come home from school, 'cause the school finished at one o'clock, from eight till one. And I don't know why, I laid there and I fell asleep.

And I had a dream that I was an old man. I tell you exactly I looked like. I looked like I am now, except skinnier, and older in the face. I must have been very old and I went back. I was away all my life. I dreamt. And I just came home, and I left all my life somewhere. I came home, and I looked at the places that we lived like relations and neighbors and things. Everywhere, I don't know the dialogue, but I knew I was asking about my family and all this, and everywhere they strange people shaking their head. Didn't know. I went from one place to the other and nobody I knew. And then after all this, it took a long time,

I remember meself walking on the street and that I was walking, skinny as anything and old, but still fit. But I walk, it was a habit at home at that time you go near the walls of the houses with back of you hand, and that's how you walked along touching the houses with you hand. And that's what I did walking from one place to the other looking for my relation or anybody I know, and I never found anybody. I been different suburbs, I been different houses I used to know, nobody.

And then suddenly I woke up. Shocked. I was shocked. It was so real. I was standing, I got up, I was only lying down, but I was all dressed like. And I stood in the middle of the room, nobody was home. And I called out "Never!" I yelled, 'NEVER! NEVER! I'LL NEVER LEAVE!" Real hysterical. I was upset, shocked. All my life somewhere else. The way I stood in that room and the way I yelled out I couldn't care if any one heard me. I remember "Never! Never!". I was thinking about it I don't know how long. And I thought "No, no, no way it's just not on". And well it end up I did spend my life…I only spent 19 years in Hungary.

I was proud of my mother, she was very good looking. When I think back, nobody give a damn even when my father died, you know, no help, assistance, advice – not assistance just advice on what she should do. And she was a good cook you wouldn't believe it. She make beautiful food from nothing, see we wouldn't have much sometimes.

September the school year started and my father died just a few days before the 4th class started. We went back the 9th of September, see, and my Dad died sometime in the middle of September. It was 1934.

My father died and they send me away to Esztergom boarding school, only a few days later. Imre bácsi, because they were still being in charge of the house and Imre took on my father's job at the age of eleven, twelve. He still went to school as normal. Irén néni went to Budapest to boarding school. I went to boarding school, I cried for one week. But I settled down.

I was at boarding school I was only there about a year and a half and my Mum made a big mistake there…perhaps just as well it worked out the way it did. Because if I had of stayed there I probably would have finished up going the high school and would have finished up in the university because from the Bishop too, there was ready help available too. And the second year I was there, Christmas time, most of the students going home for Christmas break, you know? I didn't. Only three or four hard up people they stayed on. Some well off people their kids were there, it wasn't cheap. Anyway, the nun came in, the Mother Superior came in and said

"There's a wolf under the bridge," something like that, "and Lascsik Laci is going home, requested by his Mum". It was a shock. I didn't want to go home. I felt good at that time, I settled in, I was good at school, the teacher was very good, you know?

The school was good. I was quite happy with the food that was provided and the treatment and all that.

Anyway I got home and later on she asked me, "You don't want to learn on do you?" But that's a silly thing to ask a kid because he would say for certain, "No". And that's what I said. No. So I didn't learn... I learned I took on the eight classes, it's just like ten years here...no like year eight here. And I came back to Györ and came back to school until year eight and that was the finish. And then... I became a delivery boy and then I thought I had to learn something because I remember, my father said to me, "Learn! Learn!" Because you going to become a street sweeper!" [laughs] Not only that but then I thought to myself, "You must learn something. Learn a trade. Would you like to learn that?" So after a year or so I became an apprentice.

Kis Zoli, we went to school together, and he said that he read in the paper advertising for some technical students learning in the army. And I put my application in, I had to write a real official thing and they wrote back that I had to, because of the law, have my father's military record and all that, which I did and I got part of his record. I had to prove that there was no Jew in the family background, then they write me a letter that I was accepted and then I had to go and have a medical checkup, which I did, eye test and all that and I passed it and Zoli who actually suggested to me, he didn't get in.

Well at that time in '44/45, these Hungarian Fascists they took over at that time, they took over in October I think. I heard Horthy's speech in November. He sought peace with Russia and all that and then these Hungarian Nazis took over and Horthy was under arrest they took him to jail. But anyway what was happening then they got all the young boys, took them to Germany fourteen years old boys, twelve years old boys, you know, and one among them was Kis Zoli. They were not soldiers, they were civilians and they took them into this zone. I can't tell you about that... English Zone but at that time it was

German, and they gave the excuse I know at that time well, they need boys to rebuild the country again. That's what the fascists said, the Arrow Cross Party. It's not that they wanted to go, they didn't want to go but if they didn't go they were searching in the villages, and it happened that they were hiding boys in the strawstacks, the hay stacks. And they with the swords and things they plunged them in and they got them out and they killed them and they killed their parents too.

I served my apprenticeship in Komárom. We were wearing uniform, but the tradesmen like me were civilian. The conditions weren't good. The accommodations were pretty minimal, food was very minimal. And the uniform you had to go to Tech in and work in and it was full of grease. There was no other things to wear. And the boots, you had to go up to the ceiling and get the boots and none of them was matching, you know one was size 40 and the other was 42. Things like that. I was there till the end of '44 and all the apprentices in the country was transferred to one place.

We moved a fair bit, we moved a fair bit, different places, because the war was getting very close, you know? We got passed earlier the examination for the apprenticeship; I mean the Tech was completed in 1944. I was 19 when I finished.

Apparently it was a countrywide apprenticeship scheme, army workshops and they recruited apprentices. Now what happened then after they reunited all the apprentices in the one unit, and, with a battalion from Budapest, and just that Battalion...we were with them together. I think that what they said their plan was, because they were always talking about the war and rebuilding the country and all this and I think, because so many technical crew like we were, all served their apprenticeship, like this and I think their plan was to save the skills, and save them when the war was over to use them to serve for army units to work. We weren't army; we were perhaps like a cadet. Because you weren't a soldier, soldier was

sworn in, you know we didn't have that, but we wear a uniform, yeah. They expected that when we finish the apprenticeship, we join the army, that's right. But the thing was this: my plan was when the apprenticeship finish, I just tried to get out of it, you know? And work as a civilian even in the military somewhere. Civilians, all the tradesmen were civilians, few soldiers in the workshop, also tradesmen, like, they were conscripted, like, and they were in the age, because by us, conscription started, 21 years old, see? And I was planning perhaps later when it settled down I might quit the army and just get back to civilian. Because my aim was actually to learn a trade, get it any way I could.

When I was an apprentice, the Yanks and the English started to bomb when the Germans came into Hungary officially, that was '44, March. Until then Hungary wasn't bombed but after that, incredible. Until then they flew over Hungary but they never dropped... They did drop when they were chased by German Luftwaffe, fighter planes. I must say the Yanks, they dropped the bomb but they dropped on countryside where they no buildings were. But when the Germans came and then the Yanks bombed during the day and the Pommies came at night. And the destruction was incredible. You seen Budapest on the film, Lexi, shocking and Györ was the same.

The end of 1944 as I said we were moving different villages, like, you know? And the last village was...it was in Western Hungary not far from Györ. And then the front was already only a few kilometres away, at Kisbèr, and we could hear the artillery there, it was incredible fighting Lex and the Russians and the Rumanians changed sides and the Yugoslávs and they all came. And the resistance was such on the part of the Hungarian army there was a big resistance. The casualties there were incredible on all sides, the Russians... We didn't have to go there, we were in a village so many kilometres away, we could hear the fighting and the

artillery fires and all this, but they said that the River Danube was full with blood, bodies and all this... Russian bodies, because the Russians tried to come across the Danube, and then from the south Russians and Rumanians. I was in this village there, we were quite peacefully, we were trained actually, being trained for action there. And well, every day you went for training, physical, marching and with the rifle training.

The closest I come to action, there was a big danger when we were in Germany, we were not far from Nuremberg. And they took us in an army camp and everybody was exhausted. The Hungarians were in their own unit, but we were independent. The Hungarian command ceased...when we were near Berlin. We could see air raids over Berlin, you know? March I think it was. When we were there we had technical training there we went to classes, for military training, technical for the trade.

We had an air raid that place where we were and tanks were repaired there and things like that. And they bombed it, I don't think it was that important, although lot of, as I remember a lot of military things were going on there and I didn't think it was worthwhile but they did bomb. I got that close at that time, we were sent out with the shovel to do some shovelling. And the air raid caught us in the open, well, me anyway. I was on my own, with this German, and then as the bombs were exploded, it wasn't very far and these concrete buildings where we had these workshops, and hitting the concrete and this concrete dust everywhere and you could barely see anything, you know? And front of me, there was a building between me and where the bomb went off, so twenty metres, that close, everything shaking. I didn't feel anything, no fear. Not because I was brave, I was stupid probably. I don't say I'm brave, it never occurred to me. This German, he was front of me and when the bomb fell and this concrete dust flying everywhere and I still carry, I so duty minded, I still carried the shovel. And I noticed he was carrying some shovel too, or something, and he throw away when he started to run and he was so panicked that he fell over, you know? And I had to laugh [laughs]. And I laughed, I did! And then I said to myself, "You're an idiot. People going like that and you think it so funny that the German was so frightened that he fell over". And then it caught on me and then I was frightened. And back home when the air raids were on, everybody raced to the air raid shelters, my Mum too.

I was in Germany at that training camp during March 1945... and then we were in Reisse next to Dresden, and there were congregating, I think the whole battalion, 101 battalion I think. That was a Budapest battalion and all the apprentices were with them like, you know? And when we left Reisse the Russians were already on the other side of the river. And we were there and when we there, they gave us rations for two days to eat. And of course what they give you for two days; you eat it in one meal. There was nothing much, and when we arrived in Reisse, we never had anything for two days to eat, eh? And then one night there was

an alarm and we had to assemble in one of these German military camps, in the yard and they were talking German in the dark, there was no light, everybody was alerted and why we were there, we don't know, they announced that the Russians had crossed the river, and we have to get out because we weren't a fighting unit.

And then we left there and we started to walk on the roads different places. And then my friend Karcsi his name was, he, and Zoli, that was another boy, and Karcsi was a Budapest boy and Zoli from Pécs in south western Hungary. And Karcsi suggested, he said, "This is ridiculous, we leave, we break away from everybody, and go to Prague. In Prague we do all right because it a democracy there," and all that. The Germans were there too. And then, it was very dangerous, that was very dangerous because you see you become a deserter.

And we just detached ourselves and we went out on the road, beautiful countryside, we were in uniform, and that was already in April of' 45. And we walk on the road and we come to one place and carrying our overcoat and a pack, and we had food, rice and all this. Because when we were in Reisse there was... The shops were selling out what they were selling on the ration card before... the shops were selling out because when the Russians were there they would take it anyway, abandoned the ration card, people were lining up. And in those days it started to get warm too, you

shed your army clothes, and we nearly get into trouble with that too.

We walked the road and we came into a city, we were heading to Prague, walking east, we were walking the road was beautiful, you know? Except dangerous, you see? Well, there was nothing on the road, never met anyone, although we hit this small city, and we run out of food.

We thought we can't carry on because we have nothing to eat, so we decided to go to the city command. And I said to him, we discuss it and I said to Karcsi I said, "One of us will have to go because if he gets caught then the other ones can still be free," you know? And Karcsi did go and came back with a ticket to Prague, a watchyoumacallit? Ration card [laughs] for all of us! He asked…He spoke a little bit of German, neither of us did but he was saying, "I went in and talked to the officer there and say…," and he said in bad German, "I think my battalion from Reisse departed and I don't know where they got to, I think they must have gone to Prague", and they took it! Must have been a German that wasn't going to get you shot, just a reasonable person. They issued us a ration card, and a pass for us to Prague. And the next thing we did we got on to a train, sold some things, and have a bit of money, and I don't know where we got some cigar and smoke and that was very handy, cigars, see?

And we got to Prague and we went to a hotel! Can you imagine [smiling]? And talking to this Czech there, looking for accommodation, in uniform. And to the hotel. And I laughed – in a hotel in uniform?? A Hungarian Uniform? Anyway, went in the hotel and money wouldn't be any worth, so we had some cigar, some cigarettes or something and gave

the hotelier some cigars and we got in and that was it! And then we went out! Money meant nothing.

Anyway 1st of May, I see the newspaper in Prague and it say "HITLER DEAD!" Well, Hitler died and I think what was happening the Czech leadership were worried that they never had any resistance against the Germans, they were quite adequate, safe, you know. Get the ration card, and fairly well, there was a fair bit to go around, you could get anything for the cigar, for smoke. Or for change – I had this woollen jacket, they had it in Russia, you know, and I got hold of it somehow, and exchange it for something, some food or something I don't know, and then after Hitler death when 1st May came, German tanks were on the street because they sensed it that the Czechs might rise because, see they got to make a reputation for amongst the Germans because they never done anything. The Serbs were fighting like anything, and but the Czechs didn't, see? Apparently in the last few days they had to make a show.

And then the shooting went on in the street, you could hear it. We were running out – wanted to go down the street and get some food, we had to go out, Karcsi was prepare to go out, and as I looked down from the hotel window, from the first floor, a body was hanging out, you know, halfway on the window. The Czechs got up there and this bloke they said he was a postmaster or something, they shot him dead. And he was hanging. The ladder was still there, you know where they climbed up.

These Czech civilians and they came up again to our quarters in the hotel where we were and searched again and all this and demanded that we go with them, and took us in a police riding school I think it was, inside, you know, the police headquarters, the building.

And as we walked along, the Czechs made nasty remarks about the Hungarians as we walked along and they laughing their head off and a few blokes taking us there and when we got there they took all the papers away, I never had any identification paper and they called themselves partisans and women were there too. And the blokes were very unfriendly, and pushed you with the barrel of the gun like, "Get in there," but the women were different. Do you know what they did? They were very nice, saying, "Magyári (Hungarian), Magyári!" Stroking us shoulder and all this and then Karcsi said we were hungry and she pushed in our pocket some food. And they just took us in there and showed us to do what you like, and I still had my military overcoat, and I put it down on the ground and you lie down on it. They had a gallery there on the top on the end of the thing, you kn ow and that was where the machine gun was set up, and outside too, the machine guns. It was a police place, but these were civilians. They didn't take our food away so we had something to eat and the Germans came, because this was a partisan attack, many many German lives were in danger, not only there, but all over the place.

And these German fighters came in the air and they started to attack where we were. That was the central area apparently of the uprising and dropped a bomb and it tore out the side of where the commandant was living and other officials, because we were in the other side. And they machine-gunned the area where we were too, and many of the German civilians got hurt from German fire.

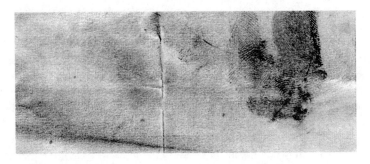

And we, well I was lucky, because what was happening I left my coat there and they took us out to do some labouring or something, I don't know what. And when the air raid came, there was a chapel there, next door or something and it had a cellar like, sort of a thing. It was very strange, as I remember and it was an opening there like a window and we wanted to jump in there because the air raid was in progress. The bombs falling, German, and the machine gun fire. They came right down, you know.

Anyway, jumped through that window and everybody jumped and I grabbed the wall and it broke away and I fell back, and this Czech, this partisan he couldn't get

in so he pushed me in and I fell right down there and then he jumped in too. And when that German air raid was over, and then we found out what was happening, that the civilian Germans had a heavy casualty from the German fire and what they did, somehow they got a white sheet and with the blood they put a great big red

cross on it, from the blood and this German came down in the plane and see this crowd there outside the building in the yard and then he went off, see, left them alone. And my coat, I left there, had bullet holes in. But they must have reported back because the next thing there a German attack came and freed these Germans. Yeah, that was on the 8th May, the day the war ended. And some people say it was the 9th but I know it was the 8th where we were, it was the 8th.

Anyway, and then the Germans had a meeting, that was towards the night and they were informed that the war was over and the Germans surrendered and all this but they made a deal with the Czechs that they let the Germans cross that bridge I tell you about, but no weapon is allowed to be carried. And so we set out, night time it was, evening, we just went, didn't ask their permission, just lined up and military units like in a war, not just like a mob, in four in a row, in formation. So we crossed the river and got on to the other side of Prague, and then we walked all the way to Pilsen.

I don't think we had anything, food. These German trucks came past, because

trucks went as well, and some of them were Hungarians, like Swábs, what do you call it? Like minority Germans ethnic Hungarian-Germans, and they tossed us chocolates. They had chocolates the Germans, in like this French cheese box? And they were in Germany, nice boys, and they chucked it from the trucks, "Hey!" The truck flying past, they knew we were Hungarian because we had the uniform on, they talking Hungarian and tossed it down, the chocolate. Never seen much chocolate when we were kids either, hard to come by, it was.

Anyway we made it to Pilsen and I thought to myself, "Well, we'll be landing into a prisoner of war camp". A few Hungarians there, was separated from the others, the Germans and the others. Apparently there was a lot of Hungarian soldiers too, and they were separated and they went into prisoner of war camp and we didn't, we seemed to be in like a refugee camp. They gave us I think two loaves of bread,

the Yanks, for 130 people, can you imagine [smiles]? Anyway that's beside the point. They came because they had to transport all these people, they couldn't walk through Pilsen and they looking for drivers. And I volunteered, Karcsi volunteered, Zoli volunteered and then they came to drive the truck and they loaded with apparently refugees, going back…I got this diesel Klöckner and I said, "This is a beauty", and mind you I'd had no experience driving, I did drive, but only the length of the yard, or things like that.

So I accepted it, but I knew a fair bit about it, the function and all this and people was, full, full of people and they took us to another area beside the river. We were staying there a few days. They gave us food, then quite sufficient. Not only that but some of these Hungarian boys, the Yanks had a food store in one of those buildings there, an air hanger, whatever it was. Food everywhere and it was guarded by military police and all this and the Hungarian boys they still got in and they got food out. Risking their lives they were. It was unreal.

And then they transferred us to an ex-German camp must have been an ex-military camp, barracks so many barracks and all that, and that's where we landed somewhere in the back. Next door Rumanians, you know and they put their flag out and all that, you know and then these Hungarians they put their Hungarians flag out and the Czechs just near the fence there were walking past and nothing worse for them than seeing a Hungarian flag.

And these were different people, French, Poles, Hungarians, Rumanians, Bulgarians…God knows how many. This was in Pilsen, not far from the airfield. We were in that barracks, military barracks until sometimes in December. And I did jobs, I did jobs for the French Red Cross, things like that and driving…it was probably November or December before we mounted these American trucks, you know? GMC? Packed up things, but we were so silly you know, could have really established myself and everybody could've done real well but we didn't think of it. But I was equipped by then, pretty well and all on the back of the truck like – to dress with, food and sugar and rice and things. But we didn't take enough, we could have loaded the truck, because no people. From Pilsen we went to Bamberg, Germany. And we were

accommodated in a house that they, the Germans were either taken away from them, or they just escaped. It was quite comfortable, there was a kitchen they cooked for us there was a German cook for us and all that, and we were in Bamberg until about next year, June 1946 I think, six months. We went to Bamberg from Pilsen because all military had to evacuate and the Russians became a satellite, they were in. From there I went to Hungary. I went, I was pretty silly because everything was good, good accommodation, but somehow… I suppose it's understandable because I never heard of my mother, or the family. I didn't know how it – I didn't know who remained alive. Irénke, or Mum or Imre, so I think that was a big contribution why I decided that I'm going home. Which I did.

The inflation was raging. Incredible, the biggest inflation anywhere in the world was Hungary. You weekly wage wasn't worth, you couldn't buy a match. Money wasn't buying anything you can only change if you had something to change like a piece of cloth. I tell you what short of: salt. You couldn't get salt and if I knew that when I left I could have brought a few kilo of salt. Well, it would have been hard to carry, and the other thing too, when we arrived back in Hungary they searched you there too. But certain things they take away.

Even though I went back '46, I wish I didn't. There wasn't much point. Not politically, financially. So I stayed there until November or December of that year, and I was very unsettled there, unhappy. It was a shit on the job in that factory in Györ, a real shit.

I decided I got to go back, to Germany. I cursed myself that I ever made home. I wanted Imre to come with me. I said, "Come on. *Gyere Imre* [Come with me Imre]". I said I can't see the point the way the Russian's were everywhere. He said, "Don't go, they going to shoot you". I said, "Don't be silly". I couldn't care less, I'm not going to put up with this shit. He wouldn't come. He said to me, because he was very well in business, "I'll buy you a second hand truck. You stay." In those days the communists weren't in power yet. I could see it coming, I had no doubt in my mind. Many of the Hungarians come out for political reasons and that, they couldn't handle the Russians sitting there, many other reasons too. I didn't like the Russians there.

And then I went down to southern Hungary, I knew people coming from west I found out that's where they take them first in the train, from American zone, English zone, things like that. And I went there and I waited there trying to find out when the next train comes with homecoming Hungarians. For some reason that's where they delivered them.

They had a few Pommie soldiers escorting the train, like. I talked to one of these Germans, he was a Berliner and I told him I like to get a trip on a train, hidden away and all that, and he hesitated. I realized he had a problem, he didn't know who I was but I couldn't speak German, only a few words. But eventually I must have made the right impression because he agreed to put me up the way back, because the train was empty. Just put me, and calls in at times, and bring me something to eat. And he did, it was good.

We got across the Austrian border and the train stopped somewhere in Austria and there were Germans in Austria they were expelled from Austria, women, children, and they had to fill up the hospital train, see. So I had to move and he was in a spot. But he took a risk, being a German, I suppose, and there were these wardrobes

sort of thing, an area that kept I don't know brooms and things, like a closet. And he put me in there and as well as he smuggled some food. It was very good of him.

And then we came to the demarcation zone between Russians and American zone…what's it called? I forgot…anyway this was in Austria. We come to the zone border between the two sections and this Berliner I knew he was in danger because what was happening that the Russian soldier checking out the train. But was happening, he made me to get out of that closet and the beds were double, and he told me, while crossing the demarcation zone and go under the bed, under one of the beds just across from the closet.

And we got to the borderline, the zone border and I got under the bed. And there was a sleeper, a railway sleeper, in the carriage. I don't know if it was the only one or under the other beds too. I don't know they use it for firewood or something. Anyway I went under the bed and he put the sleeper in front of me to cover me up, see. I went right inside as far as possible and the next thing you know, I heard steps coming, nobody was in that wagon at that time. Looks like the Russians checked them out too. These Russian soldiers came through the carriage and I could hear that Russian boot clipping. I thought, "Shit". And as he walked past on the side, I couldn't see him because I could only see the step because of the sleeper, but when he got to the end of the bed I could see his boots and he would stop. And I tried to keep my mind, not to think of it just in case it transmitting, you know that thing you sometimes transmitted? Crosses somebody's mind the same thing you thinking. I don't know whether you experienced it. And I thought at that time it's a possibility if I keep thinking 'fear' that he's here and all that he stop. And he stopped, he stopped a few steps from where I was. I couldn't see his face only his boots and I don't know what he was looking at. And I waited, and I didn't think of it I just didn't think of it, mind blank. Tried, you know, not to think. And then he restarted and he walked away, hey? God knows, I would have got taken to Russia, I don't know.

And when we crossed into the American zone I was delighted to hear the Yanky accent [smiles]. I thought this was good, they didn't check it. He came in, the German and he said, "Oh you lucky fellow!" And you know I couldn't understand German but I could understand him.

And then, we went to Nuremberg, on this train I don't know why, heading back to English zone, I suppose. I think I made a point to wear – I had some American uniform – and when I started off I wore it. We arrived in Nuremberg and the Berliner says to me, "You get out here," and I said, "That suits me," because I been to Nuremberg. And I said, "Thank you very much".

And going through the gate of the railway and of course I had no paper. I travelled with no paper or anything like that. And went through the check, through the gate and he showed his paper, good, he had an English paper, and I just walked through with him. The gatekeeper was just staggered I suppose by the time he woke up that I go through with him, we were away. And then we were through the gate and in the waiting room and he shook my

hand as I said, to get in touch with him in Berlin and then he went back. And I said, "This is alright". I went out, and that was the last time I saw Hungary until we went back in 1982.

So I set out walking, I had to get to Bamberg, see there's no way I could board a train I didn't have any papers. And I started to walk on the highway I knew, towards Erlangen. And on the side of the road this American truck came, Black American soldiers driving and I waved them down and amazingly they stopped. And they yelled out, "Where you going?" Because I understood that, vaguely, and I said "Bamberg". They said they could take me to Erlangen, that was only a section of the road and they said they'd take me to Erlangen if that would help. And I thought that would help even if I had to walk the rest of the way, that was nothing to me I walked right across Europe.

So I got off at Erlangen and I started to walk and I came to a point there was a road check there, there was American police, a German constabulary officer and a soldier. And there a fire there and they standing around a fire because at that time it was fairly cool, I stopped and started to talk. Talk, what could I talk? And could say where you going and I understood, and I told them Bamberg. And they say why am I walking? I could explain that I deliver a vehicle to Nuremberg and I couldn't get a lift back soon enough and so I decided I could hitchhike. I told them I worked for the Americans. In that time, you try to do your best and hoping you get away with it. And the officer was very good, he believe me and all this. Because he see on me American gear, and it was illegal, like, he could have got me into trouble. But the soldier he was circling me he didn't... he wasn't sure, but he couldn't overrule the officer. Very lucky he wasn't the other way around.

Anyway this German truck comes, they wave him down, identification and all that. And this German police they ask if they take me, where they going, Bamberg and all this well, could you take him, I could work it out what they say. And they refused, they can't and all this, and the Yank ripped the door open and said, "Get in!" And I jumped in. And the German were cursing, that was a German civilian

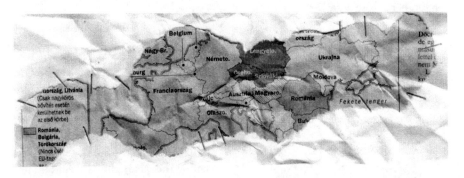

truck, see? Cursing. He took off and they were talking among each other saying that they think I'm in Berlin in with the Yanks, things like that. They never offer me a cigarette, they didn't have a nice thing to say. Describing me pretty miserable and all this, I imagine. I couldn't talk to them in German, but I knew they were discussing me, and they thought I couldn't understand. They thought I might be speaking American or something like that.

And I arrived in Bamberg at night. And I got in there and the yard was in darkness. And I knock on the door. Dead. Nothing. So what am I going to do? They weren't there any more, I could tell, it was different. And then I recalled where I worked, where the actual workshop was. So I went to the workshop where we worked and that was still working for the same mob, see? And there was a Latvian or Lithuanian night watchman and I walked in to my delight the place was still there under the control of the same unit. And I said to that guard there, the Lithuanian and I told him that I was working here in the shop and I went back home and now

I came back. And then he put on an act, you know, he was going to call the police. Because he say, "You could be a Russian spy", things like that you know. And I think I'm going to have to knock him over with a chair, something like that, I'm not going to go. And then he change his attitude, and he said he was only joking. And I thought, "You silly bastard you don't think I'm waiting here you call the police? All this way I came, I'm not going to go".

I stayed there at the workshop. Our unit went to Straubing, and I had to get in touch with them, would they make an effort to get from Straubing with a vehicle, to come and get me? I got no paper, no money, no nothing. I ended up I was able to get on the phone, I had their details to be able to ring up and I said to this other Hungarian and I told him what happened, he was begeistert [thrilled]. He said,

"Stay there Laci I'll send you a vehicle," and he sent up an American weapons carrier, a Dodge. Anyway one driver came and picked me up and took me to the new set up in Straubing. It was good.

And I went and I had no paper and I found out at that time was already, identification card was established everybody had to have it, and the refugees had to have a Displaced Person card. I didn't want that, I wanted the identity card. So I worked there for a while and done my job, travelled in the truck and worked in the workshop, and all this, and I become restless.

Everybody had this card with fingerprint, you know it was an amazing thing in Germany this identification card, and I can't see here what they have against it to use it, identifying fingerprints what's that got to do with you privacy? Then I approached Herr Moeller, Captain Moeller.

And what he did, he was in very good terms with the Military Governor, he was in very good terms with other people and he got on to one of the girls working there, a young lady, Fraulein Ushi, and Fraulein Ushi came she took me to this German office you know where they issue identification card, and I got one, eventually. It took a while because this officer, the chief of the office, he resisted and Fraulein Ushi, I can still recall her voice. Fraulein Ushi said, "Das ist sehr wichtig," this is very important, it comes from the Military Governor and so on, and if he doesn't give it me the governor going to interfere. And I don't know in what way of course, but anyway I finished up with it. He thought he had a case I won't have a photo, but I had a photo already made up, ready to go. Anyway, he took my fingerprint, he typed it out, except my name they spelt it the wrong way instead of Lascsik, they spell it Lasczik. But I said I'm not going to take it back and ask him for another one.

After a while I left, I go to Holland, I walked there. Because I was crazy! I didn't like it I was in the mines there. I had it good in Germany so I walked back to Germany. I went back to Regensburg. Because my original job was still there.

I got back to Germany in' 49. And I got back, and I crossed the border illegally. Just walking across. And then I caught a bus, and then I caught a train, and I lost everything I had. I went back to Regensburg, without identification card, and you had to had permission to stay in a certain place, city or whatever. To exist there, to live there. I went there, I was real cheeky and I went to this office and the German there, just before Christmas, a few days before Christmas and I said to him I must get an identification card and he laughed. He said, "It doesn't work that easy". I said, "I got a job here, waiting for me". He said, "What makes you think you should get the job, we'll give it to a German". I said, "That job is existing for me. If I don't get it,

there is no job. Nobody else there". And I think because it was a few days before Christmas, it might have softened his attitude. Filled out the card, picture, fingerprint. I had it again. I was lucky.

What was happening, I thought to myself, I go to America. But everybody wanted to go to America, and we were informed by the Yanks that they going home, the unit, they pulling out. And I been told what you going to do, you be without a job, this is the sort of thing that was happening. And you want to move. And again, I said, "Everybody wants to go to America," and I said, "Why not Australia?" I don't know why.

In a way it was a bit of defiance, everybody was going to America, well I put Australia and if I don't like it, I still make it to America. There was Australian commission in Schweinfurt, I had to go to Schweinfurt, and that was again a Military Camp where the Commission was. Applied, you fill out a form and you get interviewed and all this. When you come to Australia you had to have a complete record of your health, you been x-rayed, you been examined naked. And everything, you record, police, if you have any criminal record. That makes you think now, these people coming in the boats and all this, and they expect to be let free straight away. We had to go and prove it that we are

healthy, we were OK. That's fair enough, that the government wants to see that they not importing criminals, or disease or something, and spreading it here.

You had to go to the hospital, get through the test. And then they would announce if you were accepted…I think they write a letter, or they tell me when I left when to come back and report with all the things ready to leave, because from there on in they take you down to the train. All you had to do was come back, board the trucks to take you out to the railway station. Once you got everything done you pretty good. This all took a couple of weeks. Made my decision and a couple of weeks later I'm on the train. I felt alright. I said to myself, "If it doesn't work out, I just leave, I go somewhere else". I did it before, why not?

We boarded in Schweinfurt and the train took us to Italy, a place near the Adriatic Sea. And that was a camp, a lot of people there too. Refugees everywhere. In Europe at this time there were camps all over Europe. People living in them. We stayed in this Mediterranean place we were only a week, perhaps three days or four days. You had a medical examination, mainly that you had no disease, sexual disease, like. Then you went to Capua, near Naples.

In Capua, the accommodation was like a few things put together like an African… lean to [laughs]. Two or three of us were sleeping in there. But I felt good, yeah. I was 24, making a new life with no family, on my own. I didn't think it was brave. I didn't feel brave never in my life. I just took it as it comes. Just, what else could you do?

The train was going down to Naples, we got out of the train and straight onto the ship. Together there was about 4 or 5 Hungarians. And from then, we go to Naples, boarded a ship General Stewart Heinzelman, ex-USA troop transport. Well, it was very clean, very nice and the men were separated from the females. I think the ship carried on it 1100 migrants, they were all kinds. Nice facilities, shower and everything. You can clean and all that. It would be perhaps thirty to a cabin. And, when we leaved Naples, put what ever gear you had in the cabin, put on the bed. They called, we race up we leaving the Naples harbour and we raced up, watch the ship slowly move away from the side.

It was nice in a way, I wasn't greatly concerned because I was young, you see and I was…even when I was out here I wasn't very concerned because I thought whatever it is, I can handle it. I did handle other things. I didn't feel sad to be going away from Europe because I didn't think that was the final thing in my life. I thought maybe, I didn't know.

And the food was very good. You had your food standing at least the grownups did. They just had these long tables and on the tables there is plates, and you had twenty or thirty people or even more on the one table, standing up. Because there was no room to sit. I didn't mind it, that was nothing, there was plenty to eat, there was ice cream and coffee, everything. But after when the sea got rough and I reduced my intake and then I had one friend, he worked in the American kitchen too, and he bought some American food. I could eat that. Like crumbed steak and things like that, just like home.

But all the trip, I worked. I got a job and many others did too. Well the idea was they claimed at that time although the United Nations paid for that, or the International Refugees Organization it was at that time. The United Nation Relief and Rehabilitation Organization ceased, and the International Refugee Organization took over. I worked. Because the Navy claimed – I don't know whether the IRO agreed to that – if you do the work like a crew was doing, they can take more migrants, see. Instead of carrying more crew, they got migrants doing it for nothing. I mean, it would have been if they got more crew, less migrants, and they would have to pay the crew. There was people refused and they locked them up. There was mention officially that some refused, and they said they give them over to Australian authorities, they refuse work and all this.

And done painting, like it's nothing to do with... like its crew maintenance.

But still, we didn't mind. Would have been better off on the deck and watch the fish but still. We on our way.

Aranykulcs minden ajtóba beillik
A golden key fits every door
(Hungarian proverb)

ZITA (I)

I don't have any childhood memories. I was never a child. Memories of Hungary – I don't have much, a couple of things, I was only seven when we left.

I was a very disciplined child; I mean Mother let go more than I ever did, with her hands, wooden spoon, that sort of thing.

My maternal grandmother was a jolly old woman, she was tall, she had a big tummy, and I remember when she was laughing it was going up and down. There's only one photo of her somewhere, she's just accidentally in the photo. She always wore black. And a white long apron from her waist to her feet. And a scarf on her head. Her hair was white as far as I can remember, in a bun. Not very thick. She had so many kids she didn't know what to do with...she had nine children. And then they all had their children. You can imagine. She was a tall woman, probably the same as you. And she always wore black. In those days, she lived in a country place, you know, in a village, and when they got married they just all went into black. And they had a scarf over their heads, pulled their hair back in a bun, and covered up in a bloody scarf.

Actually they weren't peasants at all. My maternal grandfather worked for the railway. They were workers, they weren't land cultivators, although he did have a vineyard, it was his – he didn't work it for someone else.

My grandfather I remember just barely, he died when I was four years old. He had a moustache, a long handle bar moustache and he smoked a pipe. I can't remember him very well. I remember when he died though. Everybody got together at the house and of course they laid them out in the country, in one of the rooms in the back in a coffin with the lid off. And there was a mirror on the wall, big, and it was leaning forward and it was covered in black, and I was told not to go in there, so what do you think? I wanted to have a look at him. I wasn't scared or anything, I probably poked him. He was white as a sheet for obvious reasons, he didn't smell, he was just laid out in his best Sunday best. And there he was. Of course I got into trouble for going in, but anyway. I was always getting into trouble. I got so many hidings you wouldn't believe.

Mother didn't want to marry a village person, she wanted…see by that time, when she was a teenager, fourteen, fifteen, magazines, glamorous magazines, Budapest fashion, cars, theatre and all everything. That's what she wanted, she wanted the bright lights. So, she went when she sixteen, and then she went to, to an apprentice, dressmaker. She went to Budapest. She met someone, a girl, and I think she moved in with her. Or she worked at dressmaker or designer, it was a big place, wasn't a back yard thing. It must have been a designer that they learned from. To learn the trade.

And then she was going out with, she met, one of your grandfather's brothers, Jozsi. And then, she was quite happy with, knocking around with him, till my Dad came on the scene and poor Joe never got a look in after that. She thought Dad was gorgeous.

Under Horthy, life was pretty rotten for most people. Miklos Horthy, the regent, he was an arsehole and your grandmother worships him to this day, because he looked so nice on a white horse. Well, anyway, so the reason was that my grandmother, Dad's mum, didn't like Mother, was because Mother talked Dad into not giving his pay packet home, and of course she wasn't a Catholic. He needed some money to dress himself a little bit more respectable. So she made a glamour puss out of him. Of course he liked it. Nothing but the best after that.

I think he was a mechanic at that time, and then somehow he got that job with this aristocrat. I don't know very much about that, they didn't say very much, the only thing I know, he became the aristocrat's companion, would you believe, not just his mechanic that just looks after cars, like chauffeur, not just a plain chauffeur, not like that. They went shooting together. Shooting and rooting and whatever the case may be! [laughs]. He got used to the good life. He liked it. He was taking him everywhere that he went, Dad went. By then of course, we lived in Sölt, a little one horse town, probably about five hundred people, I never been there, but I was born there.

Your grandmother wanted a boy. Because it was the thing for the first one to be a boy. I was not wanted. She wanted a boy, with me. My father called me 'Babi' it was 'baby', that's all, it wasn't a boy's name. I was told that I was ugly when I was first born, but Mother didn't even want to look at me because I wasn't a boy, fair dinkum. And she told me this, yeah! Mother said that I looked like an ugly monkey when I was born. Anyway, but Dad said, "Ugly monkey or no ugly monkey, we're going to love her anyway". I worshipped the ground he walked on. He understood me. He and I could talk. We could talk.

Mum was on very good terms with a sister-in-law, Jozsef's wife, Dad's brother's wife, Ilonka, and they're the ones that had a girl my age, seven days older I think, my cousin. I'm not sure; I've got it written down somewhere. So anyway, they got on like a house on fire, and they were always going shopping together, and we

were kids dragged along. Plenty of money, never wanted for anything. We never wanted for anything. I mean, one thing I must admit, Mother had the best of everything. She worked, she did some sewing and I don't know how or when, I never saw her, I never saw her sewing. But she said she did, I think she did. I never wanted for anything. Dad always made extremely good money from his job. I always had lovely clothes, beautiful shoes, best of food… She was a damn good provider, she was. More so than Dad at certain times after the war…Dad wouldn't touch certain menial work.

I remember some air raids when we were perhaps gone shopping into town with Mother, in Budapest. We were going shopping in Budapest in Váci Utca [Váci Street], very upmarket. Having lunch and coffee and cakes, beautiful cakes and all

that sort of thing. The cafe scene. And then the air raids came and I remember going for shelter under Mount Gelért you know under the castle, Buda Castle?They called them bunkers, but they were cells. Not just us, you know when the sirens went and everybody had to go to the nearest shelter. I remember that. You could hear the boom, boom, boom, around them, there was bombing, there was shooting and that sort of thing. I remember coming out, the attack was over and the siren went and everybody came out...I remember, not so much in Budapest but in the country, when the planes came, the Americans and the Brits, little, tiny little planes high above you and the sun caught their wings and they were glittering in the sunlight and there were puffs of smoke around them as they discharged their guns and bombs and going and then they were gone. They were very high up, like little flies.

When they started dragging the Jews away, I remember there was an elderly Jewish couple living across the hall from us and they were dragged away and I remember they had the overcoats on, it must have been winter, and they had the yellow star patched on them. They sort of herded them. They got them all together and they were pushing them, and they virtually were gone in the clothes that they stood in. And you could see in groups of tens and twelves they were herded on the street, they were herded by somebody or other, and I don't remember whether they were Hungarian military, just men in uniform. I was so young, I was only six. But I remember that.

Dad was still in the army. He was called into the army and there again he had a bus and then he was supposed to evacuate the officers, and so forth and their family could go with them, and anyway Mother and Dad were up in Budapest and they got the city kids like us, and took them down to the country of course where it was always safer. Then they went back. It was in Györszemere, at Grandmother's mostly and even there you went into bunkers dug out in the country as well. The only thing I carried with me was that little doll, the one with the one arm. She had a flower girl dress, but that was discarded somewhere along the line. That's the only thing I have from my childhood. A little porcelain one or she's made out of plaster. I still have it. I wouldn't go anywhere without that.

I remember when we escaped being in the bus, how we got in there buggered if I know... I remember going in the bus, and I remember this German motorbike with the side car, just like you see in films, coming down towards us with the arms and legs waving, yeah they were waving, both of them. He had a pillion passenger too, sidecar passenger, whatever. And they were both waving saying, "The Russians are coming. The Russians are coming!" And I remember Dad took evasive action, and it was

winter and the fields were frozen, rock solid. It was December, I was seven and a half, it was Christmas Eve. I remember it was a moonlit night it was bright just like daylight, I think it was a full moon. And Dad drove across the field, humpity bump, and somehow we ended up at Grandmother's in Győrszemere. We were heading west, towards Vienna, heading out. And of course I think the Russians were in Vienna, weren't they? They were coming down.

And then we went across there and we, there was a little Christmas tree too in the bus 3 foot high or something like that maybe even smaller. And we spent Christmas Eve – some of Christmas in the bus. Anyway so, from the time we went across the fields I don't have recollection until we ended up in Austria, but it could have been the border to Switzerland... anyway... I remember like a horseshoe shaped quarry; tall, dugout, deep as big as the backyard, perhaps even bigger... about thirty metres long and it was protected, there was only one way in. Dad picked that because it was safe. We must have got there at night to get off the road. And, on three sides it was protected and so it was very safe. And of course he had his co-driver. I remember the next morning we woke up at dawn, and there were all these soldiers around us with guns drawn, machine guns or whatever they used. Big guns. Dozens of them, dozens of soldiers with guns drawn. I didn't think one way or the other, so Dad said, "What's this?" You know, he probably said, "Oh shit...," and they ordered the driver out and the co-driver too and there was just us. There weren't many of us. They bundled up Dad and his co-driver and they confiscated both buses, and made us get out. They wanted to take the men away.

Dad was saying to us, "What will happen to you?" And of course Mother with her big mouth, you know, saying in Hungarian of course, you know, "These are very nice looking soldiers, I don't think they going to shoot us. They look so nice and so intelligent". Turned out there was a Hungarian-American lieutenant and he understood it! Just happened to be there. For once in her life she didn't put her foot in it. So in the distance about five K's away, it was the lowlands, and in the distance you could see a farmhouse, and Dad said what's going to happen to us, his family? And Mother said, "Don't worry about us, when they let you out, you're going to find me in that farmhouse". And she pointed across the field and off we went with a small suitcase, walking across the fields. The soldiers weren't interested in us.

So what did happen... is that they took Dad away and his co-driver, I've got a photo of him somewhere, he ended up in Townsville cutting cane.... And Mother, I remember we had a suitcase, a brown suitcase of belongings, and we just started trotting across the fields. The eiderdowns and other things stayed in the bus – they

 took it, with Dad, where? Buggered if I know where, 'cause that was all luggages underneath it in the luggage compartment, wasn't in the bus. I don't know where they took Dad, away. They arrested him and took him away.

And we went across the fields, Mother and I just the two of us. She knocked on the farmhouse door and the woman who was there was about seven or eight months pregnant. I don't know where her husband was he must have been dragged away as well somewhere along the line, she was very pregnant and she needed help in the house and she gave us shelter, Mother helped with the washing and cleaning, and we lived there for a while. Probably six weeks, not for long. Mother was making her clothes and she was washing. The woman was very pregnant. I think she had the baby while we were there...and then Dad came for us in the bus, with our stuff still in the bottom of the bus – they didn't need it, why would they want poor old refugees things? So they let him go, and he came for us.

Somehow he had endeared himself with the Hungarian thing among the American military, and he probably told them he needed the buses for something or other. After they confiscated the bus they said, "Look with your bus, you are going to carry entertainers for the troops." And we fell into a pot of gold. So we went to Germany then.

So he came to pick us up and we went. And then they gave us...they took us to Weiden, and gave us a home ...I think we might have gone to Weiden first, and then to Bayreuth. We were there for five years. Mother was making clothes for the

American soldiers'...officer's wives. I was going to school in Bayreuth, in a German school; I had to learn German from scratch. You know what kids are like, if nobody talks anything else around you either sink or swim, you got to pick it up. Then, I did my entrance examination for grammar school, high school, and Dad was carting the troops entertainers, you know like Glenn Miller and Tommy Dorsey, Andrews' Sisters, all over. That McNamara he was the secretary of state or something in the Nixon administration, he was there, he was a general, he was in Bayreuth and Mother was making clothes for his wife. And all the other officers' wives.

We had heaps of stuff, papers, stockings, food and cigarettes, you know? All the things that people didn't have. In the war, people were starving and Mother and I had the best of everything. That, I cannot take away from her, the two of them. Anyway, it was fine, but there I was the foreigner, "die Ausslander" [the outlanders] they called us. We lived in that house...I'd like to go back there I still remember the house, I could find my way back there. The Haertls, they had a grocery shop, they

had a three-story house and in the roof, the top floor, like an attic apartment, we had that, we rented that off them. The address was Carl Schuller Strasse, vierundswanszig; 24 Carl Schuller Street. I like to go back there.

So we just lived there happily ever after, I mean it was the most famous musical town in all of Germany. Wagner, Liszt, all buried there.

So I was quite happy there. I really liked to live there. We used to go skiing. We went to the Black Forest mostly with Dad and the Haertls.

And Frau Haertl, she was so clean. They had wooden stairs, they had three floors, she was so clean, painfully clean, and of course they had the grocery shop downstairs, so there again, we could buy things from them, you know...at cost. And she was so clean, three stories and the stairs were about a metre wide, the wood was white, scrubbed so white. She cleaned it every week. Out of a bucket. It was so clean, you could eat off it. She also cleaned her toilets out of that bucket!

And Saturday night…the national food of Bavaria was knödle and schweinenbraten – it's like roast pork but with a dumpling. Knödle was made of potatoes, heaps of potatoes. You have to clean them, then soak them over night in water so they won't go brown. All those potatoes she'd grated it. And you mix it with plain flour and then you brown like croutons in fat, and you put it in the middle of it like a dumpling as big as your fist and then you boil it in water and it's beautiful, absolutely beautiful. But! She used the same bucket to soak the potatoes that she cleaned the loo and the stairs with! I never forget that. Oh, she cleaned it out, of course, but it was the same

bucket! She was a nice woman, she was. But she was so clean, but I mean all over. It was a big house, it wasn't one of those big houses, palatial, it was in town, they were narrow houses, tall ones, like you see in the movie, traditional German houses. The houses stuck to one another but the house next door was bombed. Like a townhouse. The house next door got a full blast, so nothing was left of it. But her house was still standing.

Immigration in Europe started all over the place. There was so many people in Germany. Everybody from the Eastern Bloc, anywhere there was a war, everybody went to Germany. It was safe. It was still the best place to go to. It's ironic, it's where everybody fled to. For the people who didn't commit any crimes, if you were not

a Jew, if you didn't steal from anyone, because that was all punishable by death, if you didn't offend anyone and you just minded your own business, life was OK. They all thought Hitler was wonderful. And they weren't Nazis. Seventy percent of the people weren't Nazis.

People were flooding into Germany from everywhere. There were camps. I think what happened then, the

Americans started to withdraw from there, and then Dad lost his job, he was without work. The Americans had withdrawn, and things changed. That particular troop had withdrawn. The type of work he wanted to do just wasn't available, and then immigration worldwide started. I had everything. Dad was doing beautifully in Germany with the Americans.

To tell you the truth, I don't know why we left. Because you know I mean, you were an outsider, they called you outsiders, here they called them migrants, there they called anybody different, "Ausslanders". Now these days they call them Guest Workers. I think they went, well just for a fresh start. Don't forget Germany was flat, it was flattened. Cologne and Bayreuth, the way it looked, it was just…pathetic. I think we would have done all right in Germany as well…life was good. People were starving, we weren't. I mean, Dad was working, Mother was working. In those days, Argentina was like Australia is now. It was the best place to go. Argentina was heaven. They were wealthy, rich and one day Australia will end just like they did, oh yes. It can't last, it never does. There was America, and Australia. All Europeans wanted to go to America. So immigration started. Then, three places Dad put in applications. One is Australia, one was Argentina one was America. Germany had to be rebuilt, there was no money, so they couldn't look after all those refugees they just couldn't. They had enough problems of their own. Which is understandable. They flattened the whole country, virtually. On the same token, Dad probably would have ended up with something there, but we went. Dad and millions of others…

The Russians were invading Hungary and we couldn't go back. Communism set in, people were murdered, they were hung, all sorts of things! All the wealth was confiscated, they stole the wristwatch off your arm, they drank out of toilets, they were pigs, peasants, they stole anything that was movable.

We waited for the emigration papers, the one that came in first and Australia came in first and that was it, simple as that. I knew nothing about Australia, I didn't even know where it was. We had to go to…Bamberg? Nuremberg? I don't know, someplace, to a holding camp. So we had to pull up sticks, put everything away and then went to a holding camp somewhere…I don't know and of course you had to be processed by the UN. And then we became DPs [Displaced Persons] officially.

And then we were in the camp. Bloody shithouse, four sheets, around you, your only privacy. Noisy. People farting and snoring, having sex, screaming. And then we were processed. Physicals, injections, interviews. Look it's not the way it is now. What they doing now it's a pushover. They were so strict, they interview you

and interview you again. All sorts of x-rays and blood tests…anyway, so then we got shipped into a train, in a cattle car! With straw on the floor? Cattle cars. No seats. And then they sent us down to Benogelia in Italy, near Naples. We met up with a lot of them. We were not in Italy for very long, only about a month. Same sort of conditions, the food wasn't so bad. I think they had not Italian food, but continental cooks, you know? All refugees, pitched in, so they could pinch something for their families, probably. Any advantage. There were cleaners, labourers…then to Naples and getting on that ship the "Fairsea". Which had an Italian crew. And they pinched all the food that was provided by the United Nations for transportation of refugees.

The quarters were excellent, there again. Most women…they were…hundred in a dormitory, men the same, hundred and twenty. Your grandmother and I were in a cabin of six. It was just, the way it turned out. And we had our own shower; they all had multiple showers, dormitory showers. We didn't have fresh water, had to shower in salt water, for a month. As I said, the crew pinched the good food and they gave us the slop. I mean it was

unedible. It was shocking. The way things were prepared was no salt, no pepper, no colour, no nothing. It was tasteless.

It was well set out, the ship was clean but the men were separated, and the women and children were separated. Half the passengers were sea sick, were vomiting right left and centre; they had diarrhoea and shit right, left and centre. Oh it was marvellous!

We saw Dad on deck, and we spent our days together and had our meals together. Actually the single men were dumped down the bottom of the ship where it was pretty bad. So, twenty eight days of that, and of course mother endeared herself with the captain…. I don't think she did anything terribly provocative. She flirted of course…. I mean she had a great wardrobe and she played it to the hilt, she would dress for the occasion, of course, amongst all the other disadvantaged, ragged displaced people, she was a fashion plate! It didn't make her very popular.

I remember the equator; that was interesting. I mean Mother made herself a three piece outfit for the sea voyage – back in Germany, she was getting her wardrobe ready, you see, for the sea voyage – shorts, a bra top and a skirt, especially for the equator thing, of course when you cross the equator by ship they have a ceremony. They cover you with foam, soap foam, they cover you in water, they toss you in the pool, all sorts of things…a celebration of the equator – they still do it! Neptune, somebody gets dressed up as Neptune. And you know it's a lot of fun. Of course there again Mother got hosed and of course what she did is ripped her skirt off dramatically, ready to throw it and there she was, in her little shorts and a bra top. Everybody else got tossed in clothes and all, and there she was, prepared. They could get her wet, she was still stylish. I remember that it was a big dramatic moment, of course. That's what Dad liked about her, her style.

I think I must have got the message that things would be alright. Couldn't get any worse, sort of thing. When we tied up in the Suez Canal, portside. Of course the Arabs were trying to sell you everything. They didn't come up on the boat. We bought a bag off one of them. I only chucked it out a little while ago…I might still have it I don't know. It smelled after fifty years, still like camels.

Lots of stairs, there was a pool for the kids but it was a canvas pool, it was a big one. They didn't have swimming pools as such, but they set one up. There was games, they tried to make it as pleasant as possible. The bad part was the food, and the people getting sick right, left and centre…and then we arrived, towards the shores of Australia, Western Australia, Indian ocean. There was a hell of a storm, oh that was a hell of a storm. I remember that of course everybody was forbidden to go on deck. We were down there and the waves were ten stories further up. It was shocking, oh yeah I was scared. I think one or a couple of engines conked out…… then we tied up at Perth. Immigration came on board and customs came on board, and they came around with us to Sydney and Newcastle, processing people the whole time.

And I had a dream that I was an old man. I tell you exactly
I looked like. I looked like I am now, except skinnier, and
older in the face. I must have been very old and I went
back. I was away all my life. I dreamt ... ust came
home, and ... somewhere. ... e, and I
looked a ... we lived like relations and
neighbour ... here, I don't know the dialogue
but I kne ... t my family, and all this, and
everywher ... le shaking their head. Didn't
know. I w ... o the other and nobody I knew.
And then ... ber
meself wa ... nny
as anythi ... s a
habit at ... the
houses with b ... ked
along touching ... t I
did walking f ... my
relation or a ... I
been different ... to
know, nobody. ... was
shocked. It wa ... was
only lying, but I was all dres ... d in the
middle of the room, nobody ... lled out
"Never!" I yelled 'NEVER! NEV ... VE!" Real
... upset, sho ... somewhere
... od in that ... elled out
... f any one ... "Never!
... king about it I don't know how long. And
... , no way it's just not on". And well it
... my life...I only spent 19 years in Hungary.

The biggest single obstacle in building a united family of the Australian nation is
the perpetuation of the mistaken belief that Australia has always been a homogenous
nation. (Grassby, 1990, p. 5)

CHAPTER 8

AUSTRALIAN IMMIGRATION

When my parents departed for Australia, their European epoch ended forever. When they entered Australia, it was an unsettling and to some, a difficult and unstable period. This chapter examines the immigration context into which my parents and other post-war migrants entered. In the following chapter, issues of ethnic identity that are pertinent to this inquiry will be discussed in order to build a contextual foundation for the second suite of narratives.

Although the context of this study focuses on immigration during the post-war period of the twentieth century, it is essential to provide a framework for the ideologies that gave rise to the political decisions of the time. What follows is a concise review of the history of Australian immigration to the post-war period, followed by a brief representation of the settling-in period for the migrants. Subsequent to that, contemporary political perspectives are discussed.

HISTORICAL CONTEXTS

Since 1788, when 160000 convicts and officials arrived on our shores, Australia has been a country populated by immigrants who have all attempted to impose their character and identity upon this, their adopted nation. The official line during colonial times was that Australia becomes 'another England', and Australian historians have persistently emphasized the notion that the First Fleet brought only Englishmen to settle in Australia (Izzard, 2011). There were in fact, twelve nationalities represented on that first fleet, including the English and Irish, and also Italians, Spaniards, Poles, Sri Lankans and Africans (Grassby, 1990). Until the 1950s, the Department of Immigration was constantly publicizing the fact that we were 98% British. This was far from the truth. German Lutherans began settling in South Australia from 1838, and later with the Gold Rush, more people arrived from Europe, the US and China. Pacific Island Kanakas came in 1863 as labourers, as did small groups of Europeans.

During the 19th century there was a significant increase in the arrival of free settlers and during the Gold Rush epoch, the Chinese were the largest non-British group to arrive (Izzard, 2011). In the 1850's there were race riots between white people and the Chinese, and the racial mixtures were seen as the likely causes (Lewis & Gurry, 2001). Decades later, Australian nationalism was based on the racial vision of people who were white, had no criminal record and no religious differences (Izzard, 2011).

The White Australia Policy was born with Federation in 1901 and was to persist for the next seventy years. It was implemented largely in order to curtail the immigration of Chinese and Kanakas. Even though politicians of the day were wholly united regarding the ideology of a White Australia, they were not in agreement regarding how to achieve this. Some wanted racial bans, and others a dictation test, while all wanted to ban natives of Africa and Asia. A dictation test was eventually introduced under the auspices of the Immigration Restriction Act. It was a fifty-word complex passage test, which the immigrant had to 'pass' in order to gain entry to Australia and persisted until 1958. It was racist in its intent and its result, since it was based upon the racial superiority of White Anglo Celtic peoples (Lewis & Gurry, 2001; Rintoul, 2002). It was used on any 'undesirable White person' and could be given in any language that they could not understand. These ideologies were also prevalent in other First World nations at this time (Colic-Peisker, 2011).

The Immigration Restriction Act appalled Japan since Japan was an ally of Britain, and saw itself as racially superior to the rest of Asia (Lewis & Gurry, 2001). All of the Kanakas, who had been introduced as cheap labour in order to cut cane in Northern Queensland for forty years, were returned to their South Sea Island homes. More than 7000 were deported until 1906 when a Royal Commission determined that some were permitted to stay (Izzard, 2011). Some Chinese who were working in Australia at this time were also allowed to stay, but at a great cost; their wives were deported. One consequence of the White Australia Policy and the subsequent removal of the Kanakas was that White labour was used on the cane fields for the first time; Australia was the first country in the world to employ white people for such menial tasks. This decision was due to the Australian politicians' distaste of the legacy of slavery that was prevalent in the United States (Grassby, 1990).

During World War II Australia had a population of only 7 million and this was a turning point for the country. Prime Minister Chifley commenced a population expansion program, nicknamed 'Populate or Perish', arguing that Australia had to grow as a nation in order to survive. The country needed to be developed and the population needed to increase, due to the rapidly declining birth-rate since the depression of the 1930s. Therefore Australia had to increase its numbers of migrants. The champion of this scheme was Australia's first Minister for Immigration, Arthur Calwell. His aim was to increase immigration by 1% per year of the total population. This meant that in 1945, the quota was about 70000 a year, and fearing a public outcry, Calwell promised Australians that migrants would only be allowed to enter if there were jobs here for them. The union movement accepted this and the 'New Australians' started to flood in. White, preferably British people were the most acceptable candidates.

At this time 90% of immigrants were from Britain, and the remaining 10% were from Northern Europe (Lewis & Gurry, 2001). There were restrictions against those from Southern and Eastern Europe until after World War II when it became clear British immigrants were scarce. The government's solution to this problem was a larger scale immigration program. This scheme, apart from the usual Anglo-Celtic immigrants included Displaced Persons [DPs] from different parts of the world. There were 8 million refugees after the war and Calwell agreed to take some of these, including my parents and grandparents. He wanted only hardworking Europeans who looked like Australians of British descent (Pagone & Rizzo, 1990).

The emphasis of this rebuilding program was on development of the country and population growth, or as it was termed then, the 'national need' (Phillips & Houston 1984). Australia needed men, especially young men, who were able to do any type of manual work. The country also needed plenty of healthy migrant children and their descendants, in order to increase Australia's population and contribute to the future of their new country (Ambrosy, 1984; Jayamaran, 2005).

To be sure that the immigrant was allocated to the right place of work according to areas of need, each immigrant had to sign a two-year contract with the Australian Government, which stipulated that the new Australian must take any type of work anywhere in the host country. In my father's case, the contract was to work in the blast furnace of the BHP in Newcastle, New South Wales (NSW), in January of 1950. My grandfather sought work independently and found it as an airplane mechanic, also in Newcastle. Such opportunities were conditional; the migrant was required to assimilate to the greater Australian society (Lewis & Gurry, 2001).

Postwar Migrants: Settling In

Calwell stipulated that Australia only wanted hard-working people from the Baltic nations of Latvia, Estonia and Lithuania. He wanted them unskilled, since their qualifications would not be recognized in Australia, and he wanted them blonde-haired and blue-eyed, so that they would look like Australians. When the migrants first arrived they were sent to migrant camps to be processed and to await their assignments. Bonegilla in Victoria was the largest of these, followed by Greta, in the Hunter Valley just north of Newcastle, NSW. The timber and corrugated iron huts were a first Australian residence for many of these traumatized people. For my mother and her family, whose first residence was indeed Greta camp, the conditions were seen as 'unliveable' and they were motivated to leave as soon as they could. My father was sent to Bathurst and received his assignment there. English lessons were compulsory, and 'Advance Australia Fair' (now Australia's national anthem) was played every morning at dawn over the loudspeakers.

The periods of confinement were variable. Some migrants left after weeks, months or even years, until they could find independent housing. The men were sent to work at various locations, and were often away for extended periods. The women stayed behind, attending English classes and school, and for the most part, running the camp. For many immigrants, arriving in a migrant camp like Greta was a relief. There was food and it was warm and comfortable. But most of all it was safe. In the case of my parents, neither of whom enjoyed camp life, they left after the shortest possible period, never to return.

The New Australian was very much the underclass of Australian society, marginalized and socially segregated. They were the 'wogs' and 'dagoes', the working class – they got the dirtiest, filthiest jobs that no one else would touch and then, worked longer, worked harder and experienced a measure of success, yet even this was resented (Tsiolkas, 2013). The wogs became second-class citizens and, "Conflicts arose, too, between immigrant parents and their children, who were carried along in the slipstream of the dominant culture and began to reject their heritage" (Powell, 2002, p. 15). In terms of acceptance by the greater Australian society, it was not a good time for the immigrant. This was certainly the experience of all of the members of my family. However, it is in no small part due to their colonizing efforts, as well as changing world views, that things slowly transformed.

Changing Perspectives

Times, society and politics were changing. By 1960, the White Australia policy was being debated on the streets and in clubs and pubs. The Colombo Plan was introduced by the Menzies government which allowed some Asian students to study at Australian universities. Students and church groups began campaigning against the White Australia policy, branding it immoral (Lewis & Gurry, 2001; Pagone & Rizzo, 1990). Australia started to forge new economic ties with its neighbours and the glaring racism of our immigration policy was at odds with this desire (Izzard, 2011). An active debate between the older and younger generations in Australia was raging.

In 1965, the Australian Labour Party finally eradicated the White Australia policy from its political platform, but the Prime Minister was still opposed to changing it completely. Racist policies were being condemned globally and the immigration policy was stealthily and gradually being abandoned without the consultation of the Australian people. The government of the time realized that if Australia was to have any future economic relationship with Asia, the White Australia policy would have to be abandoned. Australia had to make a guarantee of mutual respect, and was at risk of becoming a marginalized nation like South Africa with its Apartheid policy. Finally in 1972, the reformist Labour Prime Minister Gough Whitlam officially ended the White Australia policy.

At this time, Australia was still predominantly a White nation at the same time as the Communists were triumphing in Vietnam. Many Australians felt we had a duty to assist the refugees from South Vietnam who were fleeing their ravaged country in unseaworthy boats, since our presence in that war had contributed to their refugee status (Whitlam, 2002). These 'Indo-Chinese' as we knew them at that time, were our first boat people and during 1975 to 1995, Australia accepted 200 000 of them. We took more Indo-Chinese than other developed nations, including America, and started to accept the ideology of multiculturalism for the first time in our history. Australia's economy was thriving, our culture was being diversified and enriched, and public policy became one of inclusion rather than exclusion, of multiculturalism rather than racism. It was indeed unfortunate that the reality took longer to develop.

Immigration Policies

The policies associated with immigration throughout Australian society can be summarized as the White Australia Policy from 1901 to 1972; the Assimilation Policy from 1945 to the 1960s; the Integration Policy from the late 1950s to 1972; and the Multicultural Policy from 1972 to the present day and despite a tenuous grasp on multiculturalist ideology globally (Colic-Peisker, 2011), Australia gave it bipartisan support in February of 2011.

The White Australia policy excluded those immigrants that initially were not British and later, were not of white European descent. Asians and Kanakas were the policy's original targets and it is a guiding principle that lingered in Australian politics for the greater part of the twentieth century. It permeated later government policies of assimilation and integration, and has bled into the public consciousness, even whilst governments were proclaiming a robust multiculturalism. Most recently, the current immigration debate has been tarnished with the remnants of an idealized white Australia through the racist rhetoric of politicians during the last 20 years. The past three Coalition (conservative) governments, including the current administration, have also been sullied with suggestions of racism. Clearly White Australia is a legacy that Australians cannot easily discard.

Prior to 1972, when multiculturalism became policy, we were an inward looking nation. During the years of the White Australia policy and assimilation, many Australians referred to Britain as 'home', it was illegal to broadcast in foreign languages unless immediately translated and there was no government assistance for migrant settlers. Indeed, assimilation was not restricted to Australia, it was a fashionable concept globally from the beginning of the twentieth century, and stipulated that ethnic minorities must become like the majority or dominant culture. After World War II in Australia, this meant that all cultural baggage should be left on the docks and be completely abandoned, in order that the immigrant fit a new version of 'normal'. In particular, the immigrant was not to offend or frighten the existing citizens with peculiar customs and languages.

Australian assimilation was a very watered down version, even though there was an Assimilation Division within the Department of Immigration at the time; however it was more of a rhetorical flourish to appease the public. By 1966 Australia's manufacturing workforce was one-third migrant, but there were no interpreting services, programs or networks, and not much to prevent some migrants plunging into poverty. Assimilation was the official policy for all migrants and Indigenous peoples until the 1960s, when Australia signed the International Convention to Eradicate All Forms of Racial Discrimination. Then Indigenous policy moved towards self-determination and migrant policy moved towards Integration, and then onwards to multiculturalism (Jakubowicz, 2002).

In Australia, Integration came after Assimilation during the 1960s when the world was experiencing radical social revolutions. It was a policy whereby tolerance was expanded so that individuals were allowed to retain their group cultures, whilst simultaneously being accepted into society at large. It is suggestive of the division between the private practice of beliefs and culture and the public commitment to the greater society in its social structures. Integration assumed that the first generation migrant would have difficulties 'fitting in', but their children would be absorbed into the wider community. This put a great deal of pressure on second-generation children like myself to move from their parents' culture, since it grudgingly accepts difference and yet adds pressure to change. The policy pays lip service to cultural diversity, whilst expecting assimilation in the long term and subsequent generations. Many in Australia saw this as a good compromise.

Al Grassby was the first politician to encourage Australians to share their heritages, and it was with the Whitlam government that much changed in the Australian consciousness. Grassby said later by way of tribute, "Without Whitlam, nothing would have been possible" (in Powell, 2002, p. 15). With Gough Whitlam's recent passing (October, 2014), it was interesting to note how many tributes lauded his contributions, particularly with respect to cultural reforms. However, this was very controversial at the time, and Grassby was subsequently the only minister to be voted out at the next election in 1974.

Grassby and Whitlam paved the way for Prime Minister Malcolm Fraser to adopt multiculturalism as official policy. Multiculturalism's basis was the belief that societies operate better when all people feel that their cultural beliefs are respected, tolerated, and can be freely expressed, and that they do not have to abandon them in order to be good citizens. The reciprocal responsibility is to accept others' rights to do likewise, whilst being loyal to the structures and principles of Australian society and working in the interests of the Australian nation (Jayaraman, 2005). Under this guiding principle, many key programs and policies were established such as the Special Broadcasting Service [SBS], equity of access and equity of opportunity (Jakubowicz, 2002).

In recent years, almost one quarter of all Australians were born elsewhere, and close to half the population are second-generation migrants, with at least one parent born overseas (Jayaraman, 2005; Sala et al., 2009). Australia is arguably one of the most ethnically diverse countries in the world, deliberately created through immigration. Our migrants have traditionally been seen to be aspirational, to understand the importance of education and possess a robust work ethic. People from non-English speaking backgrounds [NESB] have traditionally been part of a low socioeconomic demographic, however in recent decades they, and their children and grandchildren, have become what one writer calls a new multicultural middle class (Colic-Peisker, 2011).

The efforts of migrants and their offspring have no doubt contributed to the energetic ethnic and assorted identities of Australia as is evidenced by the diversity of cultural practices that Australia is now fortunate to enjoy. However, it is obvious here as it is globally, that many Australians still treat its newcomers with suspicion and disdain. This reality will be more fully discussed in a later chapter, however as is illustrated in the second suite of narratives, many of the issues and experiences discussed in this chapter are indeed at least partially, our experience. Chapter 10 examines theoretical frameworks of ethnicities of first- and second-generation migrants, and when considered together, these two chapters contextualize the narratives that are positioned between them.

...when an immigrant arrives in a new country he is a stranger. One notices the way he speaks, if he speaks the language of the host country at all. He might use paralinguistic (non verbal) vocabulary in his desperation because he has been taught different mores, norms, customs and cultures in his own country.

As a consequence both the host country's people and the newcomers, feel this gap of social distance. (Ambrosy, 1984, p. 7)

GYPSY

My studies are transforming me.

I am learning so many things through my search and discovery mission that my parents and other Hungarians had learnt almost by osmosis in their lived experience of it. It feels as if I am joining them in some way, becoming more like them....

No, that's wrong. My experience is so different to theirs. Rather, it feels as though I am being stitched into them, into the complex and intricate embroidery of Hungarianness. Is that even a word? Hungarianism? Hungarianeity?

Anyway, I am a thread of an entirely different colour and texture, and although the pattern I'm creating looks similar to the traditional ones, it isn't as uniform as the other patterns. My pattern is looser, more unusual; it has elements of something other than what is normally there. It is not the traditional satin stitch that I am becoming, but I feel that I am finally allowing myself to be sewn in.

I knew that there is a lot missing, though.

Although I have been to Hungary once before with Stu, I was strictly a tourist, a complete foreigner. I need to go back and experience the place from an altered perspective. Perhaps if I take my children I will have a different appreciation of the country? I've wondered about this a lot.

But who was I kidding? I need to go with The Oldies, I need to be there with them. But Dad isn't interested, and he won't be drawn on it.

I can't speak the language so I can't read the literature or poetry that is such a large part of the Hungarian culture and which cannot be translated accurately or faithfully. I've read translations before, but something is always lost, of course. And I can't hear myself speak my heritage tongue, this complicated language that is so beautiful. Just like the embroidery, it's so extravagant.

I can do other things though, things that connect me. I listen to the stirring music and become sentimental. Brahms' Hungarian Dance #5 is a playlist top ten, and so is Hungarian Rhapsody # 2 – that's the one that really gets to me. I wonder if it's because its Dad's favorite? I'm not sure why, that piece feels like home.

I make Hungarian food, Mama taught me well. And it's when I cook that feel as though I am linking myself to the traditions of the past (not as good as Mama, but I do OK). At these times, I do feel Hungarian. And I believe that I am intrinsically Hungarian – that my inner self, the core of me is not wholly Australian. I can feel it if I cook and also if I sit particularly still. It's almost as though I can hear it. It's like an underground river that I know is there but cannot see. This has always been a part of me and it is starting to rumble, soundlessly. Like an echo. Like a ghost.

Although I really am Australian and I have thrown my lot in with the locals, that's not where I really am. I just feel too different, too disconnected. And although I know that my awareness of Australian history has certainly been raised by my recent readings, I am still not reconciled with my concrete Australian identity.

So this feeling of in-between-ness is something that I am feeling more acutely. I am betwixt and between the cerebral borders of Australia and of Hungary and this space, this no-man's-land, is a place that I cannot describe, but it's where I feel most 'present'. I don't feel like a hybrid and I don't know where I truly belong. I am starting to wonder whether the tension between these selves will ever be resolved in my head. But I do feel that my journey is as yet unfinished and that by moving forwards I am at least making some sort of psychological progress. At least I can actually mentally support the notion of what it might be like to be Hungarian and what it might be like to be authentically Australian.

What I do know (always the teacher), is that if I was ever going to embody both of these primary parts of my identity, I will have to in the first place, try to assimilate all of the information I have gathered about myself, my family and the country of my heritage. But how should I go about this? And will it work?

Assimilation, a tactic that I know well. I actively used it at the age of 5, 6 and 7 in order to sublimate the real Hungarian me and try to fit into the real Australian them. This was not as instinctive as I've supposed earlier. It is a learned behaviour, utilized in response to negative external social forces. The dictionary says it means to incorporate, to digest, to learn. And that's really what happened to me, whether I liked it or not. I learnt to incorporate myself into the fabric of the larger Australian society and in return it had, after a period of dyspepsia I suppose, learnt to digest me, and almost but not quite, swallow me whole. I am the poster child for Arthur Calwell's master plan – to become one of them (as so many Australians still desire from their immigrant newcomers), to leave the cultural baggage behind with my parents before I began my journey into the life that existed beyond the kitchen.

I thought about how I should go about this for a long time, and in the end it comes down to three things. And although the solutions seem so clear to me now, I couldn't see them at first. What I did always know was that in order for me to continue on my journey I would have to travel down some painful and difficult roads. I have to cross more borders, both metaphorical and real and I have yet more work to do.

*

It is so logical in the end, the solutions so obvious. I have spent many hours searching for answers, and they were in front of me all the time.

I have been an artist for a very long time, not so commercially successful, although I have had my share of commissions, exhibitions and sales. I just never had the time or energy to devote myself totally to my art, although it fulfils me in ways that other things cannot. My creativity has been continuously nurtured, first by my mother, later by my teachers, and later still by my students, who continue to inspire and guide me in my practice. But more than all of this, art has always been an avenue for my psyche to unburden itself, to figure out things intuitively that I consciously cannot. It is a meditative space, a salve for my soul, often revelatory and always a release. So this is where I turned, to the one place where I felt most myself, in order to find my way. I have to draw a map of my journeys, I have to document my discoveries and I have to create my own souvenirs. If I want to fully know something I have to immerse myself in it, visually.

This was my first port of call. The other two journeys seem almost impossible to contemplate and I can't even face them until I have done some 'wet work'. So I began to plan, sketch and make notes. I revisited the transcripts that I had of Mama and Dad's stories. I looked at my own.

I went back to my readings and writings about Hungary and about Australia. I thought about the courage of my parents and grandparents, and the journeys they made halfway around the world. I looked at the family photographs, tracked the family histories back to the 18th century, and I read and read and read.

When it was all in my head, I made some concrete plans. My artistic practice is usually structured in the first instance; I have always had to do my research. I have to know as much as I can before I can let go in the painting, printing and collage processes. It is during the making that I completely change my approach and allow my intuition and imagination free reign. It is at this time in the process that chance and happy accidents can be embraced.

Painting is so wonderfully wet. It is fully sensuous and in that way very liberating. It allows a quiet, meditative space to occur, a stillness that I don't ever experience at any other time or place in my life. It is this stillness that allows for contemplation and for revelation. It is the place where I have my most epiphanic moments.

And so I am able to crystallise the areas that are significant to this story of mine, which include so many stories of so many others. I started with my parents, and with myself, and created portraits in differing styles. By doing the portraits I was able to get inside the characterizations a little more. I started to see my parents and my grandparents more fully, not only as their offspring but also as an appreciative adult audience. I compared their exploits to what I was doing at similar ages and discovered some similarities. Whether these were inherited, shared or coincidental is of little importance. The events connected me to them more fully. At 22, for example, my father started to contemplate a life away from Europe. At the same age I was wandering through Africa on my own nomadic quest which would, like it had him, change me forever. The fact that my parents had had a somewhat nomadic existence resonates with me still. They traversed the world, driven by circumstance; I traverse the world driven by opportunity and desire.

It wasn't until 1991 though, that I had a glimpse of what the immigration process might have been like. It was the year that I dragged my own little family to Canada to pursue a teacher exchange experience for 13 months. To uproot Stu and our two-month-old Remy was not traumatic, since it was our choice, but the experience of living in a foreign country was trying at times, and we didn't have the language issues even in Québec. Ironically, my French is better than my Hungarian.

These thoughts are vibrating through my consciousness as I paint. I am searching for points of reference that are not tied to our ethnicity and that I can relate to as an adult. The fact that I found them is a triumph in terms of making these all-important connections. I am also creating archival documents, and I am documenting the history of my family in Australia, as well as their life before and the reasons for their journeys.

When I completed the portraits, I needed to go further with the whole portrait idea. I have painted the portraits in words, and I want to portray their stories in paint. I realize that the 'voice' of the written word differs from the 'voice' of portraiture in that the two genres communicate in different ways. I remember reading that Leonardo Da Vinci once belittled the art of writing as the inferior cousin of painting since a great painter can describe one's history in a moment. But being neither a great painter nor a great writer, I have to use both. I feel that where language fails, images will succeed. And vice versa.

So I start looking for photographs of my parents in their early twenties, when they were somewhat mature yet still youthful. I decide to recreate their images using block printing, since this is a medium I often use for its plasticity in both execution and result. The act of carving the lino block is reductive – as more is carved away, the image appears, and is finally printed. Because it is a printing process, each block can yield an infinite number of prints, and each of these can be hand-coloured and altered so that they become original works.

I played around with the differing prints until I was satisfied that they were credible likenesses. I didn't merely seek a visual resemblance, but an allegorical portrait as well. That is, the images incorporate symbols and textures, and other visual qualities that tell stories about the characters of the subjects. They profile a likeness, and point towards a life. I am satisfied that I am able to capture what I had interpreted as the essence of them, and their lives. I then turned towards myself.

I have done self-portraits before, and some were accurate likenesses, but I felt that I had to go back to my childhood, since I feel that it was the critical moment in the development of my identity. This was to be a very painful and difficult process. I had to decide what I was going to portray, and how I was going to 'say' it.

Those moments of trauma were indeed life changing for me. And even though this whole process has been somewhat healing, the demons still lurk within, and indeed govern much of my adult behaviour. I am driven because I have something to prove, over and over again. As if by doing so, by being hard-working and successful somebody important will finally take notice. Even though I realize this is somewhat pathetic, my inferiority complex is something I still carry inside of me, like a precious nugget all shiny and worn from being constantly stroked and examined. As I started to examine its roots, I think about this issue constantly.

I felt as though I had to reach out and connect myself to that 7-year-old child, and have a good look at her again. It was here that I started planning for my self-portrait. On a visit down south to my parents' house during a recent school holiday period I decided to revisit the playground of my old infants school. I took my girls and Stu into the playground that day, and I was showing them where my classrooms were, where I played and where I spent 7 years of my life.

I was quite unprepared and in good spirits when I came around the back of the toilet blocks. I turned the corner and was talking to the girls who were asking lots of questions about how I was as a little girl. I looked at Bronte, my younger daughter and realized that she was 7 years old, about the age I always see myself when I remember my childhood.

"And this is the girls toilet," I said, looking at Bronte as she was nodding, urging me to continue. "It's where I...I used to...I used to hide here...," I realized I couldn't go on. From deep within me a raw sorrow slammed upwards and into the back of my head.

As I quietly struggled with it Stu said, "Let it out Lex. Let it go. It's OK. You're safe." Always so in sync with me, Stu knew exactly what was going on.

The girls were bewildered until their father explained. "This is where your mother hid from all the kids who were teasing her when she was little, because she was Hungarian. That's right isn't it Lex?" he affirmed, watching me.

All I could do was nod. I cannot believe that more than 30 years after the events in this place that were to wound me so thoroughly, I could be so affected. Maybe it was having both my children there, but especially Bronte, who looks so like me when I was her age. In the dinginess of that shaded porch, with my hand resting on the cold metal handrail, I felt wretched and totally unprepared for the emotions that were billowing inside. I felt deep, deep sadness and dejection. I felt small. I felt sorrow and regret.

But I was also incredibly, lividly, furiously, angry. I was angry at myself for my weakness, my lack of courage. I was angry at those cruel children and their narrow-minded parents. And I was angry at the teachers for failing to take an interest, let alone protect me.

"Ah", I thought to myself upon reflection, "Now we're getting somewhere." Anger is productive.

And even though I still feel so pathetic, I realize that I need to push all of these feelings into an artwork. I need to describe them visually so I can let them go.

The painting I created is called "7 years" inspired by a Norah Jones song of the same name. It describes a little girl, innocent and alone. She looks up at the world with a mixture of pathos and expectation, already emotionally drained, so young. She doesn't necessarily mind being alone, in fact that is what she truly wants: to be left alone, to not be hassled any more. Behind her is the scene of much of her misery – the playground – with her safe haven, the porch near the toilet blocks directly behind her, standing there like a sentinel, stoic and secure. This is a portrait of not belonging, of acute alienation and of confusion.

Much of my memories of this place are sensual. I can still smell the acrid waft of urine that drifted over from the boys' toilets. I can feel the cool of the shade on the skin of my bare arms in the summer and the cold metal of the handrail under my hands. The wall of the toilet block where I used to stand, my little hand up against it, peering around the corner to make sure the coast was clear. I can still feel its texture in my memory, slightly prickly and warm, it is a vivid memory. In the painting the little girl stands resolute, resigned to her fate, miserable and completely abandoned.

Making this picture is a catharsis. Being able to visualize myself outside of myself allows me to separate my self from the issues. One of the overwhelming impressions I have is that the girl in the painting is rather a wretched figure, from the forlorn expression on her face to the crisp bows in her hair, to her undone shoelace.

Am I still seeking sympathy? Is it indeed a ridiculous notion that a woman of my age should still be so obsessed by the events of her (long past) childhood? Good questions and ones that I ponder continuously during the construction of this work. When I painted it, I wanted to do it privately, I didn't want anybody to see her and now that she is finished, I can't look at her. She now languishes, face to the wall, in my studio. One day soon, I hope I will be able to look at her without cringing.

*

With greater clarity I can now look further into the stories Mama and Dad had shared. There are several issues tickling my psyche. The first has to do with the notion of escape, of having to leave a place quickly due to dangerous forces. It isn't like running away; it is more like an exodus. In this I am specifically thinking of my father's dangerous flight from Hungary the final time. What he must have been feeling, what he was leaving behind and what he was about to confront. I hoped that his feelings of displacement and dislocation, were neatly packaged somewhere in his mind so that he could ignore them and just do what he had to do, for the sake of his sanity and his freedom. His journeys, both physical and psychological, and the fact that he never thought any of his experiences were a big deal. That the ordinariness of his young life was so obvious; I was ridiculous in exalting him to the status of the heroic, the courageous.

"They were just ordinary days Lexi. Was no big deal," he said to me often, trying to talk me down from my platform of admiration. "Was no big deal, just, what else could I do?"

Dad has always been such a humble gentleman and I want the next artwork to be somewhat elegant, to reflect this humility. The mixed media painting I made was smaller than the previous works. I wanted it to be a less permanent, more fragile medium than canvas, and one that keyed into the notion of 'papers'. Identity papers that all Europeans had to carry (but that my father had often surrendered) in order to move between places. I also wanted this work to be a more universal image, and descriptive of the transition period where Dad had to put all of his thoughts and feelings on hold and just do. This transitional period is a contested zone, a psychological no-man's-land, a place of change.

I chose feathers as a literal symbol of flight, and arranged them into organized rows to reflect stability in a changing world. The grid pattern is disrupted occasionally with other smaller grid patterns of feathers. There are real feathers stitched into the surface of the paper to hold them in place. This also relates to the craft of Hungarian embroidery and appears in a lot of my past works. The metaphors of weaving in, of being tied to something, of being stitched onto and into, of hanging by a thread, are all very rich and pertinent to the themes I am exploring. But stitching and thread are not totally secure, and if necessary can be removed, cut or easily broken in order to escape from the surface; the feathers can blow away, at will or by the will of others. Thus the work is fragile and impermanent.

The experience of journeys, passages, and moments of travel are insubstantial and do not exist as real things – they are simply virtual moments and in Dad's case, the early parts of this journey were dangerous. He could have been arrested several times, sent back to Hungary, or shot. His journey may never have happened, and his future (and my existence) surely hung by a thread.

The work I titled "Flight", flowed into the next, as my artwork often does, and the ideas emerged sequentially. I have been thinking of myself as a stubborn but persistent boundary hunter, who actively (or so it seems to me), seeks borders to cross. It is as if my acquired comfort zones are not sufficiently satisfying to warrant languishing within them for long. Living in the margins and crossing borders has become habitual for me. And I start to wonder what those in between places between the boundaries, could look like.

When I think of a 'no-man's-land' I tend to think of a dry, arid inhospitable place, like a desert, unable to sustain life for any lengthy period of time. But that is OK because most people never venture into deserts for very long.

By contrast, the spaces beyond the borders (to my way of thinking) are lush and fertile; they are the places where, if you choose, you can live forever. They are glamorous places, attractive and seductive. They are the restful places where you can relax and be complacent. They are the places of comfort, and of belonging.

Between these two areas are the borders, the edges – the doorways, portals, thresholds, entrances and exits. Access is enabled two ways – you may either be allowed to enter or allowed to leave. These borders are accessed either by a key, or by satisfying the gatekeepers or border guards, through bribery, proving your mettle or by showing your passport. Each of these things, the key, the bribe, the proof of worth and the identity documents can take many and various forms. They can be any one or combination of knowledge, language competence, appearance, tribal affinity, cunning, success, courage or acquiescence.

For me, forever in transit and between the places of belonging, the transit zone is a place of the familiar. As I said, it is like a desert. I have spent much time in some of the world's real deserts and if I had a choice, I would go back. It is true that on first glance the desert appears hellishly hot and inhospitable, but you can learn to work with the harsh conditions. You simply adjust. Apart from the odd feral insect, it is a completely hospitable place, providing you have adequate supplies and can protect yourself from the heat and light when they are at their most unkind. The sky at night is spectacular and the purity of the landscape is beguiling. Deserts are so appealing to me.

CHAPTER 9

Boundaries on the other hand, are difficult places. They have razor wire, are guarded and are notoriously difficult to cross. When Stu and I went to Hungary in 1984, the Berlin Wall was still in place, Communism had a firm grip on the country and the border from Austria was a daunting prospect. The storm fences and armed guards in watchtowers examined our every movement. We lined up for half a day watching, as the Russian border guards searched every car for contraband and then interrogated every prospective visitor. We understood that this border was the frontline to the Soviet Union from the West, but it was chilling nonetheless.

When it was our turn, we resignedly got out of the car and opened the boot for inspection. At that moment my aunt, Irén néni and uncle, Zoli bácsi, dashed up to us, hugged us and spoke in Hungarian to the border guards. They had a short conversation and then the gatekeepers allowed us to move through the frontier and into Hungary, without any further search or questioning. Our tribal affinity was established and we were simply waved through.

This was the first of many difficult borders Stu and I were to cross in our travels, but it was perhaps one of the most significant. It taught me that in order to belong one must have a connection of sorts. If I had been able to speak Hungarian myself (or Russian) the crossing would have been easier. The fact that my passport said I was Australian helped as well. Foreign currency, especially American dollars, probably would have done the trick as well.

The places in-between are becoming crowded these days, since there are so many of us languishing out here in the margins of society. We have learned to make ourselves comfortable in a seemingly hospitable place; it's busy out here now. The inhospitable margins of yesterday are the new black.

These things are in my thoughts as I sketch and make and I have also been thinking about what my mother has told me about the moments of my birth. "No wonder you came out screaming", she said, "Since you were stuck in the doorway for so long, neither in nor out". The nurses ignored her protests that it was all happening and they'd better hurry. Those particular 'gatekeepers' told Mama she was misguided, that it was not yet time and that she was imagining things.

It was such a patronizing attitude. A birthing mother, particularly one who has done it before, knows exactly what is going on when she is giving birth. How could she not? And I don't even want to ponder the dynamic of working-class-ethnic-woman and White-Anglo-nurses-more-interested-in-their-cups-of-tea than the insistence of their patient because it is too obvious to mention. But the facts of my birth have become a major metaphorical reference point for me, that of the liminal.

I feel at home in the transit area, that deserted place, because not only is it an unencumbered, quiet, pure environment that many find inhospitable, it is also anticipatory. It is a place that is full of potential and expectation; it is indeed pregnant with possibility and the promise of things to come. When will you cross the border? Will you wait patiently for the borders to change? Which border will you choose to cross?

116

All of these ponderings have ramifications not only for my own life, but for the lives of others who are out here with me, either by choice or by circumstance. I realize that I am comfortable in the transit zone, between the barriers. It is a place I know well. It is a place that accepts me.

The human spirit is resilient. It will make its home in a desert or bed of thorns or a garbage dump or tundra. Some of us will choose to stay in these unattractive places. People will always adapt, and construct a home in the absence of home. At the moment mine is here, in the transit zone, and the work I created to reflect this, entitled "Belonging" is a digital image of speed and stability. It is in movement, anchored by symbols of strength and monumentality.

By doing these artworks, my thoughts about my issues are crystallizing. I am becoming critical in a way that is neither detached nor objective. I am immersing myself in my 'truths', my 'evidence' and my 'realities', yet I am able to analyze the information through creativity, imagination, serendipity and chance. I am surrendering to these strengths, and it is very productive.

The most striking thing I notice as I am planning and executing these artworks is how sequential they become. One flows into the next and the momentum is compelling. It is all I want to do.

I was having so much success at my first port of call (my artwork), but I know I have to trek onwards to the second place. I know what I have to do next. It is the second of the three things I have decided to access as solutions to my dilemmas. If I am ever going to reconcile my selves and traverse those final borders that need to be crossed on this journey, I have to convince The Oldies to come with me, back to Hungary. I must go there with them, to experience what it is like to be in Hungary with the Hungarians that are my parents. I have to persuade my father especially, who is getting older and never, he says, wants to leave Australia again. Newcastle is where he belongs, he insists, and that's where he wants to remain, forever.

My father is a stubborn man. This is perhaps the biggest challenge yet.

ng

e girl with

alone

as a leaf
amn
ng to the g
t a

d little sn
face
little girl
g wrong
e's all alor
g
g
g
favourite
a l
wrong

and she's

I have come to learn that this sense of displacement, of not belonging…is shared by many people whose lives have not been so obviously displaced or uprooted as mine. And yet, as every migrant knows, being obliged to start again, to find that you must remake your life brings that predicament into sharper focus than might have been the case otherwise. (Riemer, 1992, p. 2)

CHAPTER 10

DISPLACEMENT, DISLOCATION AND ETHNICITIES

The stories of Zita and Laci, set within the broader contexts of Hungarian refugees and post-World War II Europe, and their subsequent migration into a white Australia, illustrate issues of identity and ethnicity with relation to both belonging and alienation. This next account examines those shifting relationships, and in particular, how an immigrant's disposition, character, and temperament can lead to either of the two extremes of belonging and alienation. I also explore the ethnicities of the migrant child, and in particular, the second-generation migrant child, since these issues are a key element of this inquiry. Further, contemporary notions of identity and multiple selves are also examined. This discussion creates a context for further discussion in subsequent chapters regarding theories of belonging and the second suite of narratives.

Identity is the foundation upon which feelings of alienation or belonging exist. The later narratives in this work attest to the existence of deep feelings of alienation, displacement and disenfranchisement, and as a consequence, a crisis of identity occurs. Therefore an examination of this core issue is essential at this stage in the tale. This story is a significant turning point in the rendering of this study.

IDENTITY: A CONTEXT

Identity is not something we have, but rather something we do (Sala, Dandy & Rapley, 2009); it is not clear, flimsy or transparent. Rather, identity is fraught with contradictions, complexities and ambiguities (Zevallos, 2008). Erikson (1968, cited in Daha, 2011) asserted that although identity formation is an individual undertaking, it is also a product of interactions with the environment. It is a multifaceted, complex dynamic, and a socially determined construct – we develop our identity in relation to others (Kim & Chao, 2009; Sala et al., 2009; Mathews, 2000; Zevallos, 2008). Identity is continuously constructed and reshaped during interaction with "outsiders, strangers, foreigners and aliens – the others. You know who you are only by knowing who you are not" (Cohen, 1994, p. 1). However, as the next suite of narratives will attest, knowing who you are not may not be helpful to a reconciled identity at all.

Many philosophers, including Hume, Locke, Descartes, Sartre and Kant have attempted to resolve the paradox of personal or social identity (Slugoski & Ginsburg, 1989). They theorize about the unity, continuity and similarities in humans as well as the qualities that make each of us unique. William James and other clinicians have recognized that the issue is highly psychological (Hart, Maloney & Damon, 1987; Slugoski & Ginsburg 1989).

The self is continuous, although it is during adolescence that a sense of continuity is resolved after faltering in late childhood, due to the many physical and psychological processes that occur during this period, as well as an increased social awareness (Gonzales-Baden & Umaña-Taylor, 2011). A sense of personal identity at this time is almost totally invested in others. This sense of an objective self, distinct from others, derives from the characteristics that one uses to define oneself, such as the physical, active, social and psychological self-features. It is this self that many describe when asked about themselves and about others (Hart et al., 1987).

The development of identity is in fact, lifelong – beginning in infancy, becoming prominent in adolescence and continuing to challenge each individual throughout her life (ibid). The foundations of identity are formed primarily when the child learns about his membership to society (Bottomley, 1976). Individual idiosyncrasies are reconciled with the greater environment to 'filter' the world in unique ways. For myself, this happened at the precise moment I entered school and had a life outside of the secure borders of the family.

Whilst class, nation and culture are influential in a collective way as a child grows, identity does not remain fixed, but rather evolves in a reflexive process as the individual experiences the world. Childhood is the most intense period of this process, the intensity diminishing as the individual develops, coinciding with the gradual relinquishment of parental influence. The self is a relational achievement and the subjectivities attained through the development of identity are the result of a multifaceted interplay between various influences and encounters (Andits, 2010). The child will also absorb negative definitions of their identities, especially if they are reinforced by strong socializers like the school, or school peers (Bottomley, 1976), as was the case in my experience. What is called 'secondary socialization' builds upon the foundations, differentiating with what already exists rather than competing with it (ibid). The ego identity, which forms itself through adolescence can only be formed through a crisis and remains constant for life (Kim & Chao, 2009; Slugoski & Ginsburg, 1989).

Identity and its formation do not exclusively occur in childhood, even though this intense period has a lasting imprint (Cohen, 1994). Childhood therefore, may not be a period of stability during which the self can be formed through significant influences from the environment, a context largely controlled by parental influence and the school. If the environment is unstable, or if the child is thrust into society unprepared, identity formation can be destabilized, thwarted or disabled. This was certainly the case in my experience.

ETHNICITY

In recent years, there has been a flurry of literature examining ethnicity and ethnic identity, particularly with respect to second-generation migrants (Andits, 2010; Chariandy, 2007; Christou & King, 2010; Daha, 2011; Dandy & Pe-Pua, 2009; DeCapua & Wintergerst, 2009; Getrich, 2008; Gonzales-Bachen, 2013;

Gonzales-Bachen & Umaña-Taylor, 2011; Hatoss, 2006; Kane, 2012; Kambaskovic, 2013; Kiang & Fuligni, 2009; Kim & Chao, 2009; Kim, Ehrich & Ficorelli, 2010; Papas, 2012; Rooney, Nesdale, Kane, Hattie & Goonewardere, 2010; Sala, et al., 2009; Sharma, 2012; Stroink & Lalonde, 2009; Trezise, 2011; Yip, Douglas & Shelton, 2013; Zevallos, 2008; 2005).

As such, it is obvious that ethnicity has been acknowledged as an identity source. The expression of difference in contemporary global society with its blurring of borders and boundaries and the expression of nationalism and ethnicity are experiencing an increased focus on identity politics (Dandy & Pe-Pua, 2009; Sala, et al., 2009). This resurgence is flourishing in an environment of mass xenophobia (Weinreich, 2009) and of political scaremongering over a diaspora that is becoming unstoppable.

The concept of self-identification on the basis of ethnic identification is not a new one (Hicks, 1977). What differs in the contemporary context is how it is being expressed, how it is being received and what implications these realities have upon society in general and education in particular. The next section explores the concept of ethnicity by way of definition and discussion as a link between identity and the specifics of migrant identity.

Although ethnicity is a relatively new term, it comes from the Greek ethnos, which means originally, heathen or pagan (Eriksen, 1996). Only Max Weber in the 1920s gave it any anthropological attention. However, it currently has had popular usage and still has an aura of minority politics and race relations. In social anthropology, however, ethnicity refers to culturally distinctive groups and the relationships between them.

Although Phinney (1992, cited in Kiang & Fuligni, 2009) asserted more than twenty years ago that there is no single definition of ethnicity or ethnic identity, not much has changed. There are myriad definitions, as there appear to be myriad constructions of ethnicity. For example, ethnic identity can be multiple, flexible, context dependent, subjective, socially positioned, unstable and negotiable (Sala et al., 2009), painful, difficult, nostalgic and inextricably entwined with memory (Christou & King 2010) and a discursive construction (Kim & Chao, 2009). In its maintenance, a constant negotiation is necessary, calling on multiple resources to create and make meaning of one's ethnic identity (Sala et al., 2009). It is related to self-esteem and linked to social identity (Rooney, et al., 2012) and is usually binary and fluid (Zevallos, 2008). Further, these positions are complicated by the notion of transnational identities, pan-ethnicity, a sense of ambiguity and the hybridity of ethnic identity, which can also be seen to be a form of resistance to power norms (ibid).

Characteristics that are shared by those of the same ethnicity include shared ancestry, whether actual or presumed, and shared memories. What categorizes one as 'ethnic' relates to cultural distinctiveness, common origins (either nationality or cultural heritage, geography, language, shared territory, genetic ancestry) and continuing loyalty to one's heritage (Gilman, 1996; Hicks, 1977).

Ethnicity affects behaviour and belief systems, and cannot be considered as some kind of neutral abstraction. Even after cultural differences have disappeared, usually through the second- and third-generations, they can be and are continually recreated. Some people regularly interact on the basis of their ethnicity, and it is these ties that affirm and strengthen the ethnic identity of the group (ibid). Ethnicity can 'feed' on itself.

Ethnic identity can be culturally exclusive since there are those who belong to a specific ethnic identity and those who do not. This belonging is most usually centred on myths of common origin, a shared history or destiny, and constant efforts and dialogues (Yuval-Davis, 1993). It cannot be reduced or defined by culture, which in itself cannot be viewed as a fixed category. The word ethnic carries with it a heavy emotional weight (Hicks, 1977) and sometimes a psychological responsibility, as it does for me.

What remains clear from the research on ethnic identity is that it remains a multidimensional construct of exploration and belonging and is an active and continuous, quest (Kiang & Fuligni, 2009). Ethnic identity is complicated with many components such as self-identification, ethnic knowledge, belonging, own attitudes to belonging and involvement in ethnic cultural practices (Andits, 2010).

Ethnic labels (such as Hungarian-Australian or Australian-Hungarian) are markers that single out and categorize individuals, a kind of shorthand explanation or symbol of one's cultural customs, behaviours and beliefs. These can be linguistically subtle, or behaviourally blatant. However, this assumption combines people together, and assumes a similarity in their natures, that is, "They act similarly because they are alike" (Hicks, 1977, p. 12). But there is also much space within a specific marker of difference that allows for more, subtle differences. Indeed, an under-researched area of ethnic identity is the diversity that exists within ethnic minority populations (Daha, 2011; Gonzales-Baden & Umaña-Taylor, 2011).

Ethnic Belonging

Generally speaking, people prefer to be surrounded by and interact with similar others and thus being with at least some ethnic peers is a powerful socializing agent, resulting in enhanced self perception (Yip et al., 2013). Ethnic belonging therefore, is about affect and based upon a sense of connectedness with one's own ethnic group (Kiang & Fuligni, 2009).

When there is contested belonging, it affects adjustment and well-being and therefore a developmental goal would be to integrate one's selves into a cohesive whole of self-consistency (Gonzales-Baden & Umaña-Taylor, 2011; Yip et al., 2013), as I am attempting to accomplish with this inquiry. According to the literature, to not do so is detrimental to self-esteem, can result in depression, confusion, psychological difficulties and poor adjustment (Kiang & Fuligni, 2009). Ethnic belonging can be more stable in context when identity is shifting between family and the outside world (ibid). Indeed a robust and resolved ethnic identity is a source of strength and resilience (Gonzales-Baden & Umaña-Taylor, 2011).

The central and original culture of the migrant and their homeland is elsewhere and therefore, their belonging to that place is now vicarious and to some extent, imagined; their identities have been complicated in the journey (Zevallos, 2008). This can be conceptualized as a 'double-voiced' homeland related discourse – that of belonging and not belonging to the homeland (Andits, 2010). As such, ethnic identity can also be located in the in-between (Christou & King, 2010; Daha, 2011; Zevallos, 2008).

Sala et al. (2009) argue that there are two parts to ethnic identity, namely developmental status and affect, for example pride in belonging. They consider that ethnic identity is a component of social identity – self concept is derived from belonging, or identifying with the group through aspects such as shared origins, history and descent. The affective part of this dynamic is the value and social significance placed upon these things. Indeed, a robust ethnic identity results in resilience to change, stress and greater feelings of belonging and may act as a protective factor against the negative effects of racial discrimination (Sharma, 2012). There is also a strong link between a truncated ethnic identity and loneliness (ibid).

Cultural Characteristics of Ethnic Identity

Identity is based upon specific cultural constructions that are idealized and as Bourdieu asserts, culture is embodied through material practices (cited in Zevallos, 2008). In the case of ethnic identity though, it is physical appearance that is linked most closely to a resolved ethnic identity (Gonzales-Baden & Umaña-Taylor, 2011), and material, cultural practices are indeed significant to a sense of ethnicity performance and belonging.

These are also 'surface pointers' used in recognition, and may include dress, tradition, physical attributes and language, with the latter carrying most psychological and social significance (Nash, 1996). Customs are linked to these surface pointers, and it is these customs that are visible and often public. Tradition implies links to survival, legitimacy, generational linkages and continuity. The preserving of traditions relies upon those who carry it to survive.

As mentioned, the most powerful of these surface pointers is that of the heritage language. As Erikson acknowledged, identity is a language game (1991, cited in Zevallos, 2008). Many writers attest to the reconciling effect upon ethnic identity that heritage language maintenances ensures (DeCapua & Wintergerst, 2009; Kim & Chao, 2009; Sala et al., 2009; Sharma, 2012; Trezise, 2011), especially into the second generation. Thus, "[w]here there is a group, there is some sort of boundary, and where there are boundaries, there are mechanisms to maintain them. These boundary mechanisms are cultural markers of difference" (Nash, 1996, p. 25). The heritage language is a powerful and obvious cultural marker of difference, and thus, an authentic ethnic identity membership includes language fluency (Sala et al., 2009).

Other cultural markers of difference include values, attitudes, behaviours, knowing about the culture, cultural practices, naming and music, to name just a few (Sharma, 2012). However, the next most significant marker of ethnicity after language is food (Sala et al., 2009, Sharma, 2012). Food and the rituals around its preparation and reception are profound expressions of ethnic identity (Papas, 2012). With respect to Hungarian society both in Australia and in the homeland, food and the cultural practices that surround it have abundant significance, and certainly did in my home when I was growing up.

Migrant Identity

What follows is an exploration into the transformation of migrant identity that occurs when the migrant leaves her own heritage culture and enters the new prevailing culture as a marginal outsider. As is apparent in the stories of my parents so far, it is a discussion that is critical to this study. This revolution of identity begs the question: "How does the "ethnic" name itself? What kind of identity is asserted through this name?" (Radhakrishnan, 1996, p. 68). Indeed, who does this 'new Australian' become?

The passage of the migrant from her homeland into a different and very new influential society, and her subsequent citizenship within the new country, means that she travels from a space where she belongs as part of the dominant majority, to a space at the margins of society, to the minorities – a place of not belonging, of alienation. Her identity, her sense of self, is transformed utterly (Radhakrishnan, 1996). This would suggest that identity shifts depending upon the exterior context, and in a didactic way is transformed, multiply positioning itself depending on the recontextualizations from within and without. How identity relates to place is the expression of a shifting equilibrium (Trezise, 2011).

Immigrants have complex ideas about their ancestry (Zevallos, 2008) and this can complicate migrant identity. During the initial phase of immigration, ethnicity is often suppressed and forgone for other characteristics in the interests of pragmatism and opportunity. Historically, in order to make progress in the new environment the ethnic must assimilate actively and suppress their ethnicity (Radhakrishnan, 1996), indeed as mentioned previously, this was policy in Australia in the post-war period. Assimilation demands the discarding of one's ethnic identity so that one can be absorbed into the dominant culture. It alludes to the melting pot theory in that all diversity under an assimilationist model is cast together into a harmonized whole, forgoing language, traditions and other cultural displays. However,

> [a]ll diasporic communities settled outside their natal (or imagined natal)
> territories, acknowledge that 'the old country' – a notion often buried deep
> in language, religion, custom and folklore – always has some claim on their

loyalty and emotions. That claim may be strong or weak, or boldly or meekly articulated in a given circumstance or historical period, but a member's adherence to a diasporic community is demonstrated by an acceptance of an inescapable link with their past migration history and a sense of co-ethnicity with others of a similar background. (Cohen, 1997, p. ix)

This view of a migrant's identity presupposes that the link to one's ancestral homeland is at the exclusion of one's present homeland, and that the allegiances to this present homeland are not as compelling or as meaningful as the other. Also, in terms of integrity, the link can be myth *or* memory, the movement traumatic *or* voluntary, natal *or* imagined natal. The criteria are so loose that they risk not hitting their mark at all. Under this definition those fifth, sixth and subsequent generations of, for example Irish Americans or British Australians, are considered to be a part of the original culture of their ancestors, even though they may have little knowledge, experience or connection to them. I find this broadly encompassing definition rather tenuous. If this were the case, then given the nature of humans in their nomadic, intermarrying and migratory tendencies, each individual would be discreetly and collectively connected to as many as twenty (or more) cultures from these five or six generations. To whom specifically then, does one owe one's cultural, ethnic or historical allegiance? What is dominant within their psyche or the associations ineffably connected by blood?

With great clarity, Kambaskovic (2013) speaks of the ghoulish categories in every migrant's life and identity when she talks about, "trauma, nostalgia, non-belonging, "ghost identities", the conflict of smugness and survivor's guilt, the need to speak up and, above all, the need to not speak up" (p. 96). Such conditions make it difficult to reconcile cultural allegiance and make it entirely tempting to suppress one's heritage identity and move on.

As can be seen historically in Australia, the migrant is compelled to attempt to belong to the prevailing and dominant culture – by suppressing their original cultural identity. When doing so, she starts to compartmentalize her life and her selves, foregrounding one identity over the other depending on the situation (Cohen, 1997; Hicks, 1977; Mathews, 2000). This life of dualism is repeated and perhaps emphasized in the lives of her migrant child, with significantly more poignancy and separatism (Mycak, Travaglia & Weiss, 1992). This tension between two histories can be agonizing. Living 'within the hyphen', where neither the ethnic nor the 'new' self assumes a hierarchical status, is the mandate for the ethnic (Radhakrishnan, 1996).

Second-Generation Migrant Identity

Radhakrishnan (1996) considered the second-generation to be the assimilated generation and it would appear that through the tensions that emerge by living a life of dualism, the second-generation may be willing to cast off its ethnic identity in order to belong. This cohort has an ill-defined and partial cultural citizenship to their heritage, framed only by their parents' experience (Sharma, 2012), with shifting boundaries of ethnic membership and personal and public anxieties regarding their identity (Getrich, 2008). Their constructs of belonging are thus multiple and layered and in this context, they will often have hybrid ideas about what it means to be Australian.

Indeed, one of the significant themes in the literature is the feeling of being alienated from the secure base of the family and a conflicted identity (Chariandy, 2007; Getrich, 2008; Loh, 1980). The ethnic identity of the second-generation is not so easily discarded, since it is in this case, inextricably linked to the primary community – that of the family. Belonging to the family unit means belonging to its histories, if not by identification, then by the undeniable fact of biology (Sala, et al., 2009).

Thus, in the second-generation, a bicultural identity is often in conflict, often more so than that of their parents. Indeed the second-generation are more likely than their parents to suffer from depression, anxiety and low self-esteem (Sharma, 2012). Biethnic adolescents are likely to have unique experiences that alter their ethnic identity formation (Gonzales-Backen, 2013).

This identity confusion appears to be constant and traumatic (Loh, 1980). Second-generation writers often express that they are torn between their parental expectations and culture, and the desire to be like their peers (Leung, 1992; Papas, 2012). Many migrant parents see as their right and their duty to impose upon their children the morals, standards, values and politics of the heritage culture, just as any parent from any cultural background might emphasize. The migrant has made huge sacrifices for their children; it's the least the parents would expect (Herne et al., 1992).

Often, these marginalized children seek solace in the solidarity that shared experiences can provide. The younger generation may resolve their ethnic identity in alliance with other ethnic minorities (Radhakrishnan, 1996). Identification with others who share similar experiences has always bonded humans together. In such a context, the second-generation child can feel safe to embrace their ethnicity (Daha, 2012). Therefore, belonging to a community of second-generation children, even if they are not of the same ethnic group, can be a source for solidarity and identification. This was certainly the case for me, as the following narrative will attest.

As previously mentioned, language is one of the most powerful links to one's identity. It is such a fundamental apsect of human identity that asking migrants and their children to give it up is akin to asking them to disable themselves in order to make them more acceptable to society at large (Browne & Magin, 1976; Hatoss, 2006). This denial of linguistic identification is prejudicial in the extreme, since retention of the first language is an indicator of the cultural vitality of the ethnic group (DeCapua & Wintergerst, 2009; Hatoss, 2006; Smolicz, 1984).

There has indeed been a significant generational decline in the use of ethnic languages (Andits, 2010; Kim & Chao, 2009; Hatoss, 2006; Papas, 2012). This linguistic erosion appears to be a common phenomenon of second and subsequent generations, but these same groups tend to retain their ethnic identity even if there is only a residual retention of ethnic language and culture, thus,

> ethnic identity is usually anchored and sustained by the ethnic family with all its extended ramifications of [relatives] and close friends. The ethnic family and a galaxy of other primary social relations, represent the bedrock for the maintenance of ethnic identity…and research shows that there has been little decline in the cohesive forces of ethnic family and primary structures to parallel the weakening of the linguistic component of ethnic cultures. The general observation, as well as research finding is that only when the children become estranged from their parents and the rest of the family that their ethnicity comes into doubt. (Smolicz, 1984, p. 133)

Most children of migrants in my generation spoke the native tongue at home, with limited literacy skills; this is consistent across almost every minority group (ibid). However, many of us worked very hard to disguise this cultural indicator and struggled to keep it hidden. Indeed, the use of the heritage language by the second-generation has been evocatively defined as the *kitchen language* (Brown & Magin, 1976).

Being marked as different, suffering from racist slurs, living a double life, without the understanding of parents on one hand (who couldn't quite relate to these particular difficulties) and teachers on the other, undoubtedly creates suffering and distress (Stroink & Lalonde, 2009). Such tensions exacerbate feelings of isolation and alienation, from both the private world of the family and the public world of school and the greater community (Brown & Magin, 1976). Yet in this country, many of these 'children' express a fierce love for Australia and a national pride in their adopted country (Mycak, 1992; Tsiolkas, 2013).

Thus, being acculturated in two cultural frameworks simultaneously, the ethnic identity of many of the second-generation is truncated, incomplete, conflicted and unresolved (Smolicz, 1984; Stroink & Lalonde, 2009). As Zevallos (2008) astutely recognizes, there are plenty of people to feel different *from*, there are few to feel different *with*. This is hardly surprising, given the hybridized contexts that second-generation children have developed within. Certainly some of my cohort of Australians feels they have been cheated out of the development of our full ethnic identity, since their Anglo-conformist schooling robbed us of it (Smolicz, 1984). We also often blame our parents for succumbing to the pressure imposed by the schools to dump our language, amongst other things. As Smolicz asserted,

> [a] young person may "feel ethnic", but cannot explain it in terms of the culture that [s/he] holds dear. This perception of inadequacy, of having failed to achieve what would be expected of [her/him] by "authentic" group members and of being cut off from the mainsprings of his culture and its literary tradition, can cause very serious resentment and anger. (1984, p. 135)

One strategy suggests that the two generations compromise – the older not to impose the authority of the heritage culture, the younger not forgetting where they come from (Radhakrishnan, 1996). However, this is unrealistic. In a context that my be highly emotionally charged (especially for adolescents), where one party has not the emotional maturity to seek compromise and the other lacks the empathy for their children's situation, compromise is unlikely. Parents may not be willing to allow their children to subsume their intellectual authority and the children may have no strategies to deal with this. Add to this the difficulties inherent in raising fully bilingual children, and the home environment can certainly become quite tense (DeCapua & Wintergerst, 2009).

So where does this leave the ethnic identity of the second- and subsequent generations? It risks being almost entirely extinguished. Social mobility and acculturation has certainly diminished the cultural and distinct values of many 'White ethnic groups', so that it would appear that by the fourth generation, ethnic identity has almost totally disappeared (Fandetti & Gelfand, 1983).

The revival and reconstruction of attention upon ethnic identities in the postmodern epoch has resulted in many previously disenfranchised ethnic children embracing their heritage and celebrating their ethnicity. Certainly, I am one of these. The struggle to belong and gain acceptance has now been been realized through the cultural capital afforded to the 'new' ethnic – where previously it was eschewed. This fetishization of difference has its problems, but it also allows for many reconciliations. Postmodernism made an indelible impact upon identity politics, and one which irrefutably transformed notions of culture and our operations within it. For this reason, a brief exploration of postmodern concepts, with respect to identity, is contextually appropriate to this discussion.

POSTMODERN NOTIONS OF IDENTITY

The emergence of a global society, a homogenous collective that has no boundaries or borders, is made possible through our essential humanism, our interdependence and our ultimate singularity – the world is one place. Our categorization into nations is weakening and goods, knowledge, images, communication, crime, culture, pollutants, drugs, fashion and belief systems all flow across borders and boundaries. In 1997, Cohen claimed we were shakily on our way towards the first global civilization, with shared values, communication and politics. It seems we have indeed arrived.

Postmodern theory assumes that the identity is never whole, but rather multiple and fragmented, depending upon a myriad of factors which interact in a reflexive way, contingent upon social, psychological and physical situations. Everyone has a psychological personal identity, but may also have several social identities that can be presented depending on the context, which influence the formation of these identities (Sala et al., 2009; Hicks, 1977; Yip et al., 2013; Zevallos, 2008) and are often socially constructed. Therefore, in such cases, identity may be imposed by others, as well as by self-identification or self-labelling (Gonzales-Bachen & Umaña-Taylor, 2011).

Ethnicities and identities are not fixed or stable but rather the result or product of several recontextualizations, displacements and travels (Radhakrishnan, 1996). In a postcolonial, postmodern and poststructuralist world, the concept of the ethnic, per se, is perhaps an archaic, modernist one. Conventional, modernist and political categories are now fossilized and are therefore unable to capture the agilities of contemporary existence. Indeed, it would appear that we have abandoned notions of class or gender as primary conceptual and organizational categories (Bhabha, 1994). The postmodern world forced an awareness of the multiple subject positions that constitute identity. Thus, focusing on the *interstitial* moments (or 'spaces') and processes where difference is articulated, where time or location is of significant impact upon the formation of identity, is entirely more appropriate when discussing constructions of identity in a postmodern world (ibid).

In a contemporary context, the modernist terms 'ethnic' and 'identity' are loaded with political structures that ignore the diversity within the contexts described by the terms. Radhakrishnan addressed the challenge of reconciling ethnic identity within the postmodern, poststructuralist and postcolonial moments, with a highly semantic yet entirely logical argument,

> [t]he constituency of "the ethnic" occupies quite literally a "pre-post"-erous space where it has to actualize, enfranchise, and empower its own "identity" and coextensively engage in the deconstruction of the very logic of "identity" and its binary and exclusionary politics. Failure to achieve this doubleness can only result in the formation of ethnicity as yet another "identical" and hegemonic structure. The difficult task is to achieve an axial connection between the historical-semantic specificity of "ethnicity" and the "posthistorical" politics of radical indeterminacy. A merely short term affirmation of ethnicity certainly leads to a substitution of the "contents" of history but leaves untouched the very forms and structures in and through which historical and empirical contents are legitimated. On the other hand, an avant-gardist advocacy of "difference as such" overlooks the very possibilities of realizing, through provisionally historical semantics, this "difference" as a worldly and consequential mode. I posit the notion of the "radical" or the "postethnic" as the moment that materializes the temporality of the "post-" as a double moment that is as disruptive as it is inaugural. (1996, pp. 62–63)

Thus, if the postmodern ethnic were purely 'just' ethnic, then she would be forever incarcerated within the many economies of repression. The postethnic on the other hand, is the moment or place that performs its own duality. As the radically ethnic, the postethnic is the last in an entire series of identities that, by virtue of choosing to be terminal in that series, inflicts fatality to the entire series and, in that very breath, inaugurates the time of the after (ibid). The time of the after is about futures where oppression will be impossible. For the radical ethnic, the politics of the 'post-' means

131

that the postethnic is produced in a non-authoritarian and non-territorial context, where boundaries are transcended and limits are transformed and accepted. Thus the postethnic is not trapped within repressive contexts and politics, but exists within a moment or place that allegorizes its own doubleness.

The migrant then, having graduated to the postethnic space, exists contemporarily in a circumstance that utterly embraces the diversity of uniqueness. Individuality in its truest sense blossoms, is realized and more importantly, accepted.

However, prior to the postmodern moment and certainly in the years that followed World War II, individual migrants experienced what is acknowledged as being a modernist experience of ethnicity. It is indeed the children of these migrants that will realize their identities as being 'post-' everything. However, their early years, and the impact that these experiences had upon the formation of the subsequent selves, is worthy of close scrutiny as occurs in this inquiry, in order to debrief these experiences and indeed provide a lens for later life.

Curiously, there has been a reassertion to localism notably through ethnicity, nationalism and religious fundamentalism, and emerging cultural identities are in transition, drawing on different traditions, harmonizing old and new without assimilation or total loss of the past (Getrich, 2008; Hall, 1993; Zevallos, 2008). This evolution of "cultures of hybridity" (Cohen, 1997) or cultural hybridity, a term posited by several theorists (Cohen, 1997; Hall, 1993; Radhakrishnan, 1996; Rushdie, 1988), is a foil to a potentially divisive ethnic revival, where the hybrid self is the ultimate decentering of all identity regimes. Theories of hybridity, most specifically in reference to Rushdie (1988), hypothesize that hybridity is subjectless and as such beheads the subject and dismisses 'identitarian' forms of thinking and belonging (ibid). Further, hybridities vary and differ, and one cannot generalize as to the nature of hybridity in a normative manner. It is conceded that there are no guarantees of identity or authenticity, and recognized thus that,

> [t]hose who oppose the [Satanic Verses] most vociferously today are of the opinion that intermingling with different cultures will inevitably weaken and ruin their own. I am of the opposite opinion. The Satanic Verses celebrates hybridity, impurity, intermingling, the transformation that comes of new and unexpected combinations of human beings, cultures, ideas, politics, movies, songs. It rejoices in mongrelization and fears the absolution of the Pure. [This is] how newness enters the world. It is the great possibility that mass migration gives the world, and I have tried to embrace it. (Rushdie 1991, p. 394)

This term 'hybridity' used by Rushdie (1988), Hall (1993) and many other scholars (Zevallos, 2008), is used to explain the emergence of dynamic and mixed cultures. An alternative term is 'syncretism' that Cohen offered as a foil to the term hybridity, which could imply sterility and uniformity (1997). These concepts fail to recognize the somewhat contested states of individual experience.

Identity can also create a burden of representation (Yuval-Davis, 1993). The presentation and representation of identity for individuals and communities as well as the differences between these, are negotiated in strange, and fluid frontlines and borderposts of identity (Bhabha, 1994). This theory demands investigation and celebration of the overlaps, ambiguities, and displacements of difference, and the mixing of cultures, religions, languages and ethnicities, beyond the scope of this study.

Mathews' reconciliation of the modern and the postmodern individual is as cogent as it is logical (2000). He asserted that it is cultures that shape selves – shape rather than transform – and these are different depending on the differences between cultures. Contemporary theorists have suggested that a postmodern self has no specific culture, but rather, many cultures, and many selves (Getrich, 2008; Gonzales-Bachen & Umaña-Taylor, 2011; Kiang & Fuligni, 2009). We continuously move through these cultures and recreate ourselves. This is largely because in contemporary society we have immediate access to any cultural moment from the past or present. Thus, we either belong to a particular place and time, or we are open and free to change. My assertion is: Why do we have to choose? Surely we can, do and be both. Mathews resolves what he calls 'this conflict' by consideration of the self and culture within a framework of how people experience their world. We are culturally shaped, even though we may well be fragmented, as the postmodernists assert. Mathew argues that underlying such fragmentation there is a 'universal basis of self' which both depends upon and is independent of our other selves. We are made from both our past memories and the anticipation of the future, which is linked to the changing present. The self is constructed through language, as Derrida (1987) asserted; it also lives in the worlds of others and in one's own psyche.

Mathews resolves both the ideology of a stable and underlying self with a postmodern tendency to choose our 'selves' from what he calls the cultural supermarket (2000). He presents the theory that there are three levels of consciousness where these developments occur. The *taken-for-granted level* (language, social practices, but below the level of consciousness) which is at the foundation level of our self, deep shaping, beyond control but with awareness; the *shikata ga nai level* ("it can't be helped" in Japanese, meaning the extrinsic forces like laws, society's rules and obligations) and cannot be resisted without a high cost to the self – a shallow shaping level, with full control and comprehension; and the *cultural supermarket level*, where the individual is free to pick and choose their identity at will. It is acknowledged, however, that choice is never free: we choose our selves through accordance with our membership to other collectives that allow us to negotiate the formation of the new selves with respect to the old or existing ones.

Although this argument would appear to be at odds with poststructuralist and postmodern definitions of the self, it actually mingles the theory with praxis. Blood and its expressions like blood ties, for example, is absorbed into the first level – something that is taken for granted, a part of one's identity that just "is" (for example, I am white and female). All other identities, that of social and legal obligations, and those through which we perform our belonging to differing and divergent social and cultural groupings, operate above the fundamental level of who we undeniably 'are'.

133

Birthplace and heritage cannot be altered and are at the foundation of who we are and become. One might choose to cast these off, but they still exist as fundamental, existential facts. Whether one chooses an ethnicity is a different argument: if your bloodline identifies you as Indigenous, for example, then you are whether you choose to recognize and embrace this part of your identity or not.

The postmodern supposition of shifting contexts and their resultant influence upon identity construction and its character as being in a constant state of flux, is most compelling. However, if this were to actually be the case, would we not be experiencing continual and constant quandaries of identity? Certainly it is obvious that within contemporary life we have myriad opportunities and access to an infinite amount of moments, experiences and choices, but do we act upon all of them all the time? Or even some of them simultaneously, some of the time? Theoretically, these options are possible, but are they likely?

In my view, having lived through the modernist moment and the postmodern moment, I find the notion of a core underlying (and not necessarily stable) foundational identity to be a logical proposition (i.e. I am a daughter of Laci and Zita). However, the notional of a stable, core self is at odds with contemporary ideology that allows for shifting identities, for fluidity, for choice. Certainly, this is at odds with my own experience and indeed why this inquiry has been realized.

Contemporary notions of identity have lost their modernist monolithic and non-hyphenated character, their singular boundaries. There are many selves and times and spaces possible, rather than a singular normative identity. However, it must be acknowledged that although postmodernism and post structuralism gave us the *permissions* to claim multiple identities, I have lived in and through the modernist epoch, which did not allow for such multiplicities, at the very time my identity was being formed in childhood. Thus, these tensions are located within my own identity conflicts and crises and indeed they expose spaces for exploration. In the three narratives that follow, which describe the migration and assimilation experiences of Laci, Zita and Lexi, these concerns will be revealed.

Bátráké a szerencse
Luck belongs to the brave
(Hungarian proverb)

LACI (II)

We came into Sydney, we came under the Harbour Bridge and somewhere in today what do you call it? Quay? Somewhere on the other side of the Harbour Bridge, I think, where the big sheds are. It was beautiful coming under the bridge. We could see some of these sailing boats and they waved, and so on. It was quite good.

And we arrived and we weren't searched. And we got there, and there was a, on the ship, there was a very casual examination, health, they had a look at you.

We waited for the train and when it came we just boarded the train, and off we were to Bathurst, and that was an ex-military camp. I didn't have any English, not a great deal. I had "Please" and all this, because I worked for the Americans. But no more than that.

Bathurst was just like an army camp, the quarters, beds all over. Barracks, wooden huts, bare timber, they used it in the Second World War. They didn't build it for us; they were just there. There about two weeks, about two or three weeks and we had a bushfire, and we went out, we put out the bushfire, things like that. We had to go through medical again. Incredible medical checks there were.

They distributed who is going where, I think. And we were sent to Mayfield camp in Newcastle. They distributed certain people they went to work for the railway; I didn't want to work for the railway. We didn't have a choice, but I arranged it so that I won't get to the railway. I said I had a defective eye. Well you gotta think for yourself!

They said I'm going to Newcastle and they wrote it, when we got to Newcastle, Mayfield and the BHP officials came there, and they sitting at the desk, taking notes, taking everything and then I get a paper that I start in January 2nd or 3rd, I don't know and it said, "Laszlo Lasczik: Blast furnace". This was January 1950 I started BHP. No choice, you had the paper and that was it.

I met a doctor, Ravazdy, and I bought him out of Prague, he's dead now. Not a long time ago. Anyway, I bought him out from Czechoslovakia from Pilsen to Bamberg. I was driving, I taught him how to drive, the GMC truck. And when I first started at BHP when I first walked in the gate, who do you think comes out from the dogwatch,

in the gate, clocking in and he's walking out from dogwatch? Because he apparently got to Australia earlier than me. There was him, Dr Ravazdy, the man I brought on the truck to Bamberg! There was very qualified men and they worked labourers and shovelling and all that. And I walk in and he walks out. I couldn't believe it. We parted in Bamberg and we met in Newcastle Steelworks. Amazing. We were speechless.

I worked in the blast furnace two years. Shiftwork, three shifts. Lived different places, I kept moving around. I couldn't…I moved around a lot I was very restless. Just wandering again, I done it so often. I mean when I kept writing a letter home, they must have been amused that every time I write I must have changed my address.

I used to go to the Greek club to eat. The food, I couldn't…I lived on

bread and milk, little bit of ham. So went to the Greek Club, near the Lyrique theatre, and there was one in King Street, but I always went to one near the Lyrique because I know the owner, Nick, Nick the Greek there, see he did alright.

After the blast furnace I went to work in the machine shop. They wouldn't recognize me as a tradesman, I had, I still got the certificate, they wouldn't recognize it. And when I wanted to get recognition, because if you didn't have recognition you couldn't get into the union, and if you couldn't get into the union they couldn't employ you. They wouldn't let me do the test, they did to some others, I don't know why they wouldn't let me. After that I know a fella there a union man in BHP machine shop, the Iron Workers Union delegate there, and he said, "Where do you work?" And I said, "Nowhere – I quit when they wouldn't recognize my qualifications". I gave my notice, and told them I had another job and they wouldn't let me go, they wouldn't pay me out. And I met this union delegate and he said, "Don't do anything I'll fix it up for you", see and he did.

I was accused for being drunk, I never had drink all day and I wasn't a real drinker unless with somebody. Coming back from Queensland by myself, and coming across the New South Wales border, New England Highway, I don't know the place name. And it was just about 11 o'clock at night, and I see a shop was still open, for late moviegoers. Couple were there, two or three people. Everything was quiet and I stopped, get meself a lemonade. And I stopped there under a light and there was a bus stop, true enough, but there no bus running by then, the whole place was quiet. I went across to the shop, small shop. I left a pound on the counter, and waited, people there. And the next thing I see this black mariah comes and stops front of my car. I had a ute, was a ute. Was a big cop, young, was fairly young, you know? And lookin' at the vehicle, and I grabbed my money and I raced outside, I said, "What's wrong?" and he walking around and he looking at the car, and I just stood there and waited. I said, "Anything wrong officer?"

He said, "Are you the driver of this vehicle?" I said, "Yes". He said, "You're drunk". "No," I said, "I'm not, not drunk. I came all the way from Brisbane". And he said, "You're drunk. You coming with me". I said, "I'm not coming with you, I

haven't had a drink and I haven't got a drink. And I just stopped for a drink here, lemonade". And he insisted, "Come with me".

And then I was, I thought to myself, "You going to pay for this. I don't care how much it's going to cost me". And he asked for driver's license, see? And I thought he takes the license, because he had a right to, I knew he had right to ask for license. And I gave him the license and I could see he was looking at it, I think he was trying to decide what to do.

139

He must have felt what I was thinking, he picked it up. I think to myself, "You taking me in, and even if I had to work 10 years pay the costs, I'm going to get…I'm going to wipe the floor with you".

And anyway, you know what he did? Suddenly, reaches out, handed me the driver's license, he jumped in the black mariah and he went off. Was lucky for both of us because I was determined. I thought to myself "You do that and I get the right people, and it doesn't matter how much it costs, even if I pay 10 years for that. You, I am going to get".

I know many others like this Polish chappy, and he was saying that they take him in and they put him in this little cage there, like you know, isolated, you visible like. And anybody gets past, any cop, and they punch him in the nose, you know? Just for fun. Who knows why, they enjoy it. I never seen it, but that's what he said. Because, I don't know, must have been savages.

There was hostile elements against newcomers, that's for sure. Picking fights at dances, that was the motorbikes. Motorbikes riding along, coming in, and creating problems, finishing up in big fights. Picking on the New Australians. It was young people, they was all young. And this Catholic dancing, oh there was big fights, the motorbikes, and they came with taxis and they attack these new Australians. They come out of the taxis and they attack as they walking home to the hostel. Oh yeah.

And I knew a fella and he was involved, I wasn't there thank God. And he had to rip out a fence paling and he was hitting them with that, because he was attacked by so many, see?

Oh, big fights and the cops came out and they separated and the cops were riding on their bikes slowly, so no more further trouble was. And the following Catholic dance, and the priest was speaking with the boys, the migrants, they turned up again, these motorbikes, and even I was there. The priest was saying to leave, there's going to be trouble, big trouble. I was there, one young Aussie fella said to me, "You better go, get your mates and go, big trouble here". And they came, you know with their collar turned up, and walkin' around there in the hall, and we just waited. You start something and there's going to be trouble. Everybody was ready, nobody said anything to them, insulting, and they didn't. I thought they saw there going to be big trouble, so they went off without anything.

See but in those days, these young people were different, 'Empire' everything. 'Empire!' Nothing counted. Any continentals, they just second-class sort of a thing. These 'excitable continentals' and all that sort of a thing. But that was only occasional. That doesn't reflect the average Australians. No, no. Just they showing off. You see that was not long after the war, 'Empire', and the winners, and I don't know what it is, I can only think. Everything the Empire, everything the English, Empire, Empire. I got no hard feeling. That's silly young people. And anything it was talking and something was misunderstanding about the Empire they were real Empire-ist, you know, and you make something that you misunderstand because you weren't slinging off you just got it wrong or something and they said, "Watch it! Watch it!" Real ugly it was, "Watch it!" Picked you on the pub.

I tell you what happen to me. Now when I worked in one place, when I was repairing this earthmoving equipment, bull dozers and mobile cranes and so on. And I got along with everyone fabulously, and there was one fella, and he, he always was unfriendly and I was always friendly to him except he, I could see it was hard for him to be friendly, you know so once I was working on a machine and he was assisting me. And just to talk about something while I was doing the job, not because I was favouring metric or decimal system, just something to think about, at that time only the imperial system was, and talking about it and with really hatred in his eyes, I never had an argument with him, real hatred, and he said, "You come here with your stupid ideas," he said, "You fucked up you country and you want to fuck our country up too". You know? And I just looked. I thought, "What happened to him?" I only brought up the subject something to talk about, might be interested. And he was real angry, like. And I wonder, he's not alive today he be dead now, but I wonder what he thought when the decimal system came through, hey?

I settled down by' 54, we had good times, outings like. Many of my friends, or some of my friends, they went down to live in Sydney. So sometimes I went down the weekend, visited. And what we did, go down and they lived on the Cross somewhere, Elizabeth Street, somewhere, I don't know. And the pub there, and spend Saturday afternoon in the pub, and bunch of Hungarians, and talking "yak, yak, yak" you know, and that was good.

I don't remember whether it was before in' 54 or after in' 56. Well, we met, your mother and me. The way I met her is I had overalls and I needed some repair. Where we went there was a Hungarian restaurant called the 'Blue Danube' in Hamilton, was owned by Stegermaier's. It was in Beaumont Street, there was the pawn shop and the Blue Danube. Hungarians, it was a quiet drink together, see? At the Blue Danube.

Sometimes they called in Gábor, Julia and the young girl, your Mum, and that's how we met. I knew that they had the shop down the road and I said that's handy, my overalls need patching and all that and perhaps they do it. I pay for it, I didn't mean for nothing, and I did, I called in one day and I took my overalls in. Washed, not dirty. I washed my overalls, hand washed downstairs. I washed my shirts and I ironed it. Except stitching.

And then when they come to Stegermaier's sometimes and we used to have a drink together with Gabby, your Nagyapa. He was a very good man. He said to me when I said something, complaining, he said, "Laci, settle down. We are here up to shit". In Hungarian you say it differently that everybody shitting on you. But it's not quite right – "We're being shat on, and you have to accept". And I said, "I don't have to accept that". Gabby, he was good. He love you very much. Sat with you on Saturdays, watch cartoons and the wrestling.

The wedding, well Reverend Keir and quite a good crowd there. We got a picture, a photo you can see it all. We had the ceremony in the Presbyterian Church. I'm a Catholic, but it didn't make any difference. The wedding reception was in the Great Northern Hotel. It was quite a show, lot of people there, and we had a bit of a dance there and then we set off.

Well, we went to Surfers Paradise, you know it, Surfers. Is much different in those days there weren't those great big buildings. We left to live with your grandparents. I didn't wanted to, because I would have been quite happy – I seen other people moving in just by themselves, just a room and a kitchen, that would have done.

And the thing was this; I was making good money, at that time. Dangerous job, unhealthy job, at that time worked this chemical where they making rayon. Courtauld's, before we were married, a few months. And the overtime, it was on. I was the only tradesman could get in there from the BHP. Many other ones they were, would have liked to move from the machine shop and other departments because the money was good.

I was making good money. I wasn't rich but I was making good wages, in those days. I worked long shifts every time I could do. Eighteen years I was there. That was good there as far as the money was concerned, but it was very destructive you health, because it was sulphuric acid and all other chemicals boiling and the whole air was full with it. I was for years oozing from that sulphuric acid and those other chemicals. Out of the ears, and the skin and hair. The fumes were deadly. And when I used to go out, we were married and this extreme strong smell, you could smell it too. And I was embarrassed in company, sitting somebody's table with you, the fume just coming out of you. Even now, it's still there. I left' 76, May or June I think.

And one day, I saved up some money for the house, enough for a block of land, I got the block of land in Clayton Crescent, £630 plus legal costs. You know how much that land cost now? About 80 000, 90 000 dollars! And then got in touch with a builder, get a quote off him, made a house. On that block of land and eventually we come to an agreement that was OK to go ahead. £3300, incredible. Sold it for $30 000 in 1979.

And I gave up smoking at that time. And I think that's how we paid the loan out because the smoking money was put on the side to accumulate and anyway it helped to pay off the land. Well, I felt the weight of the responsibility, because I know what has to be performed here. It's not only that, to move in there, but I tiled the kitchen. I hired the sanding and every room, I sanded the floor. All of this sort of things. Well I was quite happy to work, and I was happy that things went along and I knew I had to do it myself.

It was maybe 1960 when we moved in. It was a big relief, except for the debts. But we managed. And I was the only one working until you went to school, and that was a big help, but until then I was battling all by myself. But I don't complain. We managed and just struggled on. I tell you this: I was pretty strong, I was pretty you know, very confident about my strength and my ability to carry on.

Sometimes I said to you Mum, well why don't you give you a name like Marilyn, or Debra. "Oh, no," she said. You got your name because Princess Alexandra was the lady then. For me it would have been Karen, you know. Well that was the idea to blend in, to get you, you don't get a stranger name, and then you going and playing with other kids and they never heard that. I suggested one of the names, Sandra.

I didn't want too many children. Well, if you can't secure a fair go, for the kids. The responsibility, of course, of course. I said, "Well, so far so good. I'll have confidence that we can handle two", but I tell you this: I was working as I said, flat out. It was nothing unusual during the week, two, three times double shifts, or around the clock, things like that. I never felt financially all the weight off until you were grown up.

When you went to school you spoke Hungarian until you started to communicate with other kids. Once you realized that's the language here, you didn't want to talk Hungarian. I think you might have been in Kindergarten, pre-school. But as soon as you mixed with other kids you realized that's the language and if I talked to you in Hungarian, and your Mum, you answered English.

You wouldn't talk. It didn't bother us. What can you do? It's our fault. On the beszél [talking] because I didn't bring it up that you answered in English because we should have remained just talk to you in Hungarian, even if you answer in English, you would have been still familiar with the language, so I'm not blaming you. Today you would appreciate it. Well you got basic idea. If the grammar is there all you got to know is the words, isn't it? To make it to a sentence.

We wanted to see you get a fair go! And we did. You have things that you should have, like all the good things in school, going to outings and holidays, you know,

when you were at that age. And when you are little that you have love and knowing that you are loved so much.

Your mother put some effort into it. Guitar, tennis, swimming, fencing, netball. Everything, you do everything. To make you versatile. All we wanted, not for us to show you off, that wasn't the reason. But what I'm trying to say I thought for you benefit, not for us to show you off.

My idea was for you to succeed! That's all! Because you are my child! That's why! Wanted you to secure your future, that you capable of looking after you self, and you family, that was the idea! That you won't be a fool to anybody. Because I love you I want you to do well, that's why.

I was more concerned that anything else, that you find you way in life and be happy, that's was very important, that is very important even today! To be quite capable, to handle life. To have the skill and all that, what's necessary to get along and get a decent life.

Education is important. You never know what happens in life, that you be quite capable even if you left on you own with kids and things like that, like my Mum and be quite capable don't have to go…I see them, I seen women like that and I seen them, "What am I going to do? What's going to happen now?" That's what I didn't want for you, that's what! The more qualifications you get the better. That is important to me, that you get along and your children get along. And they can manage. Whatever happens they can handle it. That's very important. That's beyond everything.

We always made all the way priority that you were equipped with anything that required. That was the priority. I didn't have anything in mind about what you were going to study, because I left that to you, to feel that you wanted to do. All I feel that you find your way, your own way, and I support to achieve it.

Lexi, it's not lucky what you achieved, you put a lot of effort in. Some of the things you got involved, I never dreamt you would do, like. We are, well I am happy and pleased with your efforts and all that, and I think your mother is the same. And we still…I don't claim any credit.

You were a good kid, no hassle, none, whatsoever. As a teenager you was very bright, happy, and I never suspected anything was bothering you. You was a bit quiet. More serious, like. You were good, I never had any problems with you. Ordinary days. You done your task in school, and friends and you had your swimming, and took part in different sports too. So fairly busy, there, never had a dull moment. We made sure you be able to do anything that was on.

Coming to Australia, it's a good decision because it worked out alright, because when I came to Australia I thought to meself, I always felt confident that if it doesn't work out, well I go somewhere else. I made some moves to go to United States. I

had, in fact I had a reply my application in' 54 from the American Foreign Service that I was ready to go. And I never got in touch with them anymore, I never even replied, because by that time, four years, I settled…I didn't when we came out here, certain things just didn't…not the people, I had no problem with the people, the biggest problem for me was the food, you know, the cookings?

I realized there coming hundreds and thousands of people coming in, I can understand that might be a shock to the local population like, you know. But other than that, they…things happened that wasn't up to high standards, sometimes people's attitude and all that. On the whole, generally in the open they pretty good. When I get here, I didn't feel alienated, but I wasn't very easy at things like, you know? The only thing that probably saved me was my age, that I was young, see?

It was a good decision to come, eventually yes. If I stayed in Hungary, well, it's hard to say, I didn't like the whole thing that I could see there, you know, Russians dominating. At that time they weren't the communists weren't so powerful, but they had power. But I could see what was happening.

Of course I'm better off here. There's no risk of that, I don't regret it at all. I have no regrets, that I left Hungary, none. I don't intend to go back again.

I am a Hungarian, I always will be Hungarian. I see the faults of some of the Hungarians …they doing some stupid things like, like when Mr Menzies, and Holt and others made a statement that the foremost migrants are the Hungarians. Others did too, in fact I heard one of them remark, it was a remark, few of them made that, that we the foremost migrant. And then the Hungarians stepped in and that's a stupid thing, they said, "Because the Hungarians are the intellectuals out here". What a lot of bull! You know? Australians give credit like that, and they destroy it. It's not the Hungarians, that are the intellectuals, real bloody idiots. Oh we have bloody idiots, Lexi, don't worry about that! Because every country got idiots, not only the Hungarians, the Pommies got they heaps.

Well there's no risk I am still a Hungarian, there's no risk of that. I am a citizen. You know what Judith Cassab said? And I think perhaps it's the same thing that, or sort of closest explanation that, "I'm a Hungarian. I am a Hungarian, and an Australian", she said, "But I'm not a patriot". You know I read that, it's in the book. Well, it's a nationalistic feeling as a Hungarian; but as an Australian, not as a nationalist, just a citizen.

Oh I would do anything for this country, if I had to, you know? A loyalty, of course! I owe a lot of things like what I got or what I achieved or the setbacks, what I didn't achieve, but I don't blame the country, I blame for myself. Although there are something like the recognition of trade that was a bit of a setback, but other than that it was alright. I could have been, I could have been a lot smarter. I could have been a lot smarter by attending to some education, like first of all, to English, to language to have a good control of English, because English was harder for me somehow.

Of course I belong here. I had to belong here. I got the family here and everything, you know. I am comfortable being an Australian. I keep attention of the Hungarian affairs and I wish them all luck, and all that, the best, you know? I feel with them, for the country like. There is no conflict, you feeling doesn't have any conflict, it would have been different if two countries were opposition to each other and all this and you would have to take sides, see that would be different. But there is no such conflict, complication, there is no such opposition between the two places, Hungary and Australia. See, so what's the big deal?

Of course this is home, but I got members of my family over there too, and their descendants and all that. I suppose I feel that this is home for everybody.

Ki két nyulat hajt, egyet se fog
He who hunts two hares, does not catch even one
(Hungarian proverb)

ZITA (II)

I was a kid, I had my 13th birthday in Naples. So July 16th we were still in Naples. I think we boarded about three or four days after. We arrived here in August, August 24th, I think we got into Newcastle, and as the train was going past here and all you could see were these old, all these old battered T-Ford cars. Model T-Fords. Can you imagine in' 49 model T-Fords which came out in the '20s? We were in the train. We came in eight-ish, nine-ish was. In the morning. This is how I recall it.

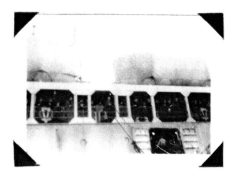

So...right, we tied up. We didn't come in the train, we tied up. And the train was on the railway track just here, old rattlers, you know the red rattlers? And of course then they put us out, we disembarked and we did it that way, we disembarked onto the trains. The luggage... they sort of came up later as far as I can recall. We had hand luggage, the things that you had with you, on board. In your cabin or whatever you call it. We were tied up for quite some time because the customs. And then of course from high up on deck we could oversee Newcastle, The Hill, we could oversee everything. The place just looked like the Wild West. I mean, all the shops had those old fashioned awnings you know with the wooden posts, and there was some...even horses tied up, because they were delivering bread and ice in horse carts in those days.

It was a country town, it was. It was very backward, as I said with T-Fords and horses and everything. I mean you just came from the other side of the world...you know Germany was fairly sophisticated even though it was flattened after the war.... Italy was sort of...Italy! Cosmopolitan, very cosmopolitan and we just thought we'd come to the end of the earth actually. We said, "Oh my God, oh shit!" You know, "We want to go back!" [laughs].

The streets were...paved, sort of. The streets weren't as well kept, as they are now, people sitting on verandas having a good old look, just like we were. They were sizing us up and we were sizing them up. And eventually I think after customs we disembarked on the train, of course going up towards Maitland. Everybody was glued to the windows, to see what the place was like. There was an atmosphere of apprehension...and of course there was a lot of empty spaces, the bush.

Well, Mother was always the optimist, she was always the optimist... I must admit, whereas Dad was sort of... "icked" at everything that was a bit substandard. He "icked" at everything. Not Mother, she didn't mind getting her hands dirty and all of that sort of thing. I must admit, the truth is the truth. She was get up and go. She said, "We'll manage". And Dad said, "Oh, God. Fancy living in this dump".

I mean you had those brown huts, it was that brown wooden hut, it was long. It was very windy. You know August, September you get the westerlies, and the westerlies, the boards, you could see through the boards of the buildings, they were all army huts, you know, underneath it was just a concrete slab with that brown building on top of it. It was really a rough army camp. Fifty, sixty people in each, no separate rooms, one long dormitory.

There's not very much I remember about the camp. I know there were westerlies and there was a lot of sand blowing into the huts. And people, you know to have a bit of privacy they hung up sheets, and things like that you know for privacy. And everything was so dusty. There blowing right, left and centre. It was a community kitchen, they cooked, they served up, so it was all wog food, bit of everything, depends who the cook was. Could have been a Russian or a Pole, so the food was quite tolerable.

There was a shower block, you had to go out, a W.C., it was outside. Like a caravan park, you know you just go out like that in the middle of the night. They had doctors, they had European doctors, of course everybody spoke German – that was the universal language, that's how we communicated. But we spoke Hungarian amongst us, that was the most comfortable of course. Doing what comes naturally.

We were there only six weeks because Dad said he couldn't put up with it, so what he actually did, because Dad didn't like roughing it, but when it come to the crunch

he couldn't stand it any longer, he took the initiative. He did. Dad said he's not coming back till he finds himself a job in Newcastle. They went from repair place, from one repair place to the other? So ended up with Hilder, in King Street. So Hilder had a repair business, a motor repair business in King Street. So they finally got in there, and Hilder was fiddling around with planes at that time. You know, I think he might have had a plane, or he was servicing plane engines, and he hired them. On the spot. And Hilder, he came up with this old dump for us in Cooks Hill, with mice rummaging through the kitchen.

I found the mice in the cooker and they, they…they were my first friends [crying]. I just let them go…. They were my pets, first friends. Talk about Cinderella! It's still upsetting. I don't know why. Don't forget we didn't have the language. It wasn't the hardship. Possibly it was about coming down in the world.

Anyway, so he found that place. And we made the best of it, so what can you do? Dad couldn't stand it in the camp, he just couldn't. You had all these aristocrats, they were cleaning toilets, my father wouldn't have a bar of it, he said he would starve first. That was their job, it was allocated, you know? He wouldn't do it. That's why he got out. Got on the train and got out. He wasn't going to do it. They were cleaning potatoes; he wasn't going to clean potatoes.

Hilder found the rental with an old man he must have been eighty if he was a day, a real old, dirty, an old widower who lived by himself with a house. He lived downstairs, he had the lounge, but oh you should have seen the place. We had two rooms upstairs. We had a kitchen, where we ate, and he had the lounge – you didn't want to go in the lounge, and then two bedrooms, I had my own room. The kitchen was downstairs; it was a place that was built onto the back of it.

We shared the kitchen, well, just the gas ring. I mean we lived upstairs and he

lived downstairs, and the place was rodent infested. Your grandmother was never a clean freak, guess who did it? She opened the business and she pissed off in the morning and leave me to it. Got myself ready, cut Dad's lunch and he went off to work at Hilder's, just down in King Street, I went to school, came home in the afternoons, start to cook the tea and she graciously did some things at the weekend. We washed the clothes by hand in an old copper, like an outhouse. A copper, there was two concrete sinks, you know those deep ones you see in the country? And the copper in the corner. You try and do it by hand! And it didn't even have a decent clothesline it was a, one of those Australian ones that tilt.

153

I did have some English. Private lessons in Germany. Dad worked for the Americans, he could make himself understood, so when we came in to Newcastle see he had an advantage over the others. Wasn't crash hot, but it was pretty good. Some German was the teacher. Plus I learned the violin, only for twelve months, basic.

Went to Cooks Hill school. But anyway, I went to school. We got the uniform...I don't recall, but obviously it was bought, she didn't make it because she didn't have a sewing machine. Cooks Hill Intermediate High. 1950,' 52,' 53. What do I remember? Not much. Give me the shits. Listen, we were the road breakers, we were the wogs and the I-ties, the migrants and all that sort of crap. I made a couple of friends, I even remember them, there was two Barbaras – yeah! I remember their surnames, how about that?

I know we played softball for sport. It was such a rotten game! [laughs] Anyway, tried to blend in as much as possible because my English was lousy. Think they probably, the first year they probably kept me in by the grace of God sort of thing, because I think probably I flunked the first time. I think they put me straight into second form, with not very much English at all. I don't recall feeling intimidated more than I already been before.

Because don't forget that's my third time around, third country. Here we go again. Just tried to live with it. And then, I had to go home to that rat hole, the one down the alley, that little house in Cooks Hill.

I was at school for two and a half years. And I left because Mother and Dad needed a bookkeeper and a housekeeper at home. They needed me, so they said, "Do you want to go on studying? But this needs doing and that needs doing". How could I? Well, it gave me the shits. I was told to do it and I did it. So much for my studies.

There was an active Hungarian community at that time, a fairly large one. We sort of got together, quite big. There wasn't a club – Stegemaiers had the 'Blue Danube' restaurant. And then they had…of course there was the 1955 floods, so they got together and had dance groups and I was one of the leading dancers. I was the soloist. Raising money, we did the performances and I was principal dancer. Hungarian dances, csárdás, pillow dance. My bridesmaid's mother was the choreographer.

The Hungarian community, well it gradually died out. There were lots of places that we went when you were little, you just don't remember. There were others, there was quite a lot of social occasions. There was dances, you know, Balls.

Well, you see Mother had the shop. And of course there were these Jewish travellers were coming around and all of that. They hired these places and they needed someone to model clothes for them. And I was it, and I was good at it too. I was really good at it. And for the clients and I think I made some money out of it, pocket money. And the bloke said, he came around quite a lot, to Mother's, selling things to Mother to sell in the shop, and he had a modelling contract that he offered me. There wasn't anything sleazy about it and he wanted me to go to Sydney. I was 19, something like that. I had been in a few beach girl competitions, came runner up. Mother convinced me that I couldn't do it, and so I stayed. I should have gone.

When we lived in Mayfield, Mother had the shop in Hamilton, she worked at nights, a lot at nights because she gossiped all day. It used to be a stopover for

every Tom, Dick or Harry Hungarian right? Including your father! So she socialized all day and of course in the meanwhile we were selling clothes too, as well as making them. She was making special orders, right? She bought stock from beautiful places. Some of those dresses that I wore, were from there. She gossiped, socialized all day, and of course a customer needed a dress, they want it next Saturday, and if she gossips all day, it has to be done…so she sewed all night.

Look, sewing is a piece of cake, providing you don't have to do any housekeeping besides. She didn't come home, she stayed at the shop. So I get sent home, I cooked the tea, I had to take cooked dinner back to the shop. To feed Mother and feed Dad and I was the one that got him ready to go on the road when he bought his truck. And then I remember before he went, he just pulled on the other side of the road near Beaumont Street at the shop, you know, pulled up with pipes and things on the trailer and said goodbye to Mother and off he went, he said, "Goodbye, look after your Mother". And I been doing that ever since.

We did have a very good relationship, Dad and I. As it happens I ended up being the son that he never had, you know, overalls, cars, working on the car, servicing, you know getting dirty. He loved it. I spent my time with him in the garage.

Oh your father was hanging around like a bad smell at Mother's, you know in the shop. He was always there. I always thought he was a sour puss, I always said so. I

mean he was pretending to come and talk to Mother, to see me. I didn't take any notice, "Oh no, not him again".

And one thing just led to another [giggles]. After a while, I sort of got to like him! [laughs loudly] he just sort of grows on you, he grows on you. He is so sweet. He just grows on you, crikey. Just so persistent. Well I was attractive! [giggles]

He wasn't good enough for Mother. I mean she tried to talk me out of it right up till the last minute. "You can still change your mind!" she said as I was dressing for the wedding. I wouldn't change my mind. I had so much drama in my life.

The wedding was in Hungarian and English. Mother's idea! Because most of the guests were Hungarians, right? And she suggested that it had to be in Hungarian, and then the two ministers almost had a bloody fight over it, about who was in charge. It was Reverend Keir's church. It was all Hungarian, the bridesmaids. I don't know how it came about, but that's the way it was.

The night you were born I was in labor for two and a half hours. Water didn't go this time. And the stupid bitch nurse. I sat there. So pregnant. Contractions. Filling out forms, for about half an hour...that stupid looking nurse asking me all those questions, which they do now, when you book into hospital, they get everything out of the way. Then, they did it when you go in. Terrific! And then I was complaining about my pains. And she said "No, no, nothing's coming yet", and then eventually they took me into the labor ward. They put me in the labor ward, with the gas, something or other there.

And they said – there's four of them – sitting in the corner having cups of tea. There wasn't anyone else, at that time; I was the only one in there. There were four beds there. I was the only one in there. They even gave me something to calm me down. They gave me a drug to shut me up, because I was complaining about it. They said, "Look, there's nothing going to happen before the morning, you might as well try and have a rest. Nothing's going to happen, try and to relax". They gave me a sleeping draught.

And these four women, nurses, they were sitting in the corner, yakking, having cups of tea or something, and I kept on, I said, "Nurse!' and they came over and "Mrs Lasczik, look…," they virtually told me to shut up. Because nothing's going to happen. They assumed it, they didn't check. They didn't. They just popped me on the table and gave me a sleeping draught, something to relax me, to shut me up, and they went and talked in the corner. Being Sunday evening, everything was very quiet, and I kept on, "Nurse, nurse!" And then finally one came over with, "Well, what is it now?" And she looked at me, and your head was out [laughs], just about out. Crowning. There you were. And you should have seen the four of them run in six different directions! Don't know where the doctor was, you should have seen them take off. "Don't even breathe, for God's sake, don't sneeze!" Anyway you came out screaming, no wonder, when you were sitting in the doorway, for so long nobody to help, not in, not out.

We stopped after you, couldn't afford any more. You can't clothe them, give them things they should have, can't let them go without. And I was so sick with you that turned me off. We just couldn't afford it, more kids. Your Dad was working so hard, and with what he was making we had to start paying the house off, we had to get a car, we couldn't afford it. We wanted for you as much as possible. I chose Kotara because it was close to Mother's, see I was still brainwashed. If we had bought  somewhere else you would have had a very different life. All around us they were working people, but they were well to do working people. Eventually we all scraped it together. Middle class area. Good middle class area.

We still got the papers for that house. It was a lot of money in those days. The electricity wasn't even on, we moved in on Christmas Eve. No electricity, no pieces of furniture. And all we had was one big rug on the floor and we had pillows, and we were sitting on the floor. Wooden floor. Polished floorboards. We had that big square that mother graciously gave, that big carpet square. And I tell you what we had fun. We were sitting on the floor by candlelight. We had a bed too. No curtains on the window, we had sheets. It was good.

Well, we wanted you not to have to do without things. Try to give you everything possible. With your names, we were arguing about it so much. I don't know why we didn't choose Karen or Sandra or Betty. Too common perhaps. Princess Alexandra was popular then. And Jacqueline Kennedy was the lady. And I tell you what, you grew into it beautifully. You had to, blend in. It wasn't a common name, it wasn't an ethnic name. They were a bit different to most.

Your Dad worked so hard at Courtauld's, and the smell and the ooze that came out of his skin…this is the first winter, because it was mostly winter, that it didn't come out in his pyjamas. This is the first winter that I haven't smelled sulphuric acid in his pyjamas. And that's twenty years after he left.

Before school you had not much English. But then you lost the Hungarian after you went to school. We didn't press it. And of course another thing too with the language, now, my head was all screwed up because of language differences. I went to a Hungarian school, OK, a couple of years. And then we left Hungary, then I had to learn German, from scratch to be able to exist. And then we came here, what did I have to do? I was getting English tuition in Germany, but you know I mean, not very much just something when we came here. But anyway, so, trying to study in three bloody different languages you were not master of any one, you were not so crash hot in any of them, but you managed.
So I scraped through everything. It was a conscious thing for you, I'm not forcing you to learn another language, I mean to keep another language, and you got to be good in this one. So you could cope, not to assimilate, just so you'd be good in your studies, because if you…I sort of had a split personality. I mean I just scraped through everywhere, but I wanted you to do better than just scrape through. So therefore I didn't force it because I know, I been through that mill three times, so I wasn't going to force that on my kids. It's our fault it's not yours that you lost the

Hungarian. It's not your fault, it's us...there wasn't a language school, there wasn't anything available in those days, in those days, there wasn't.

Education was so important for both of you...I couldn't master any of them, I couldn't master any of them. The schooling, right? I couldn't excel in anything; I was never in one place for long enough. I couldn't excel in Hungarian, when I read Hungarian I sound like a five-year-old child for a little while and then I can and it comes back. Actually, virtually didn't have a Hungarian education and 50 years later I can still talk the language. It's amazing. But anyway this is why it was very important for you to master and excel in education, in English. Because I had three goes at it and I virtually flunked at all three of them! Just scraped through. So the reason that I want to study now, is that I want to prove to myself, that if I would have had a decent chance at it, I could have done it.

As I said for years and years now, you've got to beat them at their own game. It was always a competition for me, yes. I didn't want you to be a so called as Germans called us refugees, you know, outlanders. Didn't want you to be. Well, I wanted you to blend in. Because Hungarians basically, not just you, we blend in well. It's a cultural thing, we hate each other's guts, the less we see each other, the better it is! The Greeks have their own communities. Italians as well, millions of Italians. But we didn't. Outlanders...racism I suppose, basically that's what it is...I tried to...disappear in the crowd sort of thing. I was battling. I had to be. You had to be twice  as good even to be as good. But remember I was a kid when I came here.

I think we all came out here with the same idea. I don't know about the other nationalities, hardly any of the Hungarian's offsprings don't have tertiary qualifications. You had to do better than the locals. Competitive thing, in my opinion.

There was an awful lot of racism in your primary school, and many times you came away from school and said they had problems with Mrs Port. She was very "holier than thou" with this ethnic woman, me, very self-righteous. She sort of tried to be condescending but I don't think she really succeeded, because I was never a shrinking violet either. But of course she had the power over you so I couldn't push my luck with either one of them, Miss Joseph too. She was a biddy, and so you couldn't rattle the boat, basically I knew that she had the power over you. And anyone who has the power over someone you love there's no other way out of it, you can't rub them up the wrong way too much, because they take it out on your children. It hurts terribly, when your child comes home telling you that they have been teased, racist teasing. You try to cope with it because your child can't, and it just hurts, it really hurts. It hurts more than when it happens to yourself, oh yes.

Running was your first activity. You had so many swimming lessons through sports and recreation. That's why I went to work, to afford the activities. You had tennis

lessons, had squash lessons, fencing, ballet, netball, guitar, and of course not to mention swimming costumes... tennis...cross country running, water polo, athletics club. Kotara South athletics club – that was the first thing. That was close to us too, Friday night. Yep! Make you versatile...I wanted you to have deportment...with ballet... you went to Sports and Recs camps away, you went what? All of them.

As a young woman, you know, socially we wanted you to fit in...and how do you get, you know, keep a teenager in control so that they won't get into trouble? Keep them tired. And keep them busy and tired.

For me it was very important. You *had* to excel. You had to beat them at their own game! Which you did. To me that was very important. Because you were discriminated at school, the name, the surname and you had to make them eat their words and they're still eating it. To me, that's important. To me. Perhaps not to your father. To me it's very important. Competition, yep. And it upsets me still, it certainly does. All the experiences that you had, mine was worse. Just terrible. It was just horrific at school, boys and girls, bloody new Australians and all that sort of crap!

We didn't belong. People were very rude. The things they said to us, to us, it's..., "Bloody new Australians, wogs, dagoes, why don't you go back where you came from? We don't need you here". What could you say? There wasn't anyone to go to even...now for instance, New Australians whatever, young men, seventeen, eighteen, that came out, and they were just, they weren't kicking windows they were just being rowdy or just being little bit noisy, but not being criminals, or anything like that. Just being teenagers. And the cops picked them up, any reason they picked them up, and they took them to in front of the judge and he said, "We don't do this sort of thing in Australia" and they put them in gaol to cool off, in the slammer just to cool them off overnight, or whatever the case may be.

Your Dad, his experiences, he was picked on by the cops right, left and centre. And they used to beat the new Australian boys up with telephone books, because they don't leave bruises. They used to belt them up.

I think my nomadic life, it made me strong. Adaptable, this is why I say, it doesn't matter where, you beat everybody at their own bloody game. Yep, it set me up as me against the world, that's what it did. You put this armour around yourself, you see? To protect yourself from the bullets. It wasn't a conscious thing that you did; you know, "From now on, I'm not going to let anybody else hurt me". That never even entered my head. Things just conditioned you without you even realizing. Life wasn't easy.

I still feel that I don't belong here and I don't belong there now. I'm in limbo. I feel that I don't belong here, but I don't belong there either. When we go to Hungary, you know, just when we go visiting, I'm sort of…I feel like a sociologist is supposed to feel, you come from outer space, right? And that's the way you size up the situation, you look at the natives, how they behave and all that. It's a different culture, and then you come back here and it's still a different culture [laughs]. I'm in limbo. I don't belong anywhere. But I'm here, I'm here physically, because I've got my beautiful family, right? So this is home, sort of.

I don't know, I'm very emotional about Hungary, even though I was only there six years. I can never feel that emotional here in Australia about the country. I felt that the Olympics in Sydney was a beautiful magnificent spectacle, but I didn't feel patriotic for Australia. Actually, I mean I was…we were sort of barracking for both sides – if it couldn't be one it had to be the other. Which is how it is really. Neither one nor the other.

Ár ellen nehéz úszni
It is difficult to swim against the stream
(Hungarian proverb)

LEXI

A lot of the stories that have emerged from these interviews I heard for the very first time, which is remarkable since I'd heard so many of the same stories over and over again.

All the stories that I've ever had from…or all the information that I've ever had from my parents came through storytelling and anecdotal information around the kitchen table, and later around the dining room table – when we got a dining room. It's the only way that I had any sort of contact with the family history. Indeed our grouping around the table was like a story telling circle. Everything that we ever learnt about what they considered to be home was storytelling. Completely.

So any of Dad's memories that we got, they were always fragmented childhood memories, things about the war, things about Dad's working life. And they'd come out at the strangest times and we'd hear them over and over again, repeatedly. We'd have to keep telling Dad, "Yes Dad, we've heard that", or we'd just switch off and he'd just keep telling us,

as if somehow it would make it all real to us, as if he'd forgotten that he'd told us before. As if it would connect us to his, and I suppose, our past.

I think it was his way of connecting his childhood to ours, since we had no grandparents alive to provide that function for him. So I suppose I think one of the best things about this particular experience with Dad is that for the first time in my life, I've got all the stories again, but in order. And I remember particularly how excited I was when Dad and I spent a very lucid evening in our lounge room, uninterrupted. Precious. And he put that whole war section into some sort of chronology for me.

With Mum, because of our tortured relationship with my grandmother, and the fact that she was so busy when the rest of us were sitting down for these stories, her contributions were like staccato bullets, thrown from the kitchen, mid-conversation, adding her two-cents' worth (one of her expressions) or casting us knowing or meaningful looks over Dad's head, underlining what he was saying.

Dad was sitting down telling us his stories, and Mum was usually in the kitchen, cooking the meal, or cleaning up afterwards. We didn't get nearly as much…in fact, very little if anything came through about Mum. I can't remember her talking about her life at all, except that they lived in Bayreuth. In Germany. For a long time I thought it was Beirut, you know, as kids do, not really understanding anything about Germany, and geography, or anything. I got confused. One story that was a constant from Mum was about the Germans coming down the road saying, "The Russians are coming! The Russians are coming!" which was amusing. Inappropriate I know, but funny, the way she told it.

Dad's decision to leave, I knew he wanted his brother to come, and it was a brave thing for Dad to come. The most enduring thing for me I think about that whole episode was the fact that he didn't ever

see his mother again after he left. And I remember in the seventies, I don't think I remembered when it happened, but later that Dad knew that his mother was dying and he wouldn't go, he wouldn't go back to see her. His explanation for that was that he…that we couldn't afford it and he wasn't going to deny his children anything so that he could go and see his mother one last time. By that stage his priorities were fairly firmly placed, but I knew how close he was to his mother and how much he loved her, so that must have just torn him apart. Dad always put family first, it is the most important thing to Dad. He lives that philosophy and he would have and still would make any sacrifice for us. But he bore that stoically and he accepted that he had to pool his resources into making sure that we were OK. We are everything to him. He made many great sacrifices for us. And he is just such a gentleman, as well as a gentle man, with so much dignity and endless patience. I'm so lucky to have him as my Dad. I have this impression, all throughout my early years, that they were unhappy here. It sort of settles on my childhood like a veil. I know Mum was very unhappy; she seemed to be angry all of the time. I don't know if that was because of her lack of opportunity, or her lack financial independence or her lack of wealth, or her relationship with her mother… Whether she saw that coming to Australia was a bit of a come down, that she had been used to a certain standard of living and a rather privileged childhood, despite the vagaries of the war, and she came here and was stripped of everything – money, position, not that she really had any, but her father was rubbing shoulders with a lot of famous and powerful Americans…a rosy future…I don't know. Was coming to Australia a come down? Is that what she thought?

And it's only since I had my own children that I realize that that's what it was. Mind you she was probably exhausted all the time because she was so busy being all things to all people and doing everything. I would probably have been in a bad mood too. But she seemed cranky all the time; she was a stage mother, particularly with our sports. Not with ballet so much or anything like that. Certainly with the sports. Push, push, push, push, push. Nothing was ever good enough. Nothing seemed ever good enough.

I don't remember much before school except for a couple of flashes of memory at preschool. I have only one memory of my grandfather who died when I was three, he was only 56. In my memory, I can feel him sitting behind me and I remember how he smelled. Cigarettes, because he was a big smoker, which killed him in the end.

And Brandy, which he liked Mum says. And Old Spice. That memory's particularly strong. And in tis memory, I can see the black and white TV, but I don't know what's on it, I can just feel him behind me, you know, sitting on his lap. I do feel that at this time I was secure and very loved. My parents have always been physically demonstrative – lots of cuddles and affection and I love yous.

I remember Aunty Betty from across the street. And I think it was Uncle David. They weren't really our relatives, but just good friends. I remember them, I remember Aunty Betty baby-sitting us, and I remember her bright pink lipstick, a short dark bob in a permanent wave that was always perfect. Powdered face that I could smell, cheap cologne. Smelt like something floral, and very cloying. She used to call me sugarplum and kiss me as she tucked me in. And I remember feeling really special, that this Australian lady from across the street, called me sugarplum. Made me feel special. We had a good relationship with them, and Mum and she used to baby-sit for each other. I know they came over for dinner sometimes. They had three boys, the youngest Mark David was in my class.

That's the only Australian family I remember having a close and daily relationship with except for my godparents, Lester and Shirley whom we saw on Sundays briefly after Sunday school. Lester was a friend of Mum's from way back.

I remember going onto *Romper Room* on television for two weeks, and I think that was during school time. That felt fairly special, because I recall that the other kids at school were quite envious. How did Mum get me on to that one? I still have the certificates. So positive social experiences would be things like, Australian friends that my parents had because that made me feel as if they were being accepted. There were many years there where I felt not only embarrassed about my parents (I am very ashamed to admit), because I saw them as being socially awkward, because of the language thing. I thought people wouldn't understand them, and would become irritated by their accent or lack of comprehension. I saw this sort of intolerant behaviour in many adults at this time, but also in almost all of my peers.

I was always on alert when my parents had to meet other significant people in my life, always wondering, would it go OK, or would they embarrass me? As an adolescent this got worse because not only was I embarrassed, as most teenagers are about their parents, that's pretty normal, but the cringe factor was absolutely excruciating.

When we got together with the Hungarians I didn't feel like I belonged there either. I felt like I was an impostor. Mum and Dad moved through this world easily, but I certainly did not. I couldn't speak the language and I'd go there and I'd feel totally adrift, not at all part of a supportive and like-minded community, and I felt like an impostor (and I still do), because I didn't understand anything of what they were saying. And I should have. And it was frustrating, and still is. And I remember thinking, "I don't belong here either". I didn't feel like I belonged with the Hungarians, I didn't belong with the Australians, and to some extent, I didn't feel like I belonged to my parents.

The Hungarian community...we socialized with only two families and their kids – but they were older. I remember being dragged to their places and being absolutely bored, couldn't wait to get home. We didn't hit it off; the kids really didn't hit it off. The ages were wrong. Our pastimes were wrong. Mum tells me we went to a lot of Hungarian functions when I was little and don't remember it, but by the time I was school age I can barely remember going to any

of them, so at that stage, in terms of my Hungarian identity, I suppose I still felt disenfranchized. I still remember that. It wasn't quite right.

I remember feeling very safe and very loved. I don't consciously remember speaking Hungarian and it being different. Although apparently I did speak Hungarian fluently, for years. I do remember that when I went to preschool that I wasn't struggling with the language as such, but the photos do show a very ethnic looking little girl, immaculately dressed, spotless and smart.

This is a common theme. Because Mum made all of our clothes, we always looked beautiful, but it was still all wrong. We looked too good, too different, too glamorous. Mum and Dad do tell me that once I realized that English was the language, that was it. I could not be coaxed or persuaded to speak Hungarian any more. I dropped the Hungarian completely and was not interested. They would speak to me in Hungarian and I would answer them in English. Once I'd found that that was the language that I needed to have I turned my back on the other. I don't know why. Maybe I was savvy enough at that age to even say, "Well, gotta get along here. This is what everyone else is doing". See, even at this really early age I had this…this desire to belong at the expense of my…who I was, and who my parents were. I do remember going to preschool and really liking it.

As far as my English language development is concerned I don't remember having any problems with the English language at school. I do remember going into Infants School fully formed, my English seemed as good as everybody else's. I wonder if it was.

I wonder if I caught on really quickly after a late start – learning Hungarian first and then English later – or whether I learnt both languages side by side. I know that Hungarian was spoken at home and I know that it has been a long time since I have spoken it with any confidence. I can't remember…I actually don't have a memory of speaking Hungarian at all, although it is clear that I did. I do know the words and I understand a lot of things but I can't string a sentence together and I can't remember ever doing it.

Isn't that weird? I don't have any memory of speaking Hungarian. None. And people ask me if I speak Hungarian and I say, "Yes just a little." I feel like a bit of a fraud, because I don't actually speak it. It's a very difficult language. I can say certain commands and request things and say thank you and I know the words for things, but I don't know the grammatical structure.

But on the other hand my English is great. Sacrificed one for the other. Dad tells stories about how at the age of 8 or 9, I used impossibly big words, far beyond my age, and that's true. I did. And I still love language. It's ironic I think, with this in mind that my name Lex means 'word' in Latin. I really like that. I actually have a friend who calls me lexicon. And a lot of my ethnic friends, my Greek friends, especially those whose English isn't as good as mine, and they say you can't have both with any great fluency.... And one of those friends says she doesn't speak Greek very well (to me it sounds fantastic, but anyway…it's all Greek to me!), and that she doesn't speak English very well. She says she can never find the words when she's flustered or has to make an argument. She admires me, she says, the way I can use words.

But then she did go to Greek school twice a week and I didn't do any of that. And I was glad for that when I was young, that I didn't have that ethnic pressure, even though I would have liked it now. The lack of any Hungarian community of kids my own age may not have been good for my Hungarian language development, but Mum and Dad didn't pressure me about it.

I am left feeling incredibly guilty that here I am, a good woman of pure Hungarian blood, yet I cannot speak my heritage language. I am ashamed. How can I call myself Hungarian-Australian, and not speak the Hungarian part of that equation? It is a door that is closed. Very frustrating when your grandmother launches into Hungarian because her English is failing, and you don't have a clue what she is talking about. Embarrassing, mortifying, frustrating in the extreme. And I feel as if that is utterly my fault. I was ashamed to be who I was.

I remember my first day at school – the teacher who was enrolling me had trouble with my name and asked Mum to shorten it. I was standing next to my mother. And them asking my name and them saying, "Alexandra's a little long, can you shorten it?" Didn't fit on the tag that they had to put on the desk. Already they were making us fit some certain criteria that made it easier for everybody else.

I have another Greek girlfriend, the same thing happened to her. She said that she felt ashamed that they didn't want to use her real name because in Greek, name is family honour, and she had her grandmother's name. It is part of your identity. To this day, she goes by the name "Rita" which is not her name, and she feels she has

lost who she is. Her real name is very beautiful, and she never uses it. So that's the type of thing you had to deal with in those days. So, Lexi it was and Lexi it became. Always. But that's what they called me at home. I don't ever remember them calling me Alexandra, but Lexi fit, and it stuck.

Since Mum and Dad had always called me Lexi, this was not really a problem, but my Hungarian surname was an endless source of grief to me my whole life. The mispronunciations were endless, and I always corrected people. I don't know why I did this; maybe it was just a reflex. When teachers asked me my surname, I automatically spelled it for them after I said it, always. It was less embarrassing that way. When I was older I thought how nice it would be to marry someone with a normal surname, how much easier that would be. And now I look at the trouble schools go to ensure the correct spelling of kid's names on reports and think about how many of mine were incorrect.

I don't know when I first became aware of my cultural difference. It was probably about the time I was being teased mercilessly by many of the girls in Infants School, feeling like an outcast. It was clear that I was the target of this particular type of attention because of my difference. I remember being teased by the girl bullies, about the size of my nose and the veins coming out from it. They said I had a big nose because I was a wog, or a Hungry Hungarian. I remember being teased about my name. I remember being teased about the food I had in my lunch box.

All these things, I felt, were about my ethnicity, my vast difference to everybody else. At that time there were no other ethnic children in that Infants School and so I guess we must have stuck out in that white bread suburb. I opened my Globite school case and in it were salami sandwiches on black bread. Funny that during those years, my favourite, favourite sandwich was devon and tomato sauce. And I used to beg my mother to buy devon and tomato sauce. She wouldn't. She wouldn't even buy vegemite or peanut butter like the other kids. I do remember thinking my life would be so much easier if I didn't have salami sandwiches or stinky tuna. That was the other one.

My grandmother was a force to be reckoned with. She was an incredibly dominant and manipulative mother and wife. She's mean spirited in many ways and would badmouth my mother at any given opportunity. We were estranged from her for about 10 years after my grandfather's death, and since she is the only relative we have in Australia, I felt this loss so keenly. I could never talk to my friends about visits to my grandparents or Aunty's and Uncle's, and Christmases and other family occasions were lonely. I had no cousins here, and my parents didn't socialise that much so I was very aware of this sense of being by ourselves much of the time until we were much older.

The endless bath time conversations with both my parents about what I was going to do about the teasing and how much it upset me is still a clear memory. They tried to turn it around for me. They always tried to help me, with advice. I talked about this stuff a lot to them when I was little I think. At least it feels that way.

This is really painful; reliving all of this...Wow. It still hurts.

I felt so lonely. I was so lonely. I felt so different.... It's ridiculous. Thirty-five years later it still upsets me. I didn't have any coping strategies at this point about what I could do. I just remember feeling totally, totally helpless and lonely and different. I felt very much an outsider, and I was trying to be so strong. But I was so little.

I tried to fight that feeling inside me. I thought it was unfair and unjust, but I didn't surrender to it. It did give me a whopping great inferiority complex, which I still have, but I do remember trying to fight the sadness and helplessness it gave me. Always the optimist. I wanted to convert everyone into liking me, and I did feel crushed, but not so overwhelmed that I felt like I couldn't go on. No. I fought

it with every ounce of strength and courage that I had. And I struggled on. At the age of five and six, I already recognized that life was a battlefield, and you just had to fight your way through it.

I didn't belong. I wanted to, I desperately, desperately wanted to. And I think it was probably at this stage that I opened myself up to not actively searching, but being open to the possibility of finding out how I could possibly somehow, find a way to belong. Searching for ways to minimize my difference. I think it probably happened about then. I think.

My enduring memories of Infants School are painful, cripplingly so. Infants School sticks in my memory as being such a traumatic time. Because Mum could sew, and we were poor, she would make my school uniforms. They were beautifully made, but the patterns were subtly different, not quite right, and this made me even more different. I really didn't feel like all the rest.

The Infants mistress was so nasty to me. I remember my one and only time I got into trouble. Waving at the audience during a rehearsal for a Choral Festival at the Town Hall. When we got back to school I was carpeted.

I remember clearly the headmistress saying, "I'd expect that from one of you". That hurt. I knew exactly what she meant, and I'd never even been in trouble before! And I remember thinking how unjust that was, how unjust it was. That stayed with me for a long time.

And I look back and think what an old biddy she was. How nasty and how out of touch. So if I'd been looking for help with my problems in the playground, no way I'd even entertain the idea of going to her or any other teacher, no way. No way.

Kids these days in schools are given so much opportunity to come forward with their problems, they're encouraged to discuss them. If they can't do it at school, they do it at home, and the parent feels empowered to come up to the school and speak on their child's behalf. More comfortable about going into schools than they were thirty years ago. I guess that's why. Because situations like this arose where kids felt so powerless and persecuted.

But I knew that I could go to no one, I had a sense that I could go to no one at school, not a teacher, another kid, the Principal or the Assistant Principal. I knew I had no avenue. Wouldn't have even occurred to me to do it. To tell a teacher. I was frightened of them as many kids are, and I didn't feel...I always felt that things were my fault, that I was somehow responsible for this shitty behaviour of the other kids. I had brought it upon myself somehow. I always felt there was something wrong with me and that's why this was happening. The White Anglo kids were part of some larger scheme that didn't include me and that no one would believe me. These other kids were far more wily and confident as well. And I knew no one would believe me.

By the time I left Infants School things seemed to be a little better, I was a little more confident. I was in the top 3rd class, with what I thought was the best teacher. I remember feeling a bit intelligent then. Not overtly, it was just a quiet little awareness, a realization that I felt better. I felt myself relaxing somewhat, as if I no longer had to constantly be *en garde*. At least I knew I had a brain, you know? I was in 3A; I was with the kids who were quite nice.

By the time I got into 4th class, feeling OK and starting to have a little confidence in myself, I had another reality check. I was unfortunate to have a horrifically xenophobic teacher, she was awful. She was sweaty, greasy haired. And she thought she was hot shit. But she was so rude to me, she used to tease my name, in class, in front of the others. Often. She was...what I thought even in those days, hypercritical. And aloof with me, but not with the others.

But it was in 4ᵗʰ class that I had my epiphany, and it is this one moment that really stands out, at the school athletics carnival. I had performed well, physical pursuits were easy, and I was something of a natural. This memory is crystal clear; it was one of those defining moments. The Principal was announcing the Junior and Senior boys' and girls' Athletics Champions, and I fully expected my biggest rival Cathy to win. And then he said my name. I couldn't believe it. It was me.

I was so proud, I still have that trophy. It's the only one of the hundreds that I won they I have kept. Junior Girl Athletics Champion. It was my epiphany.

Later, as I began to have more success in a variety of sporting endeavours and was recognized for these achievements, I made a very conscious decision. That

if I was going to be noticed for something or singled out, it was going to be that I was bloody good at it, so that people would admire me and envy me rather than tease me. It was a very conscious thing and that feeling remains with me: To be respected, to work hard at what I can do well so that I would be recognized, seen, acknowledged.

I don't really have many memories of being on the outer in Primary School, and things were starting to improve. I realized I had a talent for sports, athletics in particular. Mum and Dad had by that stage had already started their campaign of activities. I'd already started running. And as my athletics progressed I became quite competent, and I got to run at the Cinders Track in town. The Cinders Track was special because it wasn't grass; it was made out of cinders, of course, and it was far faster to run on than grass. Mum bought me a pair of spikes, which, I just thought were the bee's knees. A bit of a status symbol, that I had spikes to run in, and the fact that I could run, and I liked it. And the long jump and the high jump. I was a very good high jumper. Broke my arm twice doing that. But I loved the feeling of flying. They were really good times. The other kids just accepted me as another athlete, albeit with a strange name, but they never seemed to notice it.

The officials all had trouble with it in the marshalling area, stumbled over my name constantly. Later when swimming became my big thing that continued. But even though it used to shit me, I got used to it. I'm just glad that at this point in our lives, Mum and Dad expanded our social horizons.

I had school friends and swimming friends and athletics friends and I had netball as well, and later squash, tennis and water polo. Before athletics started we had fencing and ballet, so I have always had a busy, active and full life. None of the other wog kids did this. Maybe

It is herewith Certified

their parents got them into one thing, but not lots of things like us. We were really lucky that way. I didn't have a big family, but I did have my activities.

After my nasty experiences with my 4th class teacher, I went from being in her class with some of the beautiful minds in the place to being in the bottom, remedial 5th class. I don't know why that happened. And I was in there with all the dumb heads, with all the kids that couldn't read, that couldn't write. I don't know why I was put there, but there I was.

Now, my father tells a story about how good a teacher that 5th class teacher was, and how I got straight As in everything that year on my report cards, and how fabulous he was. I actually don't think it was his fabulous teaching, although I do remember him as being a kind and dignified teacher, I just think it was more the case of I was miss-placed and in the wrong class.

I went up to the top 6th class with all the brainy kids again the next year. I didn't realize it until much later that it was probably because of her, my 4th class teacher, her prejudice that put me in that class because I have since read some of my compositional writing from 4th class and it was good. Comparing them to my kids' work at the same age, and they are both bright students who write well, mine were pretty good. So I don't know what was going on there. I do remember that by the end of 6th class, I felt fairly empowered. I was a strong runner, a good netball player, I had started swimming and was having some success in that, and we had started going to National Fitness Camps in the holidays. I was really busy, we had a full life. I was starting to have some success.

By the time I got to Year 7, first form, I cut my hair off because I had started swimming training seriously, four hours a day. That was 5.30 – 7.30 in the mornings, Monday till Saturday, and then 4.00 – 6.00 in the evenings Monday to Thursday and Saturday afternoons. Club night was on Fridays, at Lambton Baths, and carnivals were most Sundays all across the state during the summer months with some winter competitions in heated pools in Newcastle and Sydney.

It was a big commitment financially and time wise for my parents, and for me. But I liked the fact that I had this other life outside of school that took up my time, with a whole different group of friends. I also loved the success and the status that came with it because it made me feel really special at school when I won. I felt that people were looking up to me, rather than down on me, and I floated above most of the petty jealousies and bitchiness of school life because in my eyes, I was a star. This success became very addictive for me and boy, was it good for my ego. Dad still tells me that when he conducts his business around town, people ask him if he is Lexi's father, people I don't even know, so I guess I must have been in the spotlight a lot. I still have swimming records at that school that stand 25 years later. Dad and Mum think that's great. I

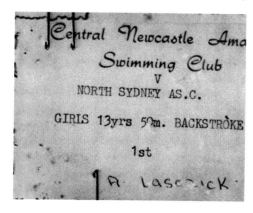

know that by the time I hit second form, Year 8, I had started to feel fit and strong and clever. I was in the top classes, when I got to high school and had made it to 7A,

I felt very proud of myself. Like I had made it. It certainly made the passage into high school very, very easy. And by that stage I wasn't suffering in terms of insults and taunts at all. Things were getting better. I do wonder if Mum and Dad realized that this sporting campaign would result in social acceptance. I'm sure that was their plan.

I do know that Dad wanted us to be socially accepted, but Mum wanted us to beat them at their own game. She knew what it was like to be in the Australian school system, that if I succeeded no one could take it away from me. It would be a concrete fact, and that was it. People could not dismiss me. She has said this to me many times. She told me that she developed this philosophy in Germany to survive. Then she got uprooted again and came to Australia and had to do it again.

So high school was better. Teachers still pronounced my name incorrectly but I'd become used to it. I was expected to complete all of high school, no questions asked. That was the only real pressure they put on me academically. That and the assumption that I would go on to tertiary study. Dad said he didn't care what we got a degree in, and what we did after college, I just had to go.

Dad was very forward thinking, he always told me that I should never have to rely on a man for anything, so I'd better be able to look after myself. In fact Dad was rather non-traditional for the time in many of his attitudes to women. He is the first feminist I ever knew, and believed absolutely in equal access for women to education, equal opportunity for all things and complete independence. Education was always critical. It was always drummed into me, how important it was.

I do remember them saying to me, "It doesn't matter what you do. It doesn't matter what you do at University, you're just bloody going". I remember that being the key. It was about power.

The only positive experiences that stand out, and I'm sure there were more, but the only positive experiences that stand out are the ones where I had success. That I earned myself, either with my brain or with my body. And I don't even know at that stage if it was conscious, I don't think that was a conscious thought when I was a child. But it was becoming that way, it was becoming conscious. So that by the time I got into high school that drive was already establilshed and I was happy as long as I could have some measure of control over the situation.

I was setting myself up for what life was going to be like I suppose. In hindsight it's very easy to see these things but I don't know how conscious it was on my parents' part. I'm sure it was. They wanted me to socially adapt. Dad always said he wanted me to fit in; I needed to fit in socially. So at this stage at high school, I did desperately want to be considered to be, and indeed felt like I was an Australian. I didn't gravitate to people who had similar ethnic identities at this stage; that came later, in college and beyond. In high school I wanted nothing to do with that.

So yes, I went onto college and gained a Bachelor of Education in Art. It was a happy time. When I finished college I didn't really have any goals. I just wanted a job as a teacher. When I got my job I was thrilled. I had a regular income, I was settled.

I knew that I wanted to get married and have children. I knew that I wanted to work. I didn't have the faintest inkling that after only two years in the job I would become a Head Teacher. Probably the youngest head of department in the state at that time, I'd just turned 25. And through various

different permutations, through Visual Arts and Creative Arts faculties, and then even sometime as a Deputy Principal I knocked myself out, before I gave it all away to study some more.

When my husband and I went to communist Hungary in 1984 after I finished my degree, we went without anyone else from my family. Mum and Dad had been back once before this. I was very apprehensive and quite nervous about it, because I knew that communication was going to be very limited, and that would be very embarrassing for me. I was hoping that when I arrived in that land of my ancestors, it would feel like home. But I was an outsider there too. Still, my family were very loving and accepting and generous, and we were there at Christmas, and it was very special. We both think it was the most meaningful Christmas we have ever experienced.

The family made all of my favourite Hungarian food, and it was an exhausting week. The enduring memory for me of the trip was Stu sitting at the kitchen table one cold morning with my Uncle. They both had dictionaries: Uncle Zoli had a Hungarian-German dictionary, and Stu had an English-German dictionary. And there they were, having a 'conversation'. It was hard work, and painfully frustrating to watch, but they were talking. That was wonderful.

It was a very meaningful time for me, and I felt the spirit of my parents draped around me like a cloak. But I was a tourist in the land of my parents, and that was confronting. One of my biggest fears is that we will never go back to Hungary as a complete family: Mum, Dad and me. We couldn't afford it when I lived at home, and I cannot talk Dad into it, he will not go back again. I feel like we have all missed out.

CHAPTER 13

The one thing I carried home with me after that first overseas trip was just how Australian I am. I was very aware of my accent, which sounded broadly Aussie next to all the other languages, and quite loud and harsh as well.

Later when we went to Canada on teacher exchange for a year, I also became very aware of all the very Australian vernacular I utilized. Things like 'crikey', 'fair dinkum' and 'struth', which I hadn't previously realized I used so frequently, brought much amused attention from the Canadians. That was enlightening on many levels. Not only had I successfully mastered the idioms of 'Australian', but also its nuanced and colourful expletives. If language was the passport to culture, then I was there: truly Australian!

I tried desperately to assimilate, I didn't know what it was called at that stage of course, but that's what I wanted. I wanted to assimilate. I wanted to be part of it, I wanted to belong, I didn't want to stand out in the crowd. Later I loved standing out in the crowd, I became a total performer. I think that is more the real me, the actress. But back then, I didn't want to be different.

And I remember the moment I turned it all around, and having at that stage some sense of acceptance. It was going to be, "OK I'm different, but I'm different and I'm better, not I'm different and I'm worse". And I'm sure that comes from Mum and I'm sure that comes from her constant dogma of beat them at their own game. You have to be twice as good to be as good, which later incidentally I embraced as a feminist. By the time I was aware of feminist issues I thought, "OK I know this battle, I've done it before", and also, "Bloody hell, not this again".

Gradually through my adult years, I've become very used to fighting battles and I am now quite comfortable in the battle zone. Even though it is quite an exhausting way to live. Life is a battlefield and I cannot stop fighting. I will always fight injustice and I will continue to question accepted dogma and norms. Because you never know,

there might be another way to do things – a different, perhaps better way, a way that might be less hurtful and damaging.

People used to say to me as I grew older, "But you don't look Hungarian," or, "You don't look like a wog". Did they, in fact, know

what other Hungarians even looked like? There are so few of us in this country, I seriously doubted it.

I had mixed feelings about those comments even at that stage. I thought, "Well, hmmmm. Does that mean that you're accepting me as an Australian?" What was a wog *supposed* to look like? Nick Giannopoulos and the whole "Wogs Out of Work" thing and other similar successes have done much to increase our acceptance whilst simultaneously fleecing the 'notwogs' of their cash – capitalising on the xenophobic experiences for fun and profit! You gotta love it. Aren't we lucky? We have a heritage different to yours, we are not associated with your convict past, and we had nothing to do with it. We can truly say we are not responsible for the atrocities of the past in this country (maybe other atrocities elsewhere, but not here). We have a heritage much richer that goes back centuries, not just two hundred years. And I'm not talking about the heritage of the land here, or the Indigenous peoples, that's different again.

I cannot relate to Australian colonial history. I can't do it. My Greek friend Karen says she does. I can't. With respect, I am sorry…. I don't get it. I feel separate to the colonial past. The only reason I feel one iota of an allegiance to that history is because my children are a part of it, and I can enter it through their family history on their paternal grandmother's side.

But then again, I don't relate to Hungarian special days either. The saints' days, I don't understand them. Mum and Dad tell me about them, but I don't feel I have the right to call that mine either. I don't know why. Sad. I really do feel like I'm between the two of them. I feel more Australian than anything else. And I think I've always felt that way. Australian with a twist of Magyar. But neither really.

I have lived a double life, it's like twin ghosts within me. I very much felt I lived in two worlds. Neither of which I felt I fully belonged to. I had a foot in each camp and I didn't like it.

I can see now, it was a blessing. I'm able to rationalize it now, that I was actually very fortunate. And I do feel very fortunate in hindsight. I feel like I belong to the ethnic population of this country and I'm glad I've got that. But it has taken me a long time to revisit that and realize that was something to be celebrated and valued.

It wasn't until I got to adulthood and at university the first time that I started to look back and try to find myself through the window of my heritage culture. I started making artworks at college that had something to do with who I was as an Hungarian woman, but I found them deeply unsatisfying as artworks. I have revisited them since. They are still unsatisfying.

I couldn't get a handle on what being Hungarian was, because I didn't really know what being an Hungarian was. And the point is, I'm not Hungarian. I have Hungarian heritage but I'm not Hungarian. And I think I feel that way because I don't have the language. The only time I feel like I'm Hungarian is when I cook. And then I really feel like I'm in touch with my heritage. It's not who I am either, but I feel in touch with where I come from. Centuries of tradition in just one pot – that's what it's like for me. That I'm in touch with centuries of tradition at that moment.

So the food motif is a really important one for me because it's the only one I can connect to. I don't like embroidery. I can't do it. I don't really like the look of it. Food I can do. But I started to reconcile my identity at college when I started making those (really awful) artworks. I see that as the start of my journey back to who I was, or who I am really. Reclaiming part of myself that I had totally rejected because of external factors that were excruciatingly painful.

And I have to credit that fact, the reason I started to do that was because I was becoming very close to a Greek girlfriend of mine who showed me that being an ethnic woman was a fabulous thing, that it was a gift. It was OK, acceptable. No, it was wonderful. She was such a catalyst in my life. It was Karen that made me really look at who I was. She and her family modelled for me, what it was like to be happily 'woggish' in Australia. But then she had such a huge family here with Aunties and Uncles and a million cousins. They got their strength from each other, and their large Greek community – they had their own newspaper, their own churches, restaurants. Goodness, they have their own Easter!

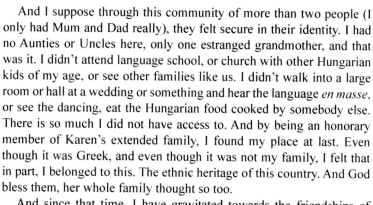

And I suppose through this community of more than two people (I only had Mum and Dad really), they felt secure in their identity. I had no Aunties or Uncles here, only one estranged grandmother, and that was it. I didn't attend language school, or church with other Hungarian kids of my age, or see other families like us. I didn't walk into a large room or hall at a wedding or something and hear the language *en masse*, or see the dancing, eat the Hungarian food cooked by somebody else. There is so much I did not have access to. And by being an honorary member of Karen's extended family, I found my place at last. Even though it was Greek, and even though it was not my family, I felt that in part, I belonged to this. The ethnic heritage of this country. And God bless them, her whole family thought so too.

And since that time, I have gravitated towards the friendships of ethnic women. Because there's a lot of stuff that is unspoken – we understand each other's formative experiences. We don't need to explain about our pasts. We know what it's like to be out here on the margins. It's crowded out here now. We have found ways to cope; we've found ways to embrace who we are.

That language loss is a huge issue for me. I don't think I'll really feel that I am reconciled until I relearn the language. It's almost like it's a closed door. And I had a closed door when I tried to walk into Australian society at the age of five. The

door was closed. I cracked it open, I pushed it open, I kicked it open. I walked in. That door to the Hungarian side of who I am is open, but it now needs to be blown open.

I absolutely do consider that my education was an assimilating mechanism, absolutely. It was the strongest assimilating mechanism that was available to me. But I also think that the other strong assimilating mechanism for me was not only my education, which gave me my equipment, armoured me with the tools to make my life, in my own way. Sport was the other one. If I hadn't had those achievements...I

wasn't strong enough or self disciplined enough at that age to throw myself into my studies so that it was all consuming, because learning didn't do it for me, it wasn't my thing back then.

I was bright but languid and immature. And I got through because I was bright, and not because I worked my slot off. I was too busy having a life of variety and balance.

I was on the go all the time, working hard, but my energies were going in several different directions at once, rather than concentrating or focusing on just one area of my life. I did work hard at times at school, but not as consistently or as focused as I could have been. And that was probably both due to a lack of maturity and all the other shit that was going on in my head. But if I hadn't had sport to empower me, I don't know what I would have done. I think I would have been a lot unhappier. Maybe I would have found other ways to cope. Maybe I would have thrown myself into my studies.

I'm just fortunate that I had skills there and two parents who believed in me. I became very good at a lot of different things. Pretty good at one of them, swimming, but not really on the top of the heap. I got what I wanted out of it so I suppose I really did succeed. That's the Australian way isn't it? Sport as the window to opportunity – becoming a sporting hero and be lauded and admired. Now that's a language the Aussies could understand.

I have made a conscious decision throughout my entire life to watch people. I guess I've always been a bit of a sociologist, always an observer. And in that way I have watched them, I have looked, I have listened, I have tried to understand how other people feel and this has been an active and very conscious behavioural trait. And I'm sure that it comes from this desperately wanting to connect with people. The fact that I am good at it, I don't know whether that's because it's an innate personality trait, whether it's because that's the way that I am, or whether its because I have developed these skills through my experiences. I think it's probably a bit of both.

I remember in the early days when talking to people that I wanted to impress or that I wanted to get along with I would sublimate myself, get them to talk about themselves, ask them questions, seem interested, whether I was or not. Quite manipulative really. I guess the fact remains that people generally like to talk about themselves. I have been a keen observer of human behaviour my whole life. It has served me very well; consequently I now have skills that I have developed over the years that I can talk to anyone if I am willing to make the effort. That coupled with my life experiences have been very, very helpful in interpersonal relationships at work and in my private life.

In this way, I have surrounded myself with lots of people in all sorts of different categories and contexts, different social circumstances to do with the activities that I was involved in and that holds to this day. I have some wonderful friends, enduring friends and I have loads of acquaintances, colleagues and mates.

Because I'm gregarious and soft and care about what people think, and how I am perceived…has that led me to an active campaign of trying to engage people and get them to like me? Now I know I've said that it's a self-serving tactic, but I don't think that that's how I am.

Did I become more gregarious, needy because of my experiences? Would we have been this way anyway? It's a question you can't really answer. All I know is the conscious things I did in order to feel acceptance. Longing to belong. That I know.

Largely because of the help of my ethnic girlfriends, I would say that I am pretty reconciled to being Hungarian-Australian. Or is it an Australian-Hungarian? I'm not sure, but I think of myself as being more of Australian than Hungarian. I have to, I've lived here my whole life, and I was born here after all.

It says 'Australian' on my passport. That's what I am. I don't know what

it's like to live in Europe. I've lived in Africa and North America, but I don't know what it's like to live in Europe. But I would say that I am an Australian, a proud Australian with an Hungarian cultural heritage. The only thing that saddens me is that once my Grandmother and Dad and Mum go, there is no one here to carry on the family names. I could have done it, I could have kept my maiden name, but I willingly shed it for several reasons. It was such an albatross around my neck. Its ethnicity when I was little was unbearable, but that wasn't an issue as I grew older. It was because of its difficulty in having to spell, write and say. But the funny thing is that I got an equally difficult married name. Hard to spell, and everybody mispronounces it.

The point is this: that before I was married, I had the cultural indicator of my name, a kind of shorthand that identified my difference, to say that I was not of Anglo Saxon descent. But once I was married, my ethnicity was veiled, and in some ways, I am ashamed to admit, that was a relief.

See, even with this stupid thing, I was desperate to belong to something other than what I really was. Some feminist I am! So my ethnicity is veiled or hidden behind an Australian name. Arthur Calwell would be proud: I am totally assimilated. The name dies out and that's it. It is sad, sad for my girls who are half Hungarian in their heritage, but are even further removed from their cultural heritage because they have this dim mother that can't even speak the language to them. I'm ashamed. So our ethnicity is veiled, theirs and mine. Unless of course I cook a Hungarian meal to an unsuspecting guest or if others meet my parents. "Are you Hungarian?" they ask. Am I Hungarian? That's a very good question. Well, genetically yes, culturally no. But the fabulous thing about this is, that I do now feel a little bit special and a little bit exotic, you know? My history is related to the history of gypsies, exotic food, fantastically spirited music, glorious literature. I wonder how I'll feel when my links to my culture are gone from this earth. If they all lose their English, and we can't communicate anymore. What a tragedy that would be.

Being a second-generation Australian has been a tremendous burden, less as I grew older and society changed and I became better equipped to deal with it. But it has also been a gift. It's made me very aware of people who are different. And very conscious of trying to make people who are outsiders feel comfortable. And I do this consciously in my teaching life, and I do it in my personal life. With my students, and my colleagues. If I can minimize people's discomfort, I will. And that extends to making people feel comfortable in my home. But Mum and Dad have always said that that type of hospitality is a very Hungarian trait. Hungarians are very hospitable, Hungarians are very generous.

So my experiences as a second-generation Australian were similar to those of other second-generation Australians in that we worked harder, because we had to. Our parents had a tremendous work ethic. If they didn't, they wouldn't have come. And they instilled those values, that bravery and that courage in their kids. We were armed to the teeth with courage and bloody mindedness because we knew we couldn't go back. We had to go forward. My parents, along with a lot of other migrants built this country, literally. By the time the sixties and seventies rolled around you could say that a lot of Australia rode on the wogs' backs, not the sheep's. But my experiences were so different....

We are the second tier; we are contributing to this country in significant ways too. Look at all the second-genno wogs in all aspects of society: we're everywhere. I'm proud of our efforts. Australia stands on our shoulders as much as anybody else's. And we have great loyalty to this place. But it was never a level playing field. And people need to understand that.

Sok jó ember elfér kis helyen.
Many good people can find room in a small space
(Hungarian proverb)

CHAPTER 14

GYPSY

It wasn't until I bullied, begged and berated my father that he agreed to go.

I had called Mama in a lather of tears and recriminations one evening after the children were in bed, and I was working on Dad's narrative.

"It's just never going to happen", I blubbered. "We'll never, ever go back to Hungary together. I'm sitting here looking through all of this Hungarian stuff, and Dad's manuscript, and I'll never see it with you!"

"Well", my mother said, used to my emotionally charged phone calls of late, "We could go together, just you and me".

We had discussed this before, Mama and me, but in my resolute bloody-mindedness, I had stubbornly refused to entertain this thought. In my opinion, it's not worth going unless both of them agree to come with me. Now I was facing the reality that I may never go back to Hungary, in my utter desperation, I reconsidered. It was better than nothing.

And so we agreed. We would go, in two months' time.

*

My father is not impressed. I try to persuade him once more.

"Why Lex? What's to be gained from all this?" he said to me, yet again. "I never want to go to Hungary again."

"Dad, can't you see?" I say, "It's just about the most important thing in my life at the moment. It's something I want to learn and share with your grandchildren... Damn it Dad, I want to know who I am!"

"You're the lovely onesie, that's who. That's who you are."

I could have screamed. When Dad doesn't want to pursue a line of dialogue, he coddles me with affection as if I were 3, not 39. I push him further.

"Fair dinkum Dad, you drive me up the wall. I'll tell you this though: If you ever decide to go back to Hungary in the future, and I have missed out because my window of opportunity is now, and I won't be able to go later, then I swear to God, I'll never forgive you!"

This last statement absolutely silences him and he just looks at me. Then he gets up from the table and walks away.

"What?" I say to my mother who is giving me her gimlet eye. *"What did I do?"* I throw my hands in the air. *"Why is he so stubborn? He won't even talk about it anymore, let alone think about it."*

"That's quite enough," Mum replies, *"We'll just go on our own."*

*

Less than a week later, Mama calls me. "Guess what?" she says, excited, "Your father has had a change of heart!"

"No!" I gush, *"I don't believe it! We're going? Really? All three of us?"*

I am astounded; he convinced me it was never possible. *"What happened? Why did he change his mind?"*

"It was that last comment you made, the one about not forgiving him? That's what did it," I can hear the smile in her voice, *"You know he never likes to let you down. He couldn't do it. So he would rather go, against his 'better' judgement. He'd rather come with us than let you down. I think he has finally realized just how important this is for you."*

In my shock and elation, this got me thinking. It is true; my Dad always comes through when I need him. He is going to come with us, even though we'd basically have to drag him there. I know though, that as soon as his beady eyes latch onto my uncle's beady eyes, he will forget his reluctance and be just as delighted to be there as me. I was so excited. At last, after a lifetime spent yearning, we are going. We are going together.

*

Dad's brother, my uncle Imre bácsi, has been searching the parish records for me as his contribution to this mission. He has managed to locate family records dating back to the early 1800s. With the documents that Nonya gave me years ago, I am getting a really good picture of my ancestry. Imre bácsi, who can appreciate my interest, is enjoying himself even though he has had to struggle with parish bureaucracy which, like many other political processes in the new Hungary, is fraught with frustrating, power hungry, mini-despots.

At the same time as my uncle is trekking all over north western Hungary on a quest instigated by this project, I am searching records in Australia. One lunchtime at work, cup of tea in hand, I decide to search the National Archives site on a whim, thinking, *"This'll be good; I bet there's no record of us here."* This is how entrenched my feelings of not belonging are – I really do not feel noticed here in Australia.

Five minutes later my cynicism is absolutely silenced. I am staring at the computer screen, as tears make an oily pattern down my face.

There they are: Dad, and on another page, Mama and my grandparents. Their names are recorded as new immigrants to Australia, in records of entry from 1949. Although they are not the original documents (copies of which I can buy if I want), I am sitting before my history, embedded into what is the history of Australia. There *it is, real and in front of me. Evidence that my parents and grandparents entered the country, the date they did so, their ages, dates of birth, languages spoken and occupations. It is at this precise moment that I don't feel so forgotten. We are acknowledged and part of the public record. And there I sit in front of that screen, feeling not so alienated after all.*

*

Up and up and up and up…

Australia is falling away behind us, we three are hurtling into the sky and an adventure 40 years in the making is beginning, at last.

I feel so lucky, a little smug and very definitely thrilled as we rise over that magnificent city I used to call home, over its sparkling harbour and its clean and splendid radiance. It is sunset, appropriately, and I look through the window into the great blue nowhere. I don't know whether it is because I am with my parents, or because of the exhilaration of take-off, but I could dance and clap and squeal with delight. As I look out of the window I can see all around me is vibrating, with the purity of the liquid golden light. I feel wonderful, I feel positively expectant, I feel new.

We chase the sunset across the great southern land – the day is behind us racing to catch up – and in front, an endless twilight. This journey has finally, finally, finally begun.

*

We are here at last, flying into Hungarian airspace as dawn breaks over the Carpathian Mountains below us. I look at my father as we both examine the video map in front of us. He is as excited as I am. Over Budapest we soar, and a few short minutes later, we touch down in Vienna. I am quite overcome with the emotion of the moment and my mother looks at me and smiles.

*

It is my intention to follow the paths of Mama's and Dad's last footsteps through Europe just prior to them leaving that final time. We will then go on to Hungary where our family are impatiently waiting for us.

My father had spent quite a lot of time working in Germany at the end of the war, and I want to see for myself where he had spent those youthful, transitional years. For some reason I can't quite explain, and that Dad doesn't understand, I want to walk those streets with my parents and listen to their stories in the places where they originally happened. For me, it is as if the circle will be closed, and I can at least join them in some new memories of these old places. For me, the concept of place has become so important.

Mama had lived in the Bavarian town of Bayreuth for about 6 years before coming to Australia, and we are going to try and find her house, if it still exists. Mama is keen to knock on that door and see if anyone knew of the family that had been their landlords, the Haertls. I'm not very optimistic about that one, but I wouldn't mind taking a peek at those very clean stairs Mama has told me about so often.

Our first stop after we cross the border into Germany is the small medieval town of Straubing where Dad had worked on two occasions. We drive through it extensively, but Dad can't recognize anything, and nothing looks familiar. It has been over 50 years after all, but I can't help feeling disappointed. We press on.

Our next stop is in beautiful, historic Regensburg. After we park the car I turn to my father.

"If I can find the old stone bridge, Lexi, I'll be able to get my bearings," he says, quite confidently.

After we visit the tourist office and acquire a map, we walk through the narrow, cobble-stone streets. The old town is so charming and historic. It is quite cold, but my father's eyes sparkle.

"There it is. That's the medieval stone bridge. I remember it. We have to cross the river; I used to live on the other side." Dad is becoming animated and excited; he has a spring in his step as he leads us to the place where he used to work.

It is quite a long walk to the old neighbourhood, over the Danube and onto an island in the middle of the river. This had been Dad's home for almost two years. We wander up the deserted suburban street, looking all around us. And then, once again, he starts to tell me stories, animated. Lots and lots of stories, in copious detail. It is as if the years fall away and he is transported to that different time in that same place. He tells me about beautiful young girls and foolish, brave boys; of swimming across the Danube and back in order to impress a certain young lady; of the work he used to do; of the laughter and the friendship and the fun.

"And this is it, Lexi. This is where the workshop was. And this next door was the tavern, like, you know, the inn. We used to get a beer here," he says.

We had walked the length of the road looking for the workshop which we finally find. A gate bars our entry to it, but on the gate is a blue and white sign that says, "31a Wohrd Strasse". It is at this address that Dad worked for the Americans for over 2 years, driving trucks and acting as a chauffeur for the officers' wives at the end of the war.

The tavern next door is closed. Even the Germans don't serve beer at 10.30 in the morning. We linger for a while taking photos and looking around. Dad doesn't want to leave, and the photograph of he and my mother in front of the gateway shows a happy man cuddling his wife, saying cheeky things to his daughter as she snaps away.

This is a priceless moment, and this day, my father gives me pearls. He shares precious nuggets of memory, and stories that mean so much more to me because he can actually show me these places of his youth. I imagine a young man standing in this spot, more than 50 years ago. I can see him in his overalls, greasy and thin, smoking a cigarette, laughing with his friends.

He takes me to the river bank and shows me where he swam. He points to the building across the street and tells me where two beautiful girls lived. We stand in front of the inn; it is the same.

This day, in this place, gives me the gift of seeing my father's eyes alive with memory and nostalgia. And in my eyes and in my imagination I see the evolving man that he once was, already wizened by the war and experience, still carefree and young.

With great difficulty, we tear ourselves away. There are more places to explore, and memories to mine.

*

The next day we head to Bamberg. Dad's grasp of German is warming up and he is quite impressive in his dealings with the locals. Mama left Germany when she was just 13, but her German is becoming more fluent the longer we are in Germany. Somehow Dad's German seems better than his English. He seems to be more easily understood here and therefore quite independent. I am starting to see my parents with new eyes. They appear to be much more relaxed, more fully functional. Europe is, or so it appears to me, more of a comfort zone even though they haven't lived here in over 50 years. I am finding this very curious.

Bamberg is yet another of those beautifully quaint and enchanting European towns that appear, in the centre at least, to have changed only slightly in 500 years. Dad spent only 6 or 7 months here, so it comes as no surprise that he remembers little. We walk through the old town and nothing seems familiar to him. He is weary from the events of yesterday and is still a little jet lagged. He rests heavily on our arms and cannot walk very fast. There is nothing here for us, and we make a hasty escape.

It is clear that we all need to take a break. We decide to go straight to Bayreuth and spend a few days resting. I am not optimistic that there will be anything of consequence to see there, but Mum is becoming excited. It is the first time she has ever been back to the town that was once her home. She recognizes the countryside as we get closer. Dad snoozes in the back of the car, oblivious. We arrive, park the car and head directly to the tourist office for a map. Mama is on a mission, she wants to find that house.

*

After consulting the map and without any hiatus we head directly to the street; it is only three blocks away from where we now stand. As we walk towards it, Mama quickly gets her bearings, and she recognizes the neighbourhood and the turn off before we are close enough to read the sign. She is determined to find the house and knock on the door. This is something she has been talking about doing for years, but never did. Mama and Dad didn't ever come back to Bavaria on any of their trips to Europe during the past 20 years. I am grateful for this as the events of this day unfold, and we three share them together for the first, and probably, only time.

Here we are: Carl Schuller Strasse. It is a narrow street, and a long one. I notice that here are two taverns at the entrance to this street, one on each corner. We start to walk down the street. Mama is looking around.

"I remember there was this bloody big hole in the block next door," she tells us as we walk, somewhat breathless. "The house next door was flattened by a bomb, and our place was freestanding after that. We lived in the mansard apartment – the attic apartment. It was quite small. Dieter, the boy I told you about, my friend, had these beautiful trains that we played with at Christmas time." She was becoming excited, the words gush out of her. We keep walking.

"It's three stories high, if you count the attic. And down the bottom was the shop, you remember I told you? The Haertls had a grocery shop. We could get everything."

"You know, Mama, it's been a long time. Don't be disappointed if it's no longer standing," I say, looking at the modern buildings interspersed with the very old ones on the street. "Do you recognize anything?" We are looking for number 24.

"That's it!" she cries, pointing across the street. "That's the one. Look! It's still got the empty block next to it. There it is!"

And there it is indeed, my mother's childhood home. I am rooted to the spot, absolutely gobsmacked. I would have been satisfied just standing looking at the space where it used to be, but there it is, intact. The shop at the bottom is no longer operating and is deserted. I am taking photos of Mum in front of the building, of the attic apartment, of the doorway. As I am composing a photograph of Mama at the front door she spins around, looking shocked. I take the photo at that moment.

"They still live here!" she whispers, astounded. "They're still here." And sure enough, there's their name on the face plate: Haertl.

CarlSchullerStrasse, 24

The same people,
a different time,
the same place.
This moment detached

by time only;
we are in the same place.

My mother's face
(more beautiful with time),

offered upwards to an old man
who dismisses us,
from a window above us,

now closing in disgust.

My mother's childhood,
a threshold

(a breath away, 3 steps).

...I have to see...

I have to see the places
of my mother's youth.

Those pale, pale stairs
from that bucket
(years of retelling this tale),
those stairs bleached white from scrubbing –
from a bucket that held cleaned potatoes on Saturday
for knodel
and for schweinbraten
made every week for that family,
that family, still there.

The button is pressed and we enter
a nervous woman dances on those stairs
(she is Frau Haertl's daughter).
And I can smell something I don't know.
It assaults me,
its acrid character I cannot define.

"Nein
nein
nicht..." she says,
dancing nervously foot to foot.
"I don't know you."
(Please. Go away)
In the next moment
the mood lifts,
and her eyes finish the dance
that her feet have started.
The mood slips sideways
to allow recognition
its space.

Enters another woman, concerned
(she is Frau Haertl's sister).
"Your mother," she says
to my mother,
about her mother.
"Your mother,
was incredibly stylish,
and very elegant."
(This mother,
my grandmother,

is half a world away at this moment.
                    She lies dozing in another place.
                              a place that is not the same,
                              a place that is internal.
                                        Spent,
                    and weary, she is elegant no more
                    and stylish no longer.
          She is just sleeping
                    and dozing
                    and dreaming. Of another time?
                         Of this place?)

But we are here
          and German is an easy language to follow
                    up those stairs
                              to the attic apartment, where I am,
          finally,
                    in my mother's childhood place.
                                        And it occurs to me,
                              that the smell I smell
                              that assaults me
          (even stronger on those stairs),
                    and makes water in my eyes –
          is the sauerkraut, and the knodel
                    for the schweinbraten.

And it is Saturday.

                         *

I have this momentous sense of time shifting, of it slipping sideways, as I stand up there in that apartment, listening to the three women talk about their shared past. I am with my Mama, making an important connection; making a memory together, my hand holding her hand, my feet here with her feet, there, in her old home.

When she lived here she was so very young. I feel that if I looked out of the window, I would see a street cobble-stoned and not paved, with gaslights lining the way, and people mostly walking, going about their business. The war was still going on when they were here; Jews were being taken away. There were shortages of food and all of the basic necessities. Yet my mother's family were safe, my grandmother was still being spoilt by her husband, Mama was enjoying her violin and English lessons, and life was very good for them. Would it ever have occurred to her that one day she would walk through those rooms with me?

It is a special time, and my mother is so moved. She discovers from the Haertls that her childhood friend, Dieter, is indeed still alive and lives nearby. His train *set is laid out on that same floor in the living room. Yes, his sister confirms, they are Dieter's trains. That Christmas Mama is to receive a card from him, their first communication in 53 years.*

We stay on the corner of that street for the next few days in one of the taverns. During our time here I jog past the house several times. It is thrilling for me to walk and to run on the very streets my mother had traversed sixty years ago, perhaps whilst holding her father's hand, or perhaps walking to school or to church, or into town to see her first opera. I walk past that skinny house again and again, and I make my own memories.

Bayreuth is a strikingly beautiful town, famous for Opera and music. Both Franz Liszt and Richard Wagner lived and worked there for a long time, and whilst that is interesting to me and to many other tourists, I will always remember Bayreuth for that very special encounter at Carl Schuller Strasse, 24.

*

During the long drive back to Vienna I have some time to think about how I feel. I am quite thrilled that I have made some important connections to both my parents, but also to their places and their memories. We share things during that week that we had not had before. These experiences also connect me more firmly to Europe and I am really enjoying being here. Of course I feel like a foreigner, but I don't feel completely outside. I am a tourist of course, but not a stranger.

The days in Vienna are glorious. Because Dad is so weary, both my parents rest in the lovely accommodations we acquire. Vienna is very expensive, but it is also very beautiful. Since Mama and Dad have decided to do less wandering I have the opportunity to fulfil a fantasy of mine, which is to ramble through a European city for hours and days on end, alone, independent and free. It is heavenly.

It is here, on my own in Vienna, that I feel fully at home; comfortable, safe and familiar. With its culture and its personality, its European-ness and its elegance, I find this place utterly captivating. But it is more than merely entertainment. I am finding German an extremely easy language to pick up and to understand, and the Austrians are very gracious and accommodating. For some reason, it all feels right. I feel European, and for a few moments at least, I feel like I belong. Maybe it is my age, maybe it is because of my interests, and maybe it is simply because Vienna was once the capital of the Austro-Hungarian Empire. Whatever it is, Vienna suits me, and it is exhilarating.

*

The final leg of this journey is to be taken by train. The short trip from Vienna to my father's home town of Györ will take only an hour and a half. We hardly have time to relax before we stop at the border town of Hegyeshálom.

My father is extremely nervous. He's been telling me for days to make sure that I behave myself, am respectful and considerate. He is so animated and his eyes, those coal black eyes, scan the landscape as he tells me stories about this town and that

*when we pass through them. The signs are in Hungarian, the landscape familiar, and
I watch my father's tension disappear.*

He is home.

*As the train pulls into the station, Dad says something to me that he had so often
in the past, but here and now it seems so much more poignant.*

*"Remember Lex, that the dust on the streets you kick with your boot, is the
remains of your ancestors," we finish the sentence together, and I have tears in
my eyes.*

*As Mum steps off the train I see her face light up. I know they are here, my
family, my own. As we all embrace and cry and laugh I think about how wonderful
this is. My family – my uncles and aunty and cousins here to greet us – they are my
family. My aunty Irén takes my hand and won't let go. She is crying and shaking and
laughing. But it is the sight of my father being embraced by his brother that brings
me completely undone.*

A moment

> *Walking skyward towards the golden sun*
> *I turn, as they appear*
>
> > > *behind me*
>
> *from that underground gloom.*
> *His eyes locked into*
> *his eyes –*
>
> > *they share the same breath,*
> > *the same blood.*
>
> > > > *Fifty years and a world apart*
> > *and they're telling their stories again.*
> > > *Again, my uncle*
> > > *again, my father*
> > *stepping up as one.*
>
> *Eyes and hands and arms connected*
> > *as they move toward me*
> > > *up those stairs,*
> > > *my mother and my aunty,*
> > > *the cousins I don't know.*
>
> *We watch them and we see*
> *an enduring, patient bond.*
> *We turn and smile and leave them*
>
> > > *until,*
> > *they emerge into the glare*
> > > *into the place they once shared.*
>
> *Silver heads aglowing,*
> > *bent together still.*
>
> > > *Two brothers*

>   *two old men,*
>   *ageless, timeless, gentle men.*
> *Furiously they absorb each other*
> *furious is their love –*
>
>   *his eyes locked into*
>   *his eyes,*
>
>   *moving as if one.*

*

They stay that way for a good half hour, on the footpath outside the train station, while we all catch up. They are totally oblivious of the rest of us; time is standing still for them.

After a while they realize that we are waiting, and we get into the cars and leave. Dad goes with his brother, and Mama and I with Irén néni and her very pregnant granddaughter, my cousin, Andika. I can understand only a little of what is being said, and Mama flips into interpreter mode – a posture she is to continue until we leave, weeks later. I know that this part of the journey will be almost entirely spent with our family, with little time alone and I am looking forward to it.

We will stay with Irén néni and her second husband, my Zoli bácsi, in their tiny two-roomed apartment. There is a kitchen and bathroom as well of course, but the apartment consists simply of a dining room and living room. It is going to be cramped but cosy, five people in a space big enough for two.

Hungary is still terribly poor. Most people live in apartments like this one that were erected quickly after the war in order to accommodate the hordes of people left homeless. This project housing dominates the city and it is only when you travel to the outskirts that you see bigger, freestanding housing. Imre bácsi lives in one of these outside of town, but it is still small by Australian standards.

It becomes increasingly obvious to me as we move through the town on our way to see relatives, shop and sightsee, that life for the average Hungarian is pretty humble. Although the supermarkets are comparable to ours in terms of the goods available, and although you can get almost anything you need, there is not the abundance of goods available, or the wide range of choice. But the biggest difference is that everything is so expensive and wages are comparatively low. Except for the beauty of the old town, the cities and towns are drab and grey, the cars rusting and old and the atmosphere is gloomy. It is exceedingly obvious that although democracy has come to Hungary and life is better, it has become extremely hard work to make ends meet. When I look around me I silently thank my parents and grandparents for their foresight and their courage. I am so grateful that I am Australian, and so appreciative that this is not my life.

There have been many times previously when I have travelled that I have felt this way, when my pride in my beautiful and wealthy country is somewhat self-congratulating. I always feel far more Australian when I leave the country than when I am living in it. My accent sounds more distinct in a sea of different voices, my attitude is more optimistic, and my nationalistic pride is continuously switched on.

As I struggle to figure this out, I also wonder why, when I should perhaps feel less foreign here and less like a tourist, that I feel more foreign here than I had in Austria. Is it the language that excludes me? I am comfortable in Austria, it feels familiar. In Hungary I stand out as being different and I feel fully Australian here. Strange. I can't help thinking that this disconnected feeling is because I don't adequately speak the language, and that I have to rely on my parents for communication most of the time; that I would feel more at home if I knew how to speak Hungarian. I am attached to Hungary through my parents, my blood and my family, but I am, very definitely, Australian.

I look closely at what my life would have been like growing up in a communist state as I talk to my cousin Laci. Laci, named for my father, is a little older than me, but a teacher as well, and I am even more appreciative of my parents' choice. He is my contemporary, we have similar careers but we are so very different. What my cousin tells me about being a child in communist Hungary makes me so grateful to have grown up somewhere else, and although my childhood was difficult and lonely, my adulthood is by far more prosperous and carefree. The benefits of working hard in a communist regime were minimal, since everybody was provided for equally, and enterprise was not rewarded or encouraged. My opportunities have been more numerous, I am prepared to work hard to capitalize on them, and my lifestyle is more comfortable. Whilst I silently offer up my prayers of thanksgiving to Australia, I realize that my country is wonderful in part because of the efforts of people from this place, Europe, who had sought a better life and made it happen.

*

When one visits family in Hungary, it is understood that much of your time will be spent indoors, around the dining room table. The rituals of preparing and consuming food are deeply entrenched in this culture, and although the food is always excellent, the ritual is not about the fare. It is of course about the loving acts that families bestow upon one another, it is about conversation and it is about catching up, talking politics and family gossip. It is about making precious connections, holding hands and laughter. Simply and elegantly, it is about család [family].

It is also understood that you never visit a relative empty handed. Gifts are given, and if you are coming from abroad, it should preferably be something exotic, expensive or distinctly in character with the country from which it comes. Mama has agonized over the gifts we brought with us, and has gone to great expense. Some are received warmly, but all are expected. It is also expected that you will contribute something to the meal, preferably alcohol. The cook of the moment takes immense pride in her work and her offerings, and will serve the most expensive and luxurious fare that she can afford. Last time I was here it was in winter and Stu and I endured many meals that started with pickled vegetables and blood pudding sausage. This time it is rántott [fried] everything, Viennese style in bread crumbs – fried veal, fried eggplant, fried chicken, fried chicken livers, fried everything. And potatoes, as many different ways of serving it as you can imagine – it is Eastern Europe after all.

I spend some wonderful time in Irén néni's small and fragrant kitchen. She shows me a few tricks and cooking tips – her meals are always wonderful and she can make a delicious dish from nothing. This is the real talent of the Hungarian cook, to use meagre ingredients to create wondrous meals. And I watch as my mother and Irén néni spend sisterly time together. They are very close, and I hadn't anticipated that. They sympathize with each other, commiserating with each other about their husbands. It's good for Mama, who doesn't have any close friends or even a sibling, to have a 'sister' that can empathize and be supportive. Sometimes they just look at each other and burst out laughing. We all talk about our husbands, and I realize how alike my aunty and I are. This is a surprise too. She is cheeky, creative and full of Hungarian good judgment.

Irénke

My aunt is old
75 years Hungarian.
Strong and robust,
vital and alive.
75 years of wisdom
passed on to me.

She whispers
through my mother's mouth:
"Have an affair
if you get the chance.

Life is long".

*

In fact it is the women in my family, I am coming to realize, that are the resilient ones. They are universally sprightly, energetic and full of beans. You'd never know that they are all close to turning 80. Their husbands all retired and slowed down – the women continued onwards at the same pace. As a result, they are without exception, vital, robust and strong. They are the backbones of their families, unassuming and modest, quietly doing what needs to be done. It is quite a legacy.

Another of these women, Irma néni, is my mother's cousin. Their mothers are sisters and they spent a lot of time together at their grandmother's home in the country before Mama fled Hungary.

"I often thought about you two," she says to Mama with tears in her eyes, "You and your mother out there in the world, just the two of you alone." She means that they did not have their very large family around them. She tells us over yet another wonderful meal about some family history.

207

"Lexi, your great aunty Mariska néni, her father-in-law's name was Jancsi bácsi. And when your grandmother came home for a visit early in 1936 with her fiancé, Jancsi bácsi could see she was pregnant. But that wasn't the scandal. The town was amazed that this skinny little peasant girl, your grandmother, managed to snare herself such a handsome and sophisticated fiancé. They didn't think it was going to last. But then she was pregnant with your mother, and they got married after all."

Such is the whimsy of fate. Had Nonya not had my mother, who knows where they would have ended up? Maybe they would have stayed in Hungary instead of fleeing in 1942. Irma néni also told us that Nonya's brother wrote and advised that they stay in Germany when Nonya asked if they should come home after the war.

"He said that they would be in danger if they came back," Irma tells us all these years later. *"Deserters were being shot at the border if they tried to re-enter the country. And your grandfather had some political involvement so they would have hung him for sure. So they stayed away. And then later they knew they couldn't come back, so they went to Australia."*

It is so interesting to hear the story from Irma néni's perspective. Mama is holding her hand and it is wonderful again to see my mother with her relatives. These two are very close; they have an enduring and very real affection between them. They seem to understand each other, and although they have a shared childhood, it bewilders me somewhat that the bond is still so strong. Is this what having a huge family is like?

I've never had these experiences with an extended family so I don't know. I watch my parents with their (very large) families and in some ways it's like seeing them for the first time, relaxed, not on their guard, fully functioning, fully in themselves, comfortable and utterly switched on. I am seeing them not as my parents, but as other people's brother, sister-in-law or cousin. Is this what it's like for other people at their family events?

To me, they look complete, and I have never felt closer to either of them. And as I watch I realize that I do have a right to claim this Hungarianness, this big part of me. I have so many family members here who love me simply because I am my mother and father's daughter, that I am család. It matters not that I live a long distance away, or that my grasp of the language is so rudimentary – these are just details. I am a part of this family whether I live here or not, and so is Stu, and so are our girls. That connection is unbreakable and real. It is enduring. When I go home, they will all still be here, with our photos, our gifts and the memories that we now share together. I belong to this family, who have always accepted this fact unconditionally, no matter where I live or what language I speak. I can claim this as mine.

*

My father is happy. He and the uncles talk for hours. He is more confident and assured than I have ever seen him. It's funny to see him being talked at for hours by Zoli bácsi who also loves to talk and has a story and opinion about everything. Zoli bácsi's sick jokes (just like Dad's) make me think that this is a Hungarian trait rather *than something peculiar to my father's personality. The three of them, Dad, Zoli and Imre, took only one hour together before they got onto discussing Trianon, and then religion, contemporary politics, gypsies and the problems of the world. Dad is in his element. He seems more independent here, and more than happy to spend time away from us.*

My mother is blossoming here too. I have never seen her more relaxed or more beautiful. I know she is tired, and constantly in interpreter mode, but she is so charismatic and charming, and all the relatives think she's adorable. I have never seen this before either. She is usually so stilted and anxious in social situations at home, like she is really uncomfortable. Here, she is herself, and it feels like I am seeing the real Zita for the first time. My cheeky uncle Imre flirts with her shamelessly, his eyes twinkling, and my alluring Mama responds wickedly. I see that all the fussing and mealtime customs that I thought was just my mother's personality are actually traditional. All the overdone, grand gestures, the ceremony, the way of eating, serving and presenting, I now understand as being Hungarian rather than just 'being my mother'. Tomatoes at breakfast, splendid affairs for every meal. Never sitting still to eat with the family, serving the men hand and foot. And yes, suffering aging husbands. All of it, all like my Mama.

*

I spoke to Imre bácsi and told him of my desire to walk the old streets and hear the stories of the three 'children' – Imre, Dad and Irén. There are a few gaps in Dad's memory that I was hoping he and their sister could fill. Imre bácsi is quite keen to help me, and more than my father he appreciates the work I am trying to do. Imre bácsi becomes my co-conspirator as we persuade the others to visit my grandparents in the cemetery and then wander through the old streets.

The bus trip to the cemetery is quite long, and we stop in town to collect flowers for the graves. We meet Imre bácsi patiently waiting for the five of us at the bus stop, and we walk the short distance past ramshackle houses to the cemetery. We find the plot, and I am surprised at the depth and intensity of feeling for the grandparents I have never known, that flows over me as I stand there in front of their black granite headstone, with their three children standing beside me. I feel the Magyar pull keenly here. I belong to them, and they belong to me. I am the daughter of their favorite child (according to both Imre bácsi and Irén néni). Their blood is my blood; I am here at last with them. I am here.

The offering

I stand in this place,
that I have seen before
but no longer recognize.
I have seen it before
through someone else's eyes.

By someone else's hand
　　　I am connected to her, not to him.
　　　　　Letters written and not read,
except by someone else,
　　their legacy half a world away –

　　　　　　　　　　　　　　　　my father.
　　　　　I knew them not,
　　　　　I knew them.
Through someone else's memories,
through someone else's mouth.
　　　　　I knew them, and
　　　　　I still cannot read the letters,
　　　　　　　that connect me
through someone else,

　　　　　　　　　　　　　　　to her.

　　　　But now I am here, and
　　　　　I stand in this place that I know,
　　but do not.
　　　　I am 30 years away from her
　　　　　　　and 67 from him.
The plot is lovingly tended to,
　　　　　and I am losing mine
　　　　　as I stand in this place,

　　　　　　　seeing it through my own eyes,
　　　　　and touch the earth with my own hands,
　　as I place
　　　　six great-grand-children

　　　　　　　　　　　　　　at their feet.

　　　　　　　　*

Imre bácsi is our self-appointed guide for the day and this is appropriate, since he is our patriarch. We leave the cemetery much subdued and I stroll into town on my father's arm. We visit their old school, the one they had attended before their *father died in 1935, when they were shipped off to various places around the country because my grandmother couldn't afford to keep them all.*

We see the church where the two boys had been altar boys, where the tobacco shop had been, the cake shop, the synagogue, where Dad had lost his money in the snow. The suburb is very run down but still quaint with many of the original buildings intact but quite weathered. It is now largely populated by gypsies.

"Can you imagine how many times I walked this street going to town? Hey?" Dad looks at me smiling.

"And now you're walking it with your middle-aged daughter," I reply.

"You're not middle-aged, you young. You're a young Mum. Well, how old are you?" When I tell him almost 40, he replies, "Well you bit older than my mother was when my father died because she was only 37."

At that moment we hear the church bells ringing. It is midday and I know exactly what it means. Dad has told me many times about the bells ringing by order of the Pope in memory of the Hungarians defeating the Turks in modern day Belgrade, once Nándofehérvár. He just looks at me and smiles. We walk on.

We stand in front of an old two story building, brightly coloured in gold and ochre, and defaced with graffiti. This is the apartment block my grandfather once managed and they all lived in. Dad points across the road, "This used to be a paper shop, Heingold, a Jewish people owned. And they took them away."

Dad pauses at this, the last sentence said with an undertone of anger and frustration, caught in his memory for a moment. We walk into the foyer of his old building and our voices echo around the concrete. Dad tells me more stories and shows me the sights. We walk through the block to the last apartments.

"I think this is it. The entry, well the door is different. This is where the cat was sitting," he says, pointing to the window sill. We walk through the rear archway to the yard outside. "We used to play here and the man upstairs, Puga bácsi, yelling at us from the window because we making too much noise." He confers with Imre bácsi and they chuckle like two school boys.

"The old impression is still there," says Imre bácsi. Dad nods to himself.

I try to convince them to knock on the door so we can have a peek inside, but they won't do it. We walk through the yard and then around the building back to the front. The ever inquisitive gypsies ask us what we are doing here. They smile and nod as we tell them and go about their business.

I take a photo of the three kids outside the old family home, and a close up of my father sitting on the step. He looks like a little boy.

"This is where I used to sit Lexi, after my father died. I would look up the street and think I see him. Someone who had the same hat or walked the same way. I thought maybe one day he would come home."

This brings me undone completely, and I am in tears. I am so tired from having to struggle to communicate, from the many emotions that have been swirling around my heart, from the changes that are happening in my psyche. I cry and cry and cannot be consoled. Iren néni reaches up and puts her arm around me and we head back into town. It's time for lunch and I can't think any more.

*

The next morning Mama and I decide to go out to Györszemere. It is the village that my grandmother grew up in and where Mama and all the other cousins including Irma néni, spent their summers, and some time at the beginning of the war because it was safer than being in Budapest. We ride the bus for about an hour, and once again the locals check us out.

The town is very small, one small shop and a dusty bus stop constitute the village centre. There is nobody on the street at 10 o'clock in the morning.

"Here we are in the wild city of Györszemere," I say into the tape recorder, "Mama's summer residence," we both giggle.

"No wonder she wanted to get out, I couldn't blame her," referring to Nonya. "There's nothing here. She brought you back here?" I ask.

"Only for holidays," Mama says. "And of course when it got dangerous in Budapest. Then she would come back and visit on the weekends. She would get some ducks and geese, put them into a milk tin, fill it up with goose fat – that was very much in demand too, you know at that time. Food was scarce. So she would close the tin and take it back to the city on the train. She would stand at the back of the train on that platform, you know on the back of it? And then she went out there presumably to get off the train, not very far from the station at the overhead bridge – and of course cars were going underneath it – your grandmother just stood in front of the tin and...," Mum mimics the action of kicking the tin off behind her. "She kicked off the tins and just casually went back inside the carriage. Your grandfather was down the bottom, collected it. It rolled down and he got it. And took it back home...," she looks at me, wide-eyed.

"And put it in the pantry? And sold it on the black market?" I ask and Mama nods. "And if she'd been caught...?" I probe.

"Would have been shot."

Mama asks a gypsy woman for directions. Once we're on track again I marvel at my Nonya's courage and resourcefulness. I suppose that's what you had to do to get by in those days. My mother is showing similar qualities as she tries to find the house we are looking for. It is on Uj Utca [New Street], but she doesn't know the number.

We pass a little girl and who says, "Keszet csökölöm [I kiss your hand]". This is a common greeting of children to their elders, but also of men to women. Men I don't even know have said this to me as I pass them on the stairs in Irén néni's apartment building, or on the street. It is a very gallant custom, and harks back to feudal times. In the villages it seems to be a more common tradition. I like it. We walk up a slight rise and Mama is in a quandary.

"I think that's it. Either that one or that." Mama can't decide between 2 houses next door to each other. She says their numbers over and over to herself and can't decide. One house has been recently renovated, the other is very run down. "Okay this is where I put my memory to work," she says, "With a bit of luck a little old lady lives there."

Having made her decision we walk through the gate. The yard is a mess and looks like a junkyard with mattresses, half a car and rubbish everywhere. There are fruit flies buzzing around us constantly. A tied up, very large dog starts barking furiously, and doesn't stop the whole time we are there. A baby starts to cry. Mama introduces us to the young girl in the doorway, another gypsy, and tells her why we are here. The gypsy girl has the most rotten teeth I think I have ever seen, and knows nothing about our family. No matter, Mama who is seeing beyond the mess and into her memory, now realizes we are in the right place. She explains where we are from and ask if we can take photos. We ask to look inside and the young girl and her cross-eyed blond daughter are very welcoming and obliging, but they know nothing. We go in and it is so small. The whole building is run down. Mama gestures to a door off to the right, and the girl says her husband is sleeping.

"That would be the bedroom where my grandfather died. This is it! She raised 9 kids here Lexi." It is a tiny house, just three rooms including the kitchen in the centre of the house where we now stand.

"It is this one, 21. It's coming back." Mama walks outside again. "There was a well there, and a dunny here. And I think there's a bunker under that mound. The way I remember the house it was bigger. But this is it." Mum is very excited and we thank the girl profusely. We ask her if there are any old people who live nearby who might remember the family. She tells us there is, across the street. We thank her again and walk over the road.

Mama rings the bell on the gate.

"The door's open!" A woman calls from the backyard. Two women are sitting, talking outside the back door. One is younger, but the other is sitting with her back to a wooden table and is very old. She is a large woman with two walking sticks at her side, her grey hair hidden under a scarf, a purple shift over a chocolate brown dress. She has large red hands with a golden ring on each, and very swollen legs. Her knees are strapped with colourful fabric as support for obviously aching joints. She has no teeth and a wrinkled but friendly face. She is a peasant woman. Mama explains why we are here, and who we are.

They talk some more and I can tell that something is familiar about her by the way both their faces have softened. She says the name of Nonya's sister, Jolán, and I ask my mother, "Do you know her?"

"We're relatives!" Mama exclaims, beaming. I can't believe it. This woman married my mother's cousin, she is Jolán's daughter-in-law and my cousin too. I can't believe it. I have family everywhere. The other woman leaves and then the néni introduces me to her son, Dénes who is also my cousin, and tells us both that we share the same great grandmother. I am speechless. All of a sudden I realise that my

family is huge. All my life it has been just us. Now I see there are so many of us, all connected, all family.

My cousin (my cousin!) invites us into her house and we have excellent coffee whilst she and Mama continue their very animated conversation. Mama interprets where she can, but generally I can follow it, my Hungarian is improving. She and Mama catch up on some ancient family gossip, and we explain the reason for our trip. We all marvel at how small the world is. She is a very gracious and friendly hostess, and proudly tells us her age halfway through our visit. She is just 69, two years older than my mother. Life is still hard in rural Hungary.

In my astonishment and exhaustion, I switch off. The néni talks constantly and I am lulled into a cocoon of warmth and security. The house is cosy, there is gulyás simmering on the stove, and the coffee is strong and sweet. I listen to their voices and the musical cadence of the language and my mind drifts off. It is almost too much for me to comprehend, and our journey has been so rushed, so action packed. I am exhausted, but I am content. There are things shifting within me. My loneliness is disappearing and things are settling in my core. Now I know why so many people search for their roots: because it is so unilaterally satisfying. For me this is much more than I had anticipated. I am seeing the places of my parents' youths and I have made connections to a family that is really mine, at last.

*

After a short visit to Budapest, it is time to go. The day of departure is gloomy, grey and damp, which suits our mood perfectly. We stand on the frigid platform realising that this leave-taking may be the last of its kind. It isn't likely that my father will ever come back. Surprisingly, he is the least affected by this.

"You can't say this is the last time Lex," he assures me the night before. "You don't know what the future holds."

He is right of course, but the rest of us aren't convinced. Irén néni can't stop crying, and Zoli bácsi is despondent. Imre bácsi seems unaffected until the end. His is the last face I see as the train pulls away. I look at him and I see that he feels the same way, if only revealing it for a moment. He looks directly into my eyes and at that moment we both know. It is the last time. We move away from each other, waving. I turn back into the carriage, miserable, and struggle to hold it in.

In this moment as I fight for composure, I think of Nagyapa. An image of him from a photograph appears in my mind. And I can hear his voice, even though I have no memory of what he sounded like.

Yet I hear him, and I hear him say three words, "Magyar, Lexi. You." And instantly the moment passes and I feel composed.

I look at my father, and I ask the question I have been waiting to ask for weeks. "Well, Dad. Are you glad we came?"

He looks into my eyes and says, emphatically, "Yes, Lexi, I am glad. Very glad we came."

That is enough for me.

I belonged to everyone, so I belong to no one…tell me, whom do I belong to? What country, what people? What family? (Tan, 1995, p. 165)

Something has
                    trembled, and uncoupled. This
                                work, this
                                        inquiry, these

            actions of
        writing and of
    making and of
        scouting and of
            exploring and of
                        travelling have
                                altered,
                                    have re*located* the places within me of
                                                    alienation, of
                                    conflict, of
                        the struggle of
        selves. The irritations have
                            altered, a
                                    re*leasing*.
                                                I am
                                                no longer my selves.
                                                I am
                                                no longer myself.
                                                I am,
                                                no longer.
                                                I am
                                                anew.

                        "There's nobody like us," says Remy, smiling, wondering...

        A suite, suite portfolio of
                                belongings, in an ecology of
                        the self and
                                other and self
                                            and others and self and
memories, feelings, experiences, languages, places, encounters and
                                                            me.

In this
        langscape,
    in this
        collective, the
                    actions, the
                        Art actions
                                are the key.

CHAPTER 15

TRANSITIONS, RESOLUTIONS AND BELONGINGS

Identities, Images and Stories

ORIENTATION

My lived experiences of belonging and not belonging with respect to the issues of ethnicity and identity are framed by both the Australian and Hungarian contexts in which I developed. These were framed by my parents' understandings as I grew up as well as their own [dis]located experiences of place. The development of my ethnic self always had a second-handedness and remains one step removed.

Until very recently, there was nothing or nobody that I could find in literature or in life that resonated with my particular experience – and how desperately I have searched. It seems as though I have hunted for most of my life to find somebody who was like me, who knew about my specific experiences of difference, without success. As Zevallos asserted, there were plenty of people to feel different from, but there was nobody to feel different with (2008). This is the essence of my alienation.

This strange, unwanted inheritance that I shared with nobody (it seemed), which I couldn't fully comprehend, has stayed with me always, although there is much I have forgotten. Being ashamed now, as an adult, of forgetting cultural things, like words to a childhood song (Papas, 2012), or a poem, or the taste of Hungarian words in my mouth, even though, "strong, long Hungarian sounds were the first human sounds I heard [and] was the language in which I stuttered my own first words" (Varga, 2004, p. 2). My persistent nostalgia for this peculiar and eccentric language, a language of endearment, intimacy, curse or joke, of parental wrath, the grandmother language I spoke haltingly and only with my elders, the resentment language which was a constant reminder that I was not a real Australian kid, the nuisance language, the kitchen language (Varga, 2004). This is the language I mourn.

It's very easy for others outside of these experiences to say (as has happened to me often), "It's only a state of mind, just fix it", or for others to presume to tell you who you are. It's not that easy (and what right do they have?) – the formative experiences of one's life are buried deep within us all, and they stay with us eternally. It's as though I have always lived with the twin identities of my physical self, occupying the places of the real, as my ghost self-occupied the places of my imagined, alternative life. This imaginary life exists in another place, in my imagination and amongst the long lost places of my parents' childhoods. I grew up with them as a constant presence, it seems. These animations, fraught and suspended in time, are a world of spirit beings that exist only in the ether of my subconscious. It is a world that I feel constant pressure to forget. As Cecil Day-Lewis so poignantly writes, it's like this,

> Move on with new desires,
> for where we used to build and love
> is no man's land; and only ghosts can live
> between two fires. (cited in Kambaskovic, 2013, p. 106)

The ghosts of my identities exist between the two flames, equally at risk of ignition. However, I cannot escape the facts of my birth, or the inescapable facts of my heritage. Nothing will ever change these things; they are absolute (Skrznecki, 2004), irrespective of whatever fashionable, contemporary theory asserts that I can alter them (Mahar, Cobigo & Stuart, 2013). These anchors to my identity are at the core of my conflicted selves.

As a child I had an all-consuming need to belong to Australia (Kambaskovic, 2013), but as strongly now, an all-consuming need to own my ethnicity and to express it culturally, to authentically demonstrate it. This paradox of where I belong or who I *really* am (Skrznecki, 2004) has driven me for decades and the ambivalence associated with it has been valuable. The trauma and the conflict have been both productive and limiting; although I cannot fluently engage in Hungarian culture as a native, the trauma is useful as an intellectual commodity (Kambaskovic, 2013), including with this work. The distress has driven me relentlessly forward.

The literature tells me that the self can be reinvented, that we can create whom we are. Our agency makes this possible; yet it is the tensions in my blood that continue to hold me back. Time has passed and the postmodern moment gave me permission to explore the multiplicities of who I am and set the conditions for these journeys and investigations. Postmodernism allowed for the possibility of theorizing about the multiplicities of belonging (Mahar, et al., 2013) and the location of my selves.

However for me, it's not really about finding *where* my identity is located, although I acknowledge this is significant. It's more to do with resolving or balancing the tensions (Bouras, 2004) between the identities I think I have, and those that were constructed for me. My shifting sense of self, something postmodernism tells me is indeed possible, has resulted in a kind of mental dysmorphia (Kambaskovic, 2013). When Barone (2001), for example, contends that memory is the glue that holds our multiple selves together, it is an elegant assertion, but one that has real problems in practice. Is it actually possible to reconcile multiple, shifting selves? I've tried to do this my whole adult life and it's done little else than make me travelsick. These states of mind and territories of being, are not about reconciliations or agreements or a settled-ness. I don't believe it is possible to be reconciled, because belonging is an unstable construct. For me, it is about resolving the tensions that I've always felt between the multiple identities I carry.

To this end and indeed with this work, things have shaken loose. In my reading, my investigations, my writing and my artmaking, I have interrogated the spaces of my identity and realized my selves in flux. I can now acknowledge that I speak an uneven combination of English and Hungarian, which are absolute opposites in every way. Varga, a Hungarian migrant writer in Australia, calls this mash up *Hunglish* (2004). In the naming of this hybrid form, she has validated it for me. Trezise (2011), another Australian writer whose mother is Hungarian, speaks of her 'discursive recuperation' with respect to her sense of belonging, necessary because her father's surname conceals a fundamental aspect of her identity. These women with similar experiences have indicated to me that I am not alone here in this place, and in this struggle. I suspect, like Varga that the, "Hungarian parts of me have always lurked in the folds of my consciousness" (2004, p. 5). I feel it most often when I am in Europe and almost never when I'm in Australia (Kane, 2012), yet as curiously not whilst I'm in Hungary.

Ultimately for me, belonging is a *process* not a consequence; it is a perpetual progression of encounter and becoming. As such, we are not ourselves (Rousell, Cutter-Mackenzie & Cutcher, 2014), but we are continually engaged in the practices of getting there. I am not yet myself.

BELONGING

The field of belonging literature has flourished over the past decade. A previously unmapped field, the multitude of inquiries in diverse arenas, whilst growing, lacks cohesive definitions and operationalizing terminology (Allen & Bowles, 2012; Mahar, et al., 2013). This is likely due to the minutiae of alienation, of agency, of place and of context.

Because belonging is a multifaceted state of being, fraught with ironies, complexities, intersections, and cultural encounters of the local and the global (Offord, 2002), it's most likely unrealistic to assume that such terminology can be consistent across diverse paradigms. Belonging is subjective – it is a perception, unique to the individual and centres on value, respect and 'fit' (Mahar et al., 2013). Because belonging is a deeply psychological construct, value and perception are both crucial – instructive reflections are an integral part of any definition of belonging (ibid). Belonging, like identity, is constructed in language and is a discursive construction (Trezise, 2011). The process of belonging is a journey of impermanent moments and interactions, "an interesting intricacy of belongingness" (Mahar et al., p. 1031). As such, the state of belonging is not a singular construct. The performativity of belonging, and of the cultural traces that contribute to it (Trezise, 2011), relies on the relationship of self to other and of self to place, shared histories, language and time. This network of interactions is more fully discussed below.

With respect to the stories of memory and experience shared in this inquiry, and particularly my own, the belongings (as both a state of being and also as possessions) are ambivalent, liminal, hidden, observable, collaborative and transitional. What follows is an exploration of these perspectives.

Belonging: Place, Language, Time, Shared Histories, Cultural Practices

The characteristics and enabling processes of belonging are socially constructed and as such, lived experiences fail to fit a normative model of belonging (Getrich, 2008). Our principal sense of belonging relies upon the culture in which we grow up, that in which we are first socialized, providing that the environment remains stable. This is different to birthright – we may be born in a place and yet be disconnected from it due to displacement at an early age, as was the case for my mother.

The bonds of shared history and memory, as well as of language, family and the shared performance of cultural practices are the ties that bind us so that we may belong together. It is the formative experiences in our 'homelands' that ensure how we move into the world and interact with others. The 'homeland' is also where we begin to practice languages, first learn about culture, become aware of place and start to create shared histories with others. As long as these factors remain stable, we are able to reconnect ourselves to these dynamics over and over again, thereby reinforcing a stable sense of self. For example, my mother was displaced from Hungary at the age of six, but because she grew up in a family of continued Hungarian activity, including the constant performance and reinforcement of the heritage language, she remains connected to the culture, if not the place. As Walton, Cohen, Cuir and Spencer, argue "[w]hen people's sense of social connectedness is threatened, their ability to self-regulate suffers" (2012, p. 513). In my case, the language and most of the cultural practices were not repeatedly insisted upon and reinforced. This resulted in an unstable sense of self for my early schooling years, until I developed coping mechanisms of my own.

There are complex issues within the concept of belonging. Firstly, there are things or people to which we simply belong, somewhat innately, through no effort of our own. We just are. For example, I am Australian-born, Female and White. These larger categories are certainly important to our sense of belonging, but these belongings can be complicated by factors that may be difficult to resolve. These can include the experience of growing up between two very separate cultural milieux, as my mother and I have; and also being displaced due to outside and sometimes incontrollable factors like both my parents' experienced.

Alternatively, the implications of belonging to a place (Offord, 2002) can be significant. An individual may not be at all troubled by not being connected to a new place because she is firmly psychologically anchored in the old (Johnston, 1976), or simply, she chooses not to belong (Mahar et al., 2013). Indeed, sometimes there are advantages in not belonging, or appearing to not belong. The individual may not be interested or motivated to seek endorsement by the dominant culture because she has little need to psychologically attach. She is gratified to move through the new world as a 'citizen', rather than as a genuine 'patriot'. This is not because she is content to be rootless, but rather because she feels as if she belongs to her heritage culture, or even somewhere else. This can be a freedom, a liberating factor. One's 'patriotism' and 'nationalism' lie elsewhere and can have its own advantages, one of which is the selective accountability to history.

Belongings can also be ambivalent, in conflict and complementary to each other. It is these binary perspectives, which have been exposed in this inquiry as notions of duality and opposition. My mother feels this keenly, as though her identities are in contrast to each other. This is also my experience, as we both had a fractured sense of self in childhood. As previously mentioned the tensions between the two are much more than a doubling of self. Ambivalence suggests a certain stillness, a static state of being. However our belongings and the states in which my mother and I exist are far more dynamic.

By virtue of the very experience of migration and displacement, belonging with respect to the immigrant is by its very nature, transitional and in flux. This is because place and belonging are intricately entwined (Schultz, 2004). The dynamism of transition is an element, which can add or subtract, be fleeting or permanent, or a vigorous interplay between enablers and barriers (Mahar et al., 2013). In any construct of transition, place and displacement are fundamental. I would argue that if an individual seeks to make a conscious transition towards a state of belonging in a foreign culture, she must be highly motivated, willing to cross borders and learn new languages. The traveller will need to be sensitive to the nuances of the dominant culture; adaptable, flexible and willing make certain transformations. In terms of my experience as portrayed in this work, it is obvious that a *desire* to belong is the necessary and proactive posture.

Languages and Belonging

The metaphor of languages that must be learnt is compelling in this context of transitional belongings. The languages may be verbal, behavioural or structural. In this sense, a language barrier is yet another border to be crossed and is achieved through the learning of new idioms. In this way, the barrier is negotiated rather than overcome.

Once in a new territory, it is vital for any newcomer to learn the multiple languages of other and of place, in order to operate fully within the new terrain. In order to belong, she must demonstrate a willingness to do so by developing dialogues in order to thrive and prosper. At this level, a degree of connectedness through shared languages is an advantage.

Languages and belonging is a critical link. Being in language is, by extension, being in place. If you speak the language of a country or a territory, you are by extension connected to the culture since language proficiency enables access. Thus, language is a gateway to culture. Although language competence does not necessarily make you a local, or assume belonging, it does allow you to occupy and engage the territory. New languages should not replace the old; rather, new languages can coexist with the old. Indeed, language and place are not as unchanging as they once were, and it is possible slip and slide between them in a way that was difficult for our parents and impossible for our grandparents (Varga, 2004). Once a semblance of language competence is established, the individual can engage with the new place, thereby demonstrating a concrete indicator of belonging. Language competence can also facilitate a psychological reconciliation between place and cultural practice. The individual becomes 'multilingual'.

It is truthful to assert that you can travel to new territories without the benefit of language competence, if you use the services of a translator. The position of the translator is pertinent in this framework, a being that can perform within more than one culture simultaneously as an interpreter. Most often unidentified, this agent is a facilitator for the two entities. However in any translation, details, subtleties and nuance will always be lost, understandings will be limited and authentic connection to culture is second-hand. Although convenient, a translator cannot fully ensure cultural empathy in each party because the translation is an interpretation, and as such does not engender a direct understanding. If authentic connections are sought, there is no substitute for being fully embodied in the language of the pertinent culture.

As this inquiry has revealed, if you do not speak the language you are powerless and mute. The words will quite literally fail you, as they have me, and without language it is almost impossible to be fully embodied in culture. In my earlier years, I couldn't speak the languages of my peers, and was quite pointedly ostracized. That my parents couldn't speak English well meant that they were socially inept, at least for a time, until they learnt the various languages, behavioural and literal, that were their passports to acceptance. If an individual does not have the language skills to transition to place independently, she will not feel as if she fully belongs to it. Since the identity in this context has no voice, no ways of expressing itself, the individual may find other ways articulate and make connections. However, since language is a primary connector, the individual will never feel fully embodied until this is comprehended. Unless the language is indeed practised and learnt, the individual will not have a resolved self and will continue to be alienated. This has been a consistent finding of this inquiry.

The notion of multivocality or multilingualism is crucial to belonging – the ability to speak many languages, with many voices makes robust connections to culture. The notion of the multilingual individual implies that she is able to assume a posture of inclusion. In this way, the self remains fluid, and emergent. Rather than being fragmented, shifting and multiple (Diamond & Mullen, 1999), the self becomes more unified. I would argue that an individual has to be reasonably integrated in order to simply operate in the world.

Liminal and Transitional Belonging

It was Barth who originally recognized the existence of margins separating people (1969). This inquiry certainly confirms that these margins exist and that they can in fact be more structured and difficult to traverse than the term 'margin' might initially suggest. Margins and borders can be actual or symbolic, visible or unseen (Cohen, 1994), but they require adroit navigation if the individual is ever able to move between them, and feel as if she belongs in either, neither or both. As the current research has suggested through the experiences of my parents and me, border crossings to places unknown can be treacherous. The border crossings shared by my family both actual and metaphorical have been unilaterally difficult. For example, when my father left Hungary for the final time, when my mother and her parents fled to Germany, when I entered school – all of these border crossings were potentially dangerous and essentially frightening. As demonstrated by this study, sometimes the old territory won't release you without a (psychological) fight. This can result in anxiety, with an identity in limbo, resolved in neither one place nor another, as my mother's story attests. These spaces in between can be described as a state of *liminal belongings*, as an existence in the in-between.

If the individual is unable to resolve these margins and borders, by inference she must become nomadic, a wanderer, constantly on the move, rootless and roaming. In this inquiry, this has been conceptualized through the metaphor of gypsy. Whilst I am aware that some may find the terminology of gypsy troubling, particularly as it relates to contemporary social and cultural tensions in Hungary, she is a deliberate construction that speaks to unresolved identity and belonging issues. In using this term, I aim to direct attention to Hungarian issues of nationhood and identity. The metaphor of the empowered gypsy has been deliberately chosen to be provocative, and to highlight issues of alienation and exclusion.

The gypsy of this tale is a survivor, empowered and confident in the liminal spaces in which she constantly finds herself. She has become comfortable in the transit zone she finds herself in again and again, because it is peaceful in these places, and she is able to abstain from the constant mêlée of alienation and exclusion she finds in other territories. When one becomes rootless, one begins to eschew roots, and therefore this gypsy constantly seeks new frontiers to conquer. I assert that it is because she does not feel fully embodied in any of these traditions, cultures and languages that she will never fully feel as if she belongs to them and them to her. She really belongs nowhere and perhaps everywhere, drifting and rootless, a constant wanderer and a boundary hunter; she goes where whimsy, circumstance and opportunity take her. She is a survivor, spirited, musical, artistic and supernatural, a spectre. She is most content in a nomadic lifestyle.

This gypsy is mysterious and never fully known. She will not be bound to one place or identity and lives a transient existence. This gypsy is always a migrant in the very real sense; she is always a guest, never a local always a 'blow in' (to use the Australian vernacular). This gypsy is a traveller rather than a tourist, who is resilient, adaptable and strong, with an arsenal of survival skills. She is ephemeral, forever in transit, with no final destination, just existing in one endless journey of learning and of life. Such is the experience of the outsider as amply demonstrated through the narratives in this inquiry.

The places between borders, the no-man's-lands, can also be places of belonging, indeed it is where I have discovered that I most often belong. It is in this metaphorical doorway that many will feel the most comfortable for several reasons. Those who cross many borders, of language, culture and place know the transit zone well. The homeland for these individuals is the in-between, the liminal, but mostly it is a transitional space. It is this notion of *transitional belonging*, of constant movement that is a central finding of this inquiry.

Belonging in the liminal and the transitional spaces, this gypsy is multivocal, adaptable and competent in all the new territories she encounters. She is an empowered figure, much like my Nonya, confident in her abilities to survive. She does not have to reconcile her belonging places in an either/or proposition because she connects to all of these places, on occasion, as she moves through them. Just as my experiences have demonstrated, this is because she no longer belongs to any one place, culture or tradition although she may at times experience moments when she feels bonded to both. It is in these situational and transitional belongings when she will experience flashes of connection. This was confirmed by my mother's experience, who claims to be 'neither one nor the other', in the liminal, yet was so comfortable and seemingly integrated during the trip back to Hungary. She belonged in Hungary fully, in that moment, even though there were times when she asserted that she felt 'outside'. The belonging moments were fleeting, ephemeral and transitional.

As my own story attests, when you belong nowhere, you seek to belong everywhere, and when you come from a heritage of enforced survival, it becomes your way of knowing. As I did, one learns to be strong, astute and creative, because this is the behaviour that was modelled to me by my parents and my grandparents. Thus, my constant experiences of rejection in the dominant culture ignited the performance of the family legacy: to fight, to adapt and to survive. In terms of the life experiences documented here, this is how I have found my own resolution of the tensions of my identity, that the many belongings (as both possessions and connections) can be maintained together, not in harmony, but in coexistence. In this way, one possesses a portfolio of belongings (rather than identities) that one is able to operate through depending on the circumstance. In this way, belonging is embodied and situational, liminal and transitional, depending upon time, moment and place.

Collaborative Belonging

As previously mentioned, belonging is a socially created construct. Feelings of inclusion do not just rely upon internal identity resolutions; they are also dependent upon the acceptance of the self by exterior forces, by dominant or 'outside' cultures, peoples and encounters. The notion of *belonging as a collaboration* between selves, others, events and cultures is an uncommon proposition.

Belonging is situated and contextual – in place, cultural practices, shared history, time and language, just as the places of not belonging, of alienation, are severed from these. Therefore, feeling as if you belong is about feeling unified with place, culture, shared history and language over time. These are not mutually exclusive, but the more of these connections that are shared the more the individual will feel integrated. Further, I argue that the individual must feel fully embodied as belonging to place, culture, shared history and/or language; and the outside place, its history, culture and/ or language must accept her as belonging to them. Therefore, the dominant culture will also be somewhat transformed through the newcomer's actions, presence and performance within it. Thus, a collaboration occurs between the individual and the collective, and also within the individual and within the collective. There must be an exchange of these interactions if belonging is to transpire. I call this the *belonging transaction* and this operation is a collaborative event.

Inherited cultures, places and histories may enhance the individual's ability to connect to homelands, but these links are largely second-hand and as such, do not necessarily facilitate belonging as is my own experience. This inheritance will indeed boost the individual's empathy and opportunity to make connections, but since the links are not direct, they risk two things. Either the individual will attempt to surrender these connections in order to facilitate belonging to an alternative place (turn their back on the parents' culture, for example), or the individual will be obligated to attempt to belong to two places, simultaneously. Both of these actions were a reality for me and both resulted in an unsettled state. Therefore a schism in the self is created that can be difficult to resolve.

Choice and power are necessary to develop satisfying and reciprocal interactions and for the individual to control to whom and what they feel they belong (Mahar, et al., 2013). This is where reciprocity or the belonging transaction must be activated. Sites of confluence between the immigrant must be sanctioned by the outside culture, so that "[b]elonging [can be] the activation of mapping landscape and territory for what is desired, what will bring security, what can be owned, that which will ensure a notion of duration or temporality" (Offord, 2002, p. 4). It doesn't take much effort by the dominant culture to achieve this, since a "mere sense of social connectedness [or mere belonging] can shape people's motivated behaviour" (Walton et al., 2012, p. 513). Such gracious gestures can have great impact.

For a migrant, especially a second-generation migrant, belonging is thus a collaboration, which relies on outside forces as well as continual transactions with the self, between the self and other, the self with place, with language, with culture, with shared history, with memory, with experience. My parents and their experiences and actions framed my belongings in both the Australian culture and the Hungarian. However, my belongings are also framed by my own interactions, which were (in childhood at least) affirming of the frameworks already established for me. This confirmed the structures that existed around me and continued to be troubling to a sense of 'citizenship' within both the dominant and the personal cultures throughout my life, but most significantly as they were established in my childhood.

Citizenship and identity are mutually inclusive terrains. Although citizenship is an incomplete term for how I theorize who I think I am, it is useful to conceptualize what it may mean for a sense of belonging. My citizenship is located in the liminal, transitional and collaborative space of binary identities, but is constructed wholly of neither, as well as both. This troubling of citizenship is further complicated by the institutional structures within which we operate.

The notion of assembling documents for a passport, for example, requires an operation somewhat external to the interior self and is wholly inert; one has to prove one's identity. We all have agency over where our citizenship may be located, but *proof of identity* is incontrovertibly linked to self and belonging – an external force that can complicate the internal. I carry with me amongst other things, an Australian passport because of my birthplace. However, I have only recently discovered that Hungarian citizenship is an inherited birthright, irrespective of the place where you are born. Lineage and national citizenship for the Hungarian is a blood truth, a blood tie. It is endowed at the moment of birth.

I feel this simple (and previously ignored) fact deeply; it hits me, hard, and shifts something within. Even as I was being continuously told I was not Hungarian, as I was struggling with my heritage, Hungary had already claimed me as its own. I find it profoundly cathartic that both Australia and Hungary acknowledge my existence, after all.

Although belonging to a certain place is complicated by the processes of globalization (Hirsch & Lazar, 2011), concrete links to place fulfil emotional, cultural and identity needs. However, belonging is far deeper than this. Coming to a state/s of belonging/s requires that a network of interactions, transitions and collaborations occur in a dynamic web of experience, place and memory. Such *ecologies of belonging* are a necessary condition for a resolved and stable suite of identities. In order to map the self, to resolve the tensions and to safely return to the metaphorical homeland within, such networks rely upon stable and productive collaborations of self and others.

Perceptions of time are critical to such collaborations, as time tolerates change and transformation. Time allows to us to see clearly backwards, through the lens of history and experience. As Papas so poignantly reveals, time is circular, it, "is beneath our feet. It is above us, around us. We carry it in our flesh…Time hovers. It haunts and teases. It is the ball we move in. It is the history we walk on" (2012, p. 12).

Reconciliations and Method

The complexity of contemplation is a minefield and a creative conundrum (Varga, 2004). As such it is appropriate to reflect upon the methods utilized in this inquiry, since the minefields, *mindfields* and creative conundrums of the research largely facilitated the forms of the representations in this work.

The self-conscious use of auto/biography and arts-based approaches within this inquiry has enabled the research to open up distinctive spaces for the understandings to emerge. These spaces rely upon both the creative agency of the artist/writer in combination with the distinctive experience of the reader. In this way, interpretation becomes a communal affair, located in the dialogue between us. As such, the interchange becomes a simulacrum of the processes of collaborative belonging, in a transaction between artist/writer and audience. When dealing with trauma and the psychology of individuated notions of identity, words in a singular portrayal remain inadequate. A proactive, self-conscious and engaged reader activates the layers of stories and images, metaphors and renderings in the deeply dialogic relationship.

The use of fiction, Art, poetry, narrative and metaphor enable an aesthetic experience in the encounter with content. Literature, fiction and the Arts are all sources for a critical perspective on notions of cultural identity (Chariandy, 2007). The form of arts-based inquiries is necessarily foregrounded in the reception of the work. The artist/writer seeks to artfully construct the 'manuscript' so that it resonates with the audience through an emotional engagement. In this way an authenticity of meaning is achieved through the experience of the encounter. Although the presence of the artist/writer is clearly within a successful text, the artist/writer herself is absent. This absent presence is a necessary tension. Even in auto/biography the author is other to the self, constructed in the text, and belongs in the narrative and not the biography (Ditlmann et al., 2010). The duality and contradictions of such stories are powerful and must be acknowledged. In this work, I have endeavoured to express all of these elements.

Arts-based research should, I believe, only be employed if the sensibility of the researcher and the requirements of the research demand it. As a pragmatist, I don't believe that this is a method that fits every type of educational research by every researcher. It is simply a matter of what works best. For me, as an artist and a teacher and a writer, this has been a good fit. Art is about the enhancement and cultivation of differences (Eisner, 2011) and thus its use in this work is in synergy with the intentions of the research. Arts-based research requires sensitivity, sound judgement, an ironic posture that doesn't take itself too seriously and a great deal of organization, rigor and discipline. It is not for the timid, and can be an extraordinary amount of work. Yet, as with the construction of most artworks, the process is delightfully perplexing, thought provoking and disobedient. It is also in itself, enormously satisfying. Although these things are not the purposes of research, they certainly motivate the researcher to continue with the work, and that in itself is a useful outcome.

The highly personal nature of this study is one of its greatest strengths – its particularity, its depth, and its accomplishment in mining these characteristics for new ways of seeing the universal have been facilitated through a particularly distinctive discourse. This has been an emotional, creative, artistic, intuitive and at times, irregular enterprise, and since these are fundamentally subjective ways of experiencing and knowing life they ought to be celebrated in research as they are in life. These ways of knowing are as significant as any other (Grumet, 1995) and voices should be encouraged and stories should be shared, in order to create noisy, tolerant and interesting societies. Accepting the creatively idiosyncratic as a discourse of knowledge is long overdue. For all the pontifications of the postmodern theorists within the academy, we have not seen much evidence of this theory in practice. If it is acknowledged that the postmodern moment was a more creative, democratic, ambiguous space, we must then accept more creative, democratic, ambiguous methods of discovery. It is these that have the potential to advance our understandings in ways never before anticipated.

In my case, the research has created many epiphanies in the process of expression. My own experience of coming to belong as a loyal Australian of proud Hungarian heritage has been facilitated through this process. My experiences as a writer have been informative and my experiences as an artist have been illuminating. The subjectivities of experience excavated in this site enlighten and enhance my practice as an educator.

In a world where knowledge is both accessible and negotiable, educators often struggle to determine what our role should be; this is certainly the case in my own teaching practice. I believe that students must learn how to interpret, deconstruct, question and analyze both what is being offered up to them as knowledge, but also what they themselves intuitively glean from their own understandings. In order to do this our students must be sensitive to otherness, to the peculiarities within difference, and to themselves. Intuition, imagination and creativity must be nurtured, not at the expense of scientific or rational thought (Eisner, 2011), but alongside it. Human experience is infinitely rich, and we operate in deeply symbolic ways. It is in this essentially human way that we are able to connect with each other. It is these skills, amongst many others, that we need to be nurturing in our students; encouraging the intuitive, the emotive and the individual. Feeling, after all, is a cognitive event.

Learning the languages of others in our societies, and being able to partake of that otherness is vital to a dynamic and productive society. Some of these languages are visual, literary, poetic, theatrical and musical. Storytelling and mythologies, especially shared stories, bind people to culture (Clandinin & Connelly, 1994; Barone & Eisner, 1997). Through the sharing of these stories we connect to each other's places, languages, experiences and histories. In this case, I concur with Kambaskovic, who asserts, "a migrant finds herself suspended between two worlds, equally comfortable and uncomfortable, in either of them. Frankly, I am beginning to see this state as a natural medium for my intellectual performance" (2013, p. 105). For me, this is an ineffable truth.

Wog, wog, why don't you go back to your country you dirty wog? (Tsiolkas, 2013, p. 22)

CHAPTER 16

AUSTRALIAN IDENTITY TODAY AND TOMORROW

Guests, Strangers and Understandings

This chapter is located in a broader context than the individual, specifically that of Australian identity, now and for the future. It is included here to infer the theories articulated in the previous chapter onto the realities of the policies and practices needed for an authentically inclusive future. Although this chapter and indeed the context for this inquiry are of Australia, many of the issues raised herein are globally relevant.

This chapter is organized into two quite distinct sections. Firstly, examinations of Australia's identity, multicultural and contemporary migration issues are articulated. Upon this foundation and in conclusion, recommendations inspired by this inquiry, as well as suggestions for further research are projected.

CONTEMPORARY MULTICULTURAL AUSTRALIA: IMPLICATIONS

Research on multiculturalism, immigration policy, national identity, race, ethnicity and whiteness in Australia is a well-populated field (Anderson, 2012). The focus for the DISCUSSION in this chapter is the understandings to be gleaned from a singular experience of alienation, within frameworks of education and contemporary experience. In order to achieve this, the Australian context will be used as a lens for the discussion.

As previously mentioned, multiculturalism in Australia has been both government policy and cultural trend during the past 25 years, and has grown in part with respect to the experiences and contributions of migrants such as my parents and grandparents. However, recent global shifts and national events have challenged Australian notions of multiculturalism. World events such as 9/11, consequent conflicts such as the bombings in Bali, London and other places, two Gulf Wars and the rise of ISIL; as well as national events like the popularity of the One Nation political party, *Tampa* and the 'children overboard' scandal, and the asylum seeker crises have all undermined the Australian public's sense of security and hard won perspectives on multicultural stability. With respect to the latter, it would seem as though previous notions of a resolved cultural identity have actually been a charade.

Such concerns, particularly with respect to a distrust of multiculturalism, are global trends shared by many western nations. International migration has dramatically

233

increased in recent decades (Jayaraman, 2005). Little more than a decade ago, 70 million people lived and work outside of their country of origin (Kelly, 2002); this has increased to 232 million (OHCR, 2014). Transnational resettlements of migrants, asylum seekers and refugees are transforming the ethnic profiles of international societies. Countries all over the world are debating these issues, and cultural pluralism, although an erstwhile political ideal, may not be desired in practice (Albrechtsen, 2002; Bita, 2002; Jayaraman, 2015; Tsiolkas, 2013). A renewed culture of assimilation and the promotion of monoculturalist values are on the ascendant, and account for the rising popularity of extreme politicians, like the Dutch politician Pim Fortuyn (who was assassinated in 2002) and the failed French right-wing political candidate Jean Marie Le Pen. Le Pen garnered much support in France by making the link between crime and immigration, as well as highlighting the failure of the French ethnic groups to assimilate culturally. In Australia, Pauline Hansen and her One Nation party held similar views asserting we were being 'swamped by Asians' in 1996. Although these politicians were controversial, they indicate an increasing mood of intolerance and frustration.

Prior to the ascendancy of the One Nation Party in Australia, many Australians (including me) arrogantly assumed that we had settled these social issues in the public consciousness. That view has exploded and a familiar disquiet has bloomed (Kelly, 2002). Hostility towards recent migration and Indigenous concerns has become a major social issue (Jayaraman, 2005). The postmodern concerns of borders blurring, globalization, the dissolution of the concept of the nation state, as well as the open endedness of cultural diversity, have all contributed to this agitation; Australians are reappraising long held assumptions (Tsiolkas, 2013).

In this unstable and insecure environment, many Australians see the 'cult' of ethnicity as threatening the ideal of 'E pluribus unum' the one culture that the many aspire to join (Albrechtsen, 2002). Together with the Australian right-wing government's present and past demonizing of refugees and asylum seekers from the very places we have joined others in invading in the guise of democratic saviours, and what seems to be a concerted campaign of divisiveness targeting our Muslim Australians, this country is on unstable, fragmented ground (Deen, 2003; Ellis, 2003; Tsiolkas, 2013; Varga, 2009). More than a decade ago, one writer predicted a global trend: the fragmentation of multicultural ideology in this century as economic forces drive a greater movement of people across borders (Kelly, 2002). It would seem that this is in fact, well underway.

Before I examine some potential possibilities to address the rising tide of xenophobic attitudes, it is necessary to reflect upon historical and contemporary notions of Australian identity and how these have developed or been surpassed, and what appears to be a racist renaissance in Australia. This will provide a context for the discussion regarding Australia's multicultural future, if indeed she is to have one.

234

National Identity

National identity is an ideology characterized by a core set of transcendent and abstract values (Ditlman, Purdie-Vaughns & Eibach, 2010). Australians seem to examine national identity endlessly in order to define whom we are, as if that will make us feel more settled and grown up (Mackay, 2000). So the question, 'What makes us Australian?' is often posed at times when we feel as if we are experiencing moments of definition. For example, in 1999 (at the end of one century and on the eve of another), in 2000 (before, during and after the Sydney Olympic Games) and in 2001 (a century of Federation). What follows is a concise outline of some of these deliberations.

Australians are united by the one fact that overrides all others: we are the quintessential immigrant nation. The only difference between us is that some of us got here before others (Hugo, 2004; McNicoll, 2000). When Governor Phillip and his unhappy band of First Fleeters landed in Botany Bay in 1788, there were about 300 000 Indigenous Australians already living peacefully, with sophisticated cultural and social structures. Given the rugged and unfamiliar landscape, the newer Australians found it challenging and in that first year many crops failed and supplies ran very low.

It was these early years, however, that began to shape the national character within White consciousness. The convicts hated all authority, and this has filtered down to today. More migrations followed due to the Gold Rush, with people coming mainly from China. The Chinese were despised because of their superior work practices and work ethic, thus causing the first anti-Asian sentiments, which persist today. If Australians massacred Aborigines on a grand scale, the attacks on these Chinese are second only to that viciousness as they were beaten, tortured and killed. The 'Yellow Peril' as the Chinese came to be known, was directly responsible for a halt to Asian immigration at the time and informed the subsequent White Australia Policy (McNicoll, 2000). This racist inheritance persisted through most of the twentieth century, peaking during post-war migration.

During Federation, journalists wrote of the Australian as a resilient bushman, and later the Anzac embodied the best of these qualities. Fostered during and after WWI, the Anzac legend is one of the strongest parts of our identity and is largely about sacrifice and participation despite the odds, on behalf of the nation and directly through one's own citizenship (Vizard, 1999). This version of the Australian assumed that our Diggers were from the bush and probably of convict heritage, laconic and resourceful with a wry sense of humour, mistrustful of bosses but absolutely loyal to his mates, awkward with women and clergy but good with children and merciless towards bullshit. This was the gospel of Australianism and particularly of mateship (Bolton, 2001).

The Australian man was traditionally defined as someone who believed in a 'fair go' and fought regimentation of authority and corruption; was bawdy, vulgar and anti-sophisticated, much like our frontier people; was heroic and stoic, a battler, an underdog, a larrikin. Much of this imagery comes from our colonial and rural past and portrayed as thus in our Arts forms; these were qualities Australians developed in order to survive. Women were also depicted as forthright, bold and resourceful, feisty and rebellious, also striving for a fair go. However, these rural images are less relevant as our archetypes, as Australia is becomes increasingly urbanized and cosmopolitan.

The Australian vernacular, with its flattened vowels and seesawing inflections as well as its unique words is a significant part of the national identity. It is a rich, witty and colourful language, quite foreign even to English speaking migrants. Throughout our White history over the past 230 years, rich and colourful abuse, some of it friendly and some of it malicious, has peppered our history. As previously observed, language is a cultural indicator of belonging. Almost impossible to mimic by the non-Australian, the dialect is one that you need to grow up with to fully conquer.

Sport is probably the foremost arena where Australian identity-hunger has prowled (Smee, 1999). We like to look successful in the eyes of the world, as if we have something to prove, but the pervasiveness of Australia's sporting culture is easy to understand. The early settlers found themselves in the midst of bounteous space and constantly sunny weather, free of European class distinctions; everybody could play anything (Devine, 2001). It was commonly understood in 1901 that strenuous activity, especially team sports, produced muscular Christianity in people and should therefore be encouraged (Denney, 2001). Women too, were encouraged to take part in sport to become strong and morally upright. Bonding on sporting arenas has been essential in the building of our national character and style; Australians have been historically very good at it and have revelled in the successes. Australians like to think of themselves as winners, and every small sporting victory is celebrated to near hysterical terms (Leunig, 1999). As through my own experience, sport has a vital role in human relations in Australia; indeed sport was essential in my process of coming to belong. In Australia, as my parents so shrewdly recognized, there can be no substantial social life without either competence in sport or enthusiasm for it; preferably both (Devine, 2001).

The notion of the 'fair go' runs throughout the Australian character but can manifest itself as a resentment of those who achieve more, and as envy of those who are more successful than the locals. This was evident during the last century when European migrants started to achieve a measure of economic success. As my father reports, the resentment manifested in racist, intolerant behaviour from workmates and authority figures, like the police, and in my case, teachers. Such behaviour is at odds with another element of the national character – that of our willingness to (and that everyone should) 'have a go' (Healey, 2000).

There are very many ways to be Australian and there are many things Australians do well. Our character is evolving and clearly traditional definitions are inadequate for contemporary Australians especially women, but also migrants, the Indigenous and the urbanized, as most of us are (Bolton, 2001). Australians today are not monochromatic, but many have clung to the bush legend in the face of change and variety. Globalization has frightened many into thinking we are losing our Australian identity, and some cling to the archetypes even though the ideology of a rural Australia is becoming a lost world.

Before a consideration of the prospects for a contemporary Australian identity is possible, it is timely to explore Australia's recent re-emergence as an insular, inward-focused and somewhat prejudiced people. The trigger for this renaissance can be attributed to the ideology and maiden speech in Parliament of the Member for Oxley, Ms Pauline Hanson.

Hanson and Howard

When Hanson made her maiden speech in September of 1996, the nation's consensus on multiculturalism appeared to be more fragile than we had previously realized (Healey, 2000). Hanson was the first politician to openly attack the policy and for some she became a folk hero, a national icon. Photographed draped in the Australian flag, her platform included a position for a White Australia, the abolition of multiculturalism, the cessation of Asian, and then later, all immigration and the abolishment of programs for Indigenous people. Labelled a racist, which she consistently denied, she was seen by some as being a puppet for far more subversive racist groups. Hanson went on to set up her own political party called One Nation, which won 23% of the vote in the Queensland state election in June 1998, and 11 seats in state Parliament. This was a substantial victory, given that she was both novice and latecomer to the political process.

One Nation has done significant damage to this country (Tsiolkas, 2013; Varga, 2009). Their policies were unworkable and short-sighted and based upon inaccurate statistics. At the time, out of 29 million refugees worldwide we accepted a mere 12 000 of the most desperate (The Age, 1998). The things that drove support for Hanson were a widespread insecurity caused by the perception that the public, especially those in country seats, were not having their interests represented; the previously mentioned and long established culture of racism and a lack of political leadership and vision by the other political parties (Mackay, 1998). The rise of One Nation's popularity was commensurate with the public's resentment and fear of globalization combined with Hanson's inflammatory rhetoric. One Nation shrewdly articulated the public's (especial rural and regional Australian's) quite valid concerns regarding the pace of economic changes, by directly accessing a working class desire to repeal the previous economic reforms (Tsiolkas, 2013). Hanson acquired significant voter support because there was a segment of Australian society who felt that they had been left out and left behind, that multiculturalism had been driven by the cities, by the professional classes, and ordinary, country folk had been ignored (Rothwell, 2002). It is these country electorates who have not traditionally supported a racially varied society, probably because they do not live in one – much of the immigrant

237

population in Australia is centred around the largest cities. At such times, many will seek refuge in the simple, and such a time is made for the emergence of right wing extremists. Unfortunately, the groundswell of support for Hanson did not disappear with her demise. It took root and was nurtured by the Howard government's continuous demonizing of refugees, as well as by world events.

In 1996 when Hanson attacked multiculturalism, Prime Minister John Howard was quietly ambivalent and refused to commit to Aboriginal reconciliation. Howard asserted that Hanson was 'appealing to the edge' on issues of Asian immigration, Aborigines and anti-globalization (Megalogenis, 2002, p. 21). Yet he very cleverly manipulated the entire situation, lying in wait until it was time to use some of those same policies in a different guise, thereby courting the Hanson vote and giving the impression that he sympathized with those who opposed migration (Steketee, 2002; Tsiolkas, 2013). Although this wasn't explicitly stated, many government policy decisions mirrored the controversial One Nation statements. Howard rode the tide of xenophobia and the subsequent mood One Nation cultivated, through wedge politics and brought Hanson's followers into his right-wing Coalition fold. It was a tacit endorsement of Australian parochialism and racism and was achieved for political and self-sustaining reasons.

Then *Tampa* happened. Just one year after the furore of national pride over the Olympics in Sydney 2000, an election was held where the electorate was so terrified by the manufactured stories (by the government and the media) of the Tampa affair, it was seduced into a deceitful narrative of fear. In August 2001, it was alleged that the passengers on the Tampa, anchored in Australian territorial waters, were prepared to throw their children overboard in order to gain access to the country as asylum seekers. It was of course utterly false, but Australians panicked thinking that a few-thousand asylum seekers threatened our borders (Roach, 2002). The catch cry of 'stop the boats' alluding to asylum seekers coming by way of people smuggling schemes on small boats through Indonesia, became part of the Australian vernacular and a potent political platform for more than a decade, continuing today. Fear, a powerful device, was used expertly in the 2001 federal election by the Howard government in a bid to be returned to office. It worked. Two months after 9/11, Australians "allowed themselves to be duped" (Marchetta, 2002, p. 12) and permitted politicians to convince them with a fabricated story that a refugee was a terrorist who would throw her child overboard for their own sanctuary (Deen, 2003; Roach, 2002). The then leader of the Labour opposition, Kim Beazley, displaying a lack of leadership to which Australians were becoming accustomed, colluded with Howard to demonize asylum seekers, and the atmosphere of hysteria and misinformation drove the nation's mood. This sentiment lingers.

The government's poor treatment of asylum seekers was central to the debate and divided the nation's opinions (Rintoul, 2002). Howard, whose previous opinions had cost him his job as Liberal leader, stalked the votes of Hanson. Both he and Phillip Ruddock, one of his Ministers for Immigration are both to this day, derided and admired for their tactics. The government called for tolerance, and then actively vilified the character of the asylum seekers (Saunders, 2002). In particular, Ruddock's controversial use of the vernacular such as *rejectee* denoting those remaining in detention centres, *illegals* and *queue-jumpers* meaning boatpeople whom he has likened to thieves because they have 'stolen' places from others in legal immigration queues, and the transformation of the term *asylum seeker* into a derogatory slur, gained momentum. Ruddock attempted to manipulate popular opinion on these issues with his derogatory and dehumanizing rhetoric (ibid). On one hand, he publicly criticized queue jumpers and labelled them as such, and then on the other, supported them by allowing them to jump the very queues he professed to support (Saunders, 2002). Ruddock used disdainful and negative arguments against what he called *these people* and shamefully, this found traction with the Australian public. The scaremongering worked.

In Howard, a mood of public scepticism found a mouthpiece. Middle Australia, their preferences and mood nicely tweaked by the normalizing of the Hanson rhetoric, and frightened by recent terrorist events, rejected in part at least, concepts of republicanism and reconciliation and with them multiculturalism. Howard's vision of a new Australian Multiculturalism was about shedding its sharper edge and becoming cleverly eclectic, was more akin to Integration (Rothwell, 2002). This was the public policy, but it would seem that the actual political practice was flagrantly subversive.

In the post-Howard epoch, the media began to rally and middle Australia began to think again (Varga, 2004), but this was to be short-lived. Between 2007 and 2013, a Labour government was returned to office twice. Amongst their social reforms, in 2008 Kevin Rudd the then Prime Minister, made a national apology to the Stolen Generation of Aboriginal people in the spirit of reconciliation. Sorry Day was a watershed moment in Australian history, with many Australians hoping that the racist tide had turned. However, when Julia Gillard controversially assumed the leadership of the party and subsequently became Australia's first female Prime Minister, she continued with a political agenda that had dealing with asylum seekers as a major focus. Meanwhile, Indonesia continued to turn a blind eye to people smuggling, thereby enabling asylum seekers to funnel through their borders freely and onto unsafe boats. There was a sharp increase in boat arrivals, the Global Financial Crisis happened and then the subsequent economic downturn (Varga, 2004). Although theirs was a more compassionate approach, like Howard both Rudd and Gillard struggled and failed to 'stop the boats'. People continued to die at sea in the small, leaky boats that carried them and their fragile optimism (ibid). Meanwhile, the electorate were unrelenting in their support for a scheme that would end the arrival of asylum seekers by boat.

When Tony Abbott came to office as Prime Minister in 2013, it was on a platform that had 'stop the boats' high on the agenda, helped along by the perceived instability and leadership woes of the previous incumbents. Within a year, he 'accomplished' this goal, however the collateral damage has been enormous. The expense and pandemonium is overwhelming, briefing and reportage by journalists forbidden, the conditions for detainees appalling, the methods irresponsible; Australia's compliance with international law in the past year has been tenuous. At time of writing, there were almost 2500 people in offshore detention, with an uncertain future, their human rights being violated on a daily, monthly, yearly basis (Gibson, 2005). The Kafkaesque system that was created to manage asylum seekers and the banal evil of the appeals process undermines our claim as a civilized nation (Tsiolkas, 2013). All of this, despite the fact that 85% of all asylum seekers to this country have been deemed to be genuine refugees and that we are obliged, as a signatory to the UN Refugee Convention to accept them (ibid).

The bitter irony is that as we have always done, Australia needs immigration if we are to have an economically and socially sustainable future. This country is underpopulated, with an untenable welfare system and a rapidly aging community. This is not an isolated Australian problem; all social democracies are indeed experiencing a demographic and economic shift (ibid).

Throughout the first decade of the 21st century and beyond, successive governments have supported offshore processing and long-term detention of asylum seekers, including children. It has been a central issue in the electorate during this time, ignited by cunning rhetoric of Hanson and Howard. September 11, the GFC, anti-Asian and anti-Muslim sentiment are all contributing factors to the contemporary mood of insularity in most western nations, however these factors may not have stirred such xenophobia in Australia had not One Nation opened a Pandora's Box of racist sentiment. It is an ugly time in our history, and once again race is at the core. As it so often does, history has repeated itself.

Whilst the asylum seeker issue is indeed highly complex, in the first instance it would seem that the electorate has forgotten our migration history within the current global context of war, terrorism, diaspora and economic instability. Australians have overlooked the overwhelmingly positive impact of post-war migration and the gentle presence of our earliest boatpeople in the 1970s, Buddhists from Vietnam. Perhaps it is because many of the recent refugees are Muslim that is the defining issue, that this is a difference that is too acute to be comfortably tolerated (Laurie, 2002). This certainly seems to be the case in other western democracies (Gibson, 2005; Izzard, 2011).

Contemporary Australian Identity: The Challenges

As is evident in the reading, Australia is suffering its own identity conflict. Over recent decades, it's clear that Australia has struggled with and resisted resolving pertinent global issues like multiculturalism, immigration, asylum seekers, refugees and cultural identity. Although these are also global anxieties, of particular concern to Australia is the expanding political and social divide between the two major factions in this country, namely the urbanized, cosmopolitan inner-city dwellers and the conservative, traditional and isolated regional residents. It has been obvious throughout the past decades that there are great cultural fault lines between these two disparate factions, each chafing against and irritating the other, primed to explode (Deen, 2003). The result has been divisiveness, encouraged by the wedge politics of previous governments. In my view, this has been exacerbated, indeed encouraged, by politicians with myopic and self-serving agendas, but perhaps more critically, in the absence of daring political and social leadership there is a mood of fear and ignorance. Australia today is bereft of long term vision.

We must all belong to our histories and to each other, united by our shared humanity. Australia is in desperate need of sustainable social cohesion if she is to face the difficulties to come. Australia has significant infrastructure challenges ahead and immigration is going to need to increase further, in order to rectify a shrinking population (Tsiolkas, 2013). Transnational migration and the increase in movement of refugees across the world are shaping the ethnic profiles of global societies, including Australia (Jayaraman, 2005). Thus, cultural pluralism and how we respond to immigration is a pressing concern, which will need proactive and elegant policy solutions.

Such solutions must be driven by astute and socially sensitive political vision, enacted through vigorous and courageous leadership. A very public social and political dialogue on racism, multiculturalism and identity must be the first item on any transformation agenda. Australians, and indeed all nations in the same situation, need to have a courageous multicultural conversation (Tsiolkas, 2013). It is indeed possible for cultural traces and emerging identities to be woven together in order to make a richer, more nuanced and united ensemble of identities; a contemporary Australian one. In order to resolve these tensions and make astute decisions regarding immigration, the treatment of asylum seekers and reconciliation (for example), an open and transparent public discourse must occur first. This is certainly a challenging proposition and will require authentic leadership unsullied by the personal agendas of politicians and their partisan priorities. The question remains, however: Will anyone in Australia have the courage to ignite this dialogue? Our own history has demonstrated that racial politics are not fixed and unchanging, and it is imperative that Australia take the lead on confronting xenophobia, racist anxiety and cultural ignorance through coherent and unflinching political and social leadership.

The irony is that the Australian population benefits greatly from an increasingly global community through their beloved technology and their ubiquitous propensity to travel far, wide and long. Immigration has also been a resounding success in Australia (Hatoss, 2006; Sata et al., 2009; Zevallos, 2005). One only has to look as far as the widespread proliferation of cafes, coffee culture and the myriad choices of international cuisine now so prevalent in this country to see an immediate and obvious immigrant footprint. In many ways, migrants colonized Australia through food, coffee, wine, the Arts and inspiring their new friends to travel. The bush legend does actually demonstrate that circumstance and environment shape national character; they are doing so now.

Both Australia's Indigenous past and immigrant stories are a collective history of a nation and all citizens share in it. I assert that we need to own these things and be grateful that we have a history and cultures that are so rich, complex and interesting. We must live our lives as forward-looking, energetic achievers. But I would also argue that we also need to understand our lives by looking backwards, so that we learn from our triumphs, and more importantly, from our mistakes.

Hugh Mackay asserted 15 years ago that our youth as a nation and our absence of a clear definition of our identity is actually our strength; because we are traditionally flexible and open to new ideas, our society is thus hybrid, fluid, and displays fresh thinking, tolerance, and a healthy scepticism (2000). Australians have historically demonstrated a capacity to learn from past mistakes and rectify them (Jayaraman, 2005) but we must remain ever vigilant. If this is the case, why do we treat our newcomers so abhorrently? And why have we done this consistently for more than two centuries? If we are indeed far more than a mob of yobbos and hedonists, why don't we support the underdog, when it is an animal of a different colour, race or creed? Clearly these are issues that need to be addressed, head on.

Social democracies, indeed most countries, must develop new conceptualizations and understandings regarding the increasingly polyethnic traits of countries in the era of globalization. In Australia, immigration has been resoundingly successful (Tsiolkas, 2013) and although in recent and historical times our nation has been guilty of bigotry, the sunny nature of the Australian temperament and belief in a fair go for all, are at odds with such wrongdoings.

Once the cultural conversation has been ignited, Australians can begin to reconsider policy regarding asylum seekers, refugees and immigration as a whole. I believe that in Australia, multicultural ambivalence can indeed be transformed into vigorous and humane policy. If as a nation, we continue to commit to certain quotas of refugees, I argue that we must fund the entire scheme adequately so that the programs will be effective and respectful. Certainly, the methods by which we process refugees and asylum seekers need to become more humanitarian, streamlined and cost effective. We must abolish mandatory detention of children, at the very least. If we continue to detain refugees, it ought to be for a minimal period of time, before releasing the 'possibles and probables' into the community under supervised programs, which would be more cost effective than detaining them indefinitely. I would suggest that rural incentive schemes, for example, be developed into successful programs for our newest residents. Immigrants in Australia have traditionally been highly motivated and hardworking. Asylum seekers could contribute to a revival of regional Australia – so called 'illegals' could be bonded to work in development schemes and fulfil commissions for the benefit of the whole country (Tsiolkas, 2013), rather than languish in offshore detention centres, going slowly mad (Varga, 2009). A more humane system to mitigate asylum seekers arriving by boat is a pressing need and a regional solution is essential. Indonesia, too, must assume some responsibility as they have covertly legitimized the practice of people smuggling (Tsiolkas, 2013).

All who decide to come to Australia must embrace this new country as their own, without rejecting their heritage cultures; because they enrich us, as has been repeatedly demonstrated in the nation's experience. Of course, migrants must find ways to reconcile the new world and the old, in order to bind themselves to this nation in productive and mutually satisfying ways.

Education, in both formal and informal settings, is absolutely necessary if these reforms are to take hold, as is concrete, sustained and accessible support from our governments in the form of social programs and institutions. Migrants must have direct access to free assistance, encouragement and support in the learning of English as their second language. This is because as has been previously asserted, language access allows entry to culture. If we expect our migrants to be fully participant in the life of their adopted nation, we must make it possible for them to do so. Bilingualism in schooling (including Indigenous languages) is also a desired outcome. The ability to operate in several languages not only makes our society more socially and culturally aware, but also more tolerant. In our seemingly isolated state in the southern hemisphere, we must endeavour to connect ourselves to other nations, both in this region but also elsewhere.

Many global societies see the concept of inclusiveness as a goal (Jakubowicz, 2002). If a democracy is going to function authentically, all need to feel included, recognized and respected; the dominant society is transformed. Concurrent with this, there is also an expectation that the newcomer must accept and respect the differences of others and then they are also transformed; such is the belonging transaction. If the multicultural ideal is to be a lived truth in our society, we must find a way to exist together peacefully with respect and tolerance. All Australians, from all cultural backgrounds must commit to Australia's interests, without forgoing their heritage cultures. A population with a variety of customs and traditions cannot avoid enriching the community, and can make valuable contributions to culture and to knowledge. As one writer puts it, in terms of loyalty, being an Australian who was born elsewhere is like having two children: you love them both (Deen, 2003). In fact, research demonstrates that if people value their heritage, they will participate more successfully in the dominant culture than someone who has had to reject or deny a substantial part of who they are (Hardgrave, 2002).

Surely, reconciliation must be placed firmly on the forefront of the national agenda. We cannot go forward as a country until we reconcile the past. Ideally, all people should be given a say and the opportunity to speak, even the smallest of voices. As the great and glorious St Istidán, Hungary's first king said, "A nation of one language is weak". We can learn from the lesson he taught his son Imre, to make welcome those "guests and strangers" because they will make the nation resilient and vibrant. We all need to speak our own 'languages' within a common language framework, so that we can build shared histories and create our own, unique Australian culture, in this, our place.

A FINAL WORD

I am a teacher: it is my mission and by most accounts, I do it well. My abilities as a teacher have been supported and indeed developed by the formative experiences of my life. Because I have felt like an impostor and a pretender my whole existence, I have been hyperaware of others who do not feel or look or act as if they belong. These outsiders, foreigners, unknowns, interlopers, strangers, gypsies and aliens are my belonging group. They have included other migrants, of course, but also Indigenous people, the disabled, GLBTQI folks, the fringe dwellers, the lonely, the disenfranchised. To be an outsider has been the most precious of gifts, as teacher, parent, friend, artist and writer. It has forced me to look more closely at difference, to move past my ignorance to understanding and onwards, to appreciation. It informs all of my actions and dealings with others.

In my teaching, it has made me responsive to and appreciative of individuality. It has made me consciously and subconsciously cater for individual student need, utilizing curriculum and reflexive pedagogy to that end both as a secondary teacher and now in the higher education context. It has made me exceptionally aware of the classroom dynamic and observant of human behaviour. This hyperaware state has been of great benefit to my teaching and to the learning of my students. My experiences with difference have made me the inclusive teacher that I am.

The research reported in this work has used one Hungarian migrant family's experience in Australia at its core, but it has revealed issues much more significant and universal. The experiences that my family endured in our shared past can be utilized as a lens through which we can gaze at the present, and beyond it, to the future. More than this, we can look outwards to society at large and apply the lessons learned from these experiences to a multitude of contexts – sociological, educational and political. The individual experience can and should inform more universal and public concerns and agendas. Micro-history is as relevant as the grand narrative, in its feminizing, individuating character. Small voices must be heard and respected if we are to fully accommodate all within the greater framework of society.

The experiences of my family are relevant on many levels, but what are of the most compelling significance are the questions they raise in terms of inclusiveness and belonging. Surely this is an ideal for any civilized culture. The instigation of new conversations between 'differents' is essential if we are to face the challenges of contemporary life in ways that are incisive, visionary and imaginative. It is our core humanity that links us as people, even though there are many differents and differences between us. This is the beauty of diversity, and of the unique.

Clearly, policy makers must drive these initiatives, but they also must be actively and enthusiastically implemented by willing educators who as role models, demonstrate inclusiveness in their teaching practice and curriculum development. In order to do this, they must be supported by an appreciative and encouraging society that appreciates the demands and rigors of such an undertaking. It must begin with the teacher, who is the direct link between the policy makers of today and the contributing, influential society members of tomorrow, supported by the community and most particularly, by parents.

If we demystify difference and learn to accept and understand it, if we refuse to submit to a monocultural hegemony and celebrate, perform and express our distinctiveness, we are able to reconcile these differences within our individual cultures rather than fear them. A worst-case scenario would be the eradication of cultural differences through the promotion of a sameness of language, appearance and ritual. Individuality and its examination have ramifications for social governance and policy. This inquiry has aimed to compel society to look more closely at what difference means.

LIMITATIONS AND SUGGESTIONS FOR FURTHER RESEARCH

In any study of this nature, there will always be constraints on time and funding, and this inquiry is bound by both. Clearly, there is a need for further work on identity politics within a global context, with a view to transforming understandings of culture and multiculturalism. One of the most significant findings of this type of individualized, peculiar and idiosyncratic research is the questions that it raises, not only for the artist/writer, but for the active reader. Those questions will also be somewhat individualized, peculiar and unique. Yet from these come more universal concerns, worthy of continued and robust inquiry.

In this case, some of those questions point towards a more concentrated study of the varied nature of difference, and how it is articulated. Aggressive and passive individualities make societies interesting, so the notion of extreme difference is worthy of further investigation, yet beyond the scope of this inquiry.

The notion of ethnic identity through the generations, from the third to subsequent generations of migrants, but also to those of mixed heritage, warrants scrutiny. Concepts of veiled ethnicities touched on in this study could be further explored, as should the notions of dualities. To which culture does one choose allegiance, when both are somewhat removed from everyday experience? This inquiry examines similar concerns, but only in the first- and second-generations. A similar study of their children, grandchildren and beyond would be significant to a nation such as Australia that is so culturally diverse.

Viewed this way, this study has been critically useful in the opening of doors either previously blocked or ignored. Specifically, the idiosyncratic nature of the research method utilized in this investigation can, I hope, inspire further unique and distinctive research projects. In such a way, new knowledge is created, old assumptions are challenged and new forms of tenaciously critical discourses evolve. The pursuit of new ways of knowing should be the goal of any educator if we are to understand the vagaries of contemporary society. Change in this context is an absolute certainty and archaically traditional ways of knowing and representing are no longer adequate, nor desirable.

This has been a joyous experience, a productive adventure. It has been transformative and unique, and unlike any other research journey I have ever made. My intuition and imagination, as well as serendipity and chance have been my guides; my subjective selves were the fundamental drivers of this work. In this way, I have aimed to present, represent and re-present lived experiences, memory and time, in order to construct a body of research to be experienced with you, my travelling companion.

Magyar vagyok Magyar
Hungarian, Hungarian am I
Magyarnak születtem
I was born Hungarian
Magyar nótát dalolt a dajka felettem.
My sweet nurse sang Hungarian songs to me.
Magyarúl tanított imádkozni anyám
My mother taught me to pray in Hungarian
És szeretni téged, gyönyörű szep hazám!
And to love you my magnificent beautiful homeland!

Magyarnak születtem, Magyar is maradok
I was born Hungarian and I"ll remain Hungarian
A hazáért, ha kell meg is halok!
If need be I will die for you my homeland!
Ringó bölcsőm fáját Magyar föld termette
My rocking cradle"s timber was grown in Hungarian soil
Koposóm fáját is Magyar fold nevelje!
The timber for my coffin is being nurtured in Hungarian soil!

by Sandor Pétöfi

EPILOGUE

The last time I saw my grandmother, she bit me.

And it was indeed the last time I saw my grandmother alive. Although she had been unyielding in her grip on life, she passed peacefully months after our last meeting. Mama, as ever, was stoic.

"She's gone," Mama says simply, after I answered the phone one Sunday evening. "I'm going up to see her, and make sure everything is organized."

That's my mother. Always competent, always capable, strong and enduring like her mother, like me. And as I sat there that evening, trying to digest the significance of Nonya's passing, it occurred to me just how far she had come, and how resolutely she had brought us with her. Nagyapa is in that equation as well, and I can sense his presence with me nowadays. It gives me solace.

As Nonya spent her last moments on this earth, 89 years after being born a peasant in a tiny nondescript village in western Hungary, one of 9 children, her great granddaughters were competing at a surf carnival on the archetypal Australian beach, Byron Bay, half a world and a lifetime away from her beginnings. I thought this was a fitting tribute to a woman whose tenacity ensured that her descendants would be fully participant in the life and culture of her adopted country, the one where she had spent most of her life.

As I read through the transcript of the only interview I ever did with her, my mother was seeing her for the last time. I heard Nonya's voice in my head as I read, forever muted, lilting and exotic; and rich, like chocolate.

Her great granddaughters, our daughters, are fully assimilated. They have a surname that has endured for six generations or more in this country. They are accepted, involved, and flourishing Australians. They participate in cultural and sporting activities that are a long way from that little landlocked country of my grandmother's birth. They are not gypsies; they belong here.

But they have another heritage, a veiled ethnicity. It is as tangibly a part of them as their Australianness, even if they don't yet fully realize it. The blood of the fierce and valiant Magyars flows through their veins, diluted, but still there.

*

On the day of Nonya's funeral, I dress in a black wool bocskai [nobleman's jacket] I had bought in Budapest just months ago, in her honor. A bocskai is a dignified, military, traditional garment, ornately braided; this black one is a stylised version of the original. It's an appropriate mark of respect to my Nonya, a little Magyar lady, to her style, her dignity, her class.

The funeral is the first Hungarian cultural event in which Remy and Bronte have ever consciously participated. They have been to Hungarian fêtes before, but they don't remember them. And this is certainly an event.

249

The service is completely bilingual; the minister Hungarian and magnificent in his own ornate black robes. In true Hungarian style, he is also embellished with braiding and embroidery. The coffin has a spray of colour atop of it; red, white and green, the colours of the Hungarian flag. The hymns are all sung in Hungarian, by our family and the few remaining Newcastle Hungarian friends Nonya had.

But unbeknownst to me, it is the order of service that will cause my unravelling.

This is also decorated with Hungarian flowers, and it isn't until I realize what I am looking at that I lose my composure. The minister, bless him, has attempted to make the service as authentically Hungarian as possible. In doing so he has included by way of further decoration, what look to be long columns of patterns. And then it hits me – these are Hungarian burial poles, the kind that used to traditionally adorn all graves in Hungarian cemeteries. They are not unlike carved bedposts or slender totem poles, and if it wasn't for the journey I have been making into the past at Nonya's inspiration, I would never have known what they are. I had read just months ago that they are rarely seen in Hungary these days, except for in that last bastion of traditional folk culture, Transylvania. When Stu gently asks me what is wrong, I can barely get the words out.

"They're...they're burial poles," I stutter and then lapse into a stunned silence.

At that moment I feel a huge jolt. It is my Nonya and my Nagyapa, calling me and connecting me to their history. Had it not been for them, I may never have felt compelled to search for my self, my place and my history. This was them again, forcing me to pay attention.

"Lexi!" they say, a sharply upward accented inflection on the second syllable.

"I hear you," I answer this time. And I do, at last.

250

AFTERWORD

The events captured in this book took place more than ten years ago. Since that time, there have been many changes to our family.

My much-adored Dad left us forever in the middle of 2012. How sad it is to write those words. However it was an expected, serene and very dignified passing. Mum and I were so grateful to be with him at the very end.

Dad would say his life was an ordinary life. To me, it was and will always be extraordinary.

In the years since I completed the original research, Imre bácsi, Zoli bácsi, and Irén néni have also left us. The Lascsik kids are all gone now. Of the Hungarians, Mum and my cousins are the only ones left. Mum and Irma néni remain bright, energetic and as always, confident. Whenever they are together, they giggle like teenagers.

More recently, our daughters have grown and left us. They are building their lives as proud, contributing Australians. They are travellers too and plan to live and work abroad as soon as they get their Hungarian passports. Having grown up in a postmodern world, the notion of borders and nationhood matter less to them; they are universal citizens with a truly global perspective. They have embraced both their Australian and Hungarian identity without issue, acknowledge them, are proud of them and have no qualms about where they belong in the world. They are far more confident and settled about their identities than I have ever been.

I saw a t-shirt on Facebook the other day. It said, "Made in Australia with Hungarian parts". Such a profound and simple statement. I think that says it all.

REFERENCES

Albrechtsen, J. (2002, May 8). The cultural divide: No mincing of words, just sacred cows. *The Australian* [Newspaper], p. 11.

Allen, K. A., & Bowles, B. (2012). Belonging as a guiding principle in the education of adolescents. *Australian Journal of Educational*, 108–119.

Altorjai-Albury, B. (1998). *Hungarian sunday: Tales from the corner shop* [Play]. Performed at the Belvoir Street Theatre, Sydney, by Company 2a, October 6 – November 1 1998.

Ambrosy, A. (1984). *New lease on life: Hungarian immigrants in Victoria assimilation in Australia*. Adelaide, South Australia: Dezsery Ethnic Publications.

Anderson, Z. (2012). Borders, babies, and "good refugees": Australian representations of "illegal" immigration, 1979. *Journal of Australian Studies, 36*(4), 499–514.

Andits, P. (2010, July). The politics of hope and disappointment: Ambivalence in the post-1989 homeland-related discourses among Hungarians in Australia. *Journal of Ethnic and Migration Studies, 36*(6), 989–1008.

Australian Bureau of Statistics. (2011). *Census data: Topics @ a glance – Migrant and ethnicity releases*. Retrieved September 8, 2014 from www.abs.gov.au/websitedbs/c311215.nsf/web/ Migrant+and+Ethnicity+-+REleases+-+Census+Data

Barone, T. (1995). The purposes of arts-based educational research. *International Journal of Educational Research, 23*(2), 169–180.

Barone, T. E. (2001). *Touching eternity: The enduring outcomes of teaching*. New York, NY: Teachers College Press.

Barone, T., & Eisner, E. (1997). Arts-based educational research. In R. M. Jaeger (Ed.), *Complementary methods for research in education*. Washington, DC: American Educational Research Association.

Barone, T., & Eisner, E. W. (2012). *Arts-based research*. Los Angeles, CA: Sage.

Barth, F. (1969). (Ed.). *Ethnic groups and boundaries: The social organisation of culture difference*. London, England: Allen & Unwin.

Barthes, R. (1994). *The semiotic challenge*. Berkeley, CA: University of California Press.

Battiste, M. (2011, January). *Cognitive imperialism and decolonizing research*. Key note address at the Narrative, Arts-Based and "Post" Approaches to Social Research Conference, Arizona State University, Tempe, AZ.

Benstock, S. (1988). (Ed.). *The private self: Theory and practice of women's autobiographical writings*. London, England: Routledge.

Berger, J. (1972). *Ways of seeing*. London, England: Penguin.

Bergland, B. (1994). Postmodernism and the Autobiographical subject: Reconstructing the other. In K. Ashley, L. Gilmore, & G. Peters (Eds.), *Autobiography & Post modernism*. Amherst, MA: University of Massachusetts Press.

Bhabha, H. (1994). *The location of culture*. London, England: Routledge.

Bita, N. (2002, May 8). The Cultural Divide: Storming of fortress Europe leads to the death of goodwill. *The Australian* [Newspaper], p. 12.

Blackburn, R. (1980). In search of the Black female self: African women's autobiography and ethnicity. In E. Jelinek (Ed.), *Women's autobiography: Essays in criticism*. Bloomington, IL: Indiana University Press.

Blaise, C. (1996). Your nearest exit may be behind you: Autobiography and the Postmodern moment. In M. Rhiel & D. Suchoff (Eds.), *The seductions of biography*. New York, NY: Routledge.

Bottomley, G. (1991) Representing the second generation: Subjects, objects and ways of knowing. In G. Bottomley, M. DeLepervanche, & J. Martine (Eds.), *Intersexions: Gender/class/culture/ethnicity*. Sydney: Allen & Unwin.

Bouras, G. (2004). Like mother, like son. In *Our global face: Inside the Australian diaspora* (6th ed.). Meadowbrook, QLD: Griffith Review .

255

REFERENCES

Brettell, C. B. (1997). Blurred genres and blended voices: Life history, biography, autobiography and the autoethnography of women's lives. In D. E. Reed-Donahy (Ed.), *Auto/ethnography: Rewriting the self and the social*. Oxford: Berg.

Brians, P. (2000). *The enlightenment*. Retrieved September 19, 2000 from http://www.wsu.edu/~brians/hum_303/enlightenment.html

Britton, B. K., & Pellegrini, A. D. (Eds.). (1990). *Narrative thought and narrative language. A publication of the Cognitive Studies Group and the Institute for Behavioural Research at the University of Georgia*. Hillsdale, NJ: L. Erlbaum.

Browne, R. K., & Magin, D. J. (Eds.). (1976). *Sociology of education: A source book of Australian studies*. Melbourne: Macmillan.

Bruner, J. (1990). *Acts of meaning*. Cambridge, MA: Harvard University Press.

Carr, D. (1986). *Time, history and narrative*. Indianapolis, IL: Indiana University Press.

Carter, K. (1993). The place of story in the study of teaching and teacher education. *Educational Researcher, 22*(1), 5–18

Cassab, J. (1995). *Diaries*. Sydney: Random House.

Chariandy, D. (2007). The fiction of belonging: On second-generation black writing in Canada. *Callaloo, 30*(3), 818–829.

Christou, A., & King, R. (2010). Imagining 'home': Diasporic landscapes of the Greek-German second generation. *Geoforum, 41*, 638–646.

Clandinin, D. J., & Connelly, F. M. (2000). *Narrative inquiry: Experience and story in qualitative research*. San Francisco, CA: Jossey Bass.

Codrescu, A. (1994). Adding to my life. In K. Ashley, L. Gilmore, & G. Peters (Eds.), *Autobiography & postmodernism*. Amherst, MA: University of Massachusetts Press.

Cohen, R. (1997). *Global Diasporas: An introduction*. London, England: University College London.

Colic-Peisker, V. (2011, Fall). A new era in Australian multiculturalism? From working-class "ethnics" to a "multicultural middle-class". *International Migration Review, 45*(3), 562–587.

Connelly, F. M. & Clandinin, D. J. (1985). Personal practical knowledge and the modes of knowing: Relevance for teaching and learning. In E. W. Eisner (Ed.), *Learning and teaching the ways of knowing: Eighty-fourth Yearbook of the National Society for the Study of Education, Part II*. Chicago, IL: University of Chicago Press.

Connelly, F. M., Clandinin, D. J., & He, M. F. (1997). Teachers' personal practical knowledge on the professional knowledge landscape. *Teaching and Teacher Education, 13*(7), 665–674.

Conway, J. (1998). *When memory speaks: Exploring the art of autobiography*. New York, NY: Vintage Books.

Craig, C. J., & Huber, J. (2006). Relational reverberations: Shaping and reshaping narrative inquiries in the midst of storied lives and contexts. In D. J. Clandinin (Ed.), *Handbook of narrative inquiry: Mapping a methodology*. Los Angeles, CA: Sage.

Curtis, D. (2001). *Someone is watching over me: The story of a Hungarian refugee*. Fyshwick, Australian Capital Territory: Panther Publishing and Printing.

Cutcher, A. (2013). [In]accessibilities: Presentations, representations and re-presentations in arts-based research. *Creative Approaches to Research, 6*(2), 33–44.

Cutcher, A. (2014). Performing the text, texting the performance: Presentations, representations and re-presentations. In R. Ewing, A. Cole, & J. G. Knowles (Eds.), *Performing scholartistry*. Halifax, Nova Scotia, CA: Backalong Books.

Cutcher, A. J. (2001, September). A small voice in the making of a nation: Autobiography and the self-portrait. *Oral History Association of Australia Journal, 23*, 85–89.

Cutcher, A. J. (2004). *The Hungarian in Australia: A portfolio of belongings* (Unpublished PhD thesis). University of Sydney, New South Wales, Australia.

Daha, M. (2011). Contextual factors contributing to ethnic identity development of second-generation Iranian American adolescents. *Journal of Adolescent Research, 26*(5), 543–569.

Dandy, J., & Pe-Pua, R. (2009). Attitudes to multiculturalism, immigration and cultural diversity: Comparison of dominant and non-dominant groups in three Australian states. *International Journal of Intercultural Relations, 34*, 34–46.

256

De Daruvar, Y. (1976). *The tragic fate of Hungary: A country carved-up alive at Trianon*. Center Square, PA: Alpha Publications.

DeCapua, A., & Wintergerst, A. C. (2009). Second-generation language maintenance and identity: A case study. *Bilingual Research Journal, 32*(1), 5–24.

Deen, H. (2003, August 2). Rethinking Australia. *Byron Bay Writer's Festival*.

Denzin, N. K. (1997). *Interpretive ethnography: Ethnographic practices for the twenty first century*. London, England: Sage.

Derrida, J. (1987). *The truth in painting*. Chicago, IL: University of Chicago Press.

Dewey, J. (1934). *Art as experience*. New York, NY: Minton, Balch & Co.

Diamond, C. T. P., & Mullen C. A. (1999). (Eds.). *The postmodern educator: Arts-based Inquiries and teacher development*. New York, NY: Peter Lang Publishing.

Diamond, C. T. P., & Mullen, C. A. (2000). Rescripting the script and rewriting the paper: Taking research to the "Edge of the Exploratory". *International Journal of Education and the Arts, 1*(4). Retrieved October 5, 2000 from http://ijea.asu.edu/vln4/

Ditlman, R. K., Purdie-Vaughns V., & Eibach, R. P. (2010). Heritage- and ideology-based national identities and their implications for immigrant citizen relations in the United States and in Germany. *International Journal of Intercultural Relations, 35*, 395–405.

Eisner, E. (2006). Does arts-based research have a future? *Studies for Social Justice, Equity and Excellence in Education, 46*(1), 135–149.

Eisner, E. (2008). Art and knowledge. In G. Knowles, S. Promislow, & A. Cole (Eds.), *The handbook of the arts in qualitative research*. Los Angeles, CA: Sage.

Eisner, E. (2011, January). *The contours of arts based research*. Key note address at the Narrative, Arts-Based and "Post" Approaches to Social Research Conference, Arizona State University, Tempe, AZ.

Eisner, E. W. (1991). *The enlightened eye: Qualitative inquiry and the enhancement of educational practice*. New York, NY: Macmillan.

Eisner, E. W. (1995). What artistically crafted research can help us understand about schools. *Educational Theory, 45*(1), 1–6.

Eisner, E. W. (1998, January). Does experience in the arts boost academic achievement? *Art education, 51*(1), 7–15

Esterhazy, P. (1990, Summer). God's hat. *Partisan Review, 57*(3).

Fandetti, D. V., & Gelfand D. F. (1983). Middle class white ethnics in suburbia: A study of Italian-Americans. In W. McCready (Ed.), *Culture, ethnicity and identity: Current issues in research*. New York, NY: Academic Press.

Firestone, S. (1970). *Dialectic of sex: The case for feminist revolution*. New York, NY: Morrow.

Fischer, M. (1994). autobiographical voices (1,2,3) and mosaic memory: Experimental sondages in the (Post) modern world. In K. Ashley, L. Gilmore, & G. Peters (Eds.), *Autobiography & post modernism*. Amherst, MA: University of Massachusetts Press.

Friedan, B. (1963). *The feminine mystique*. Harmondsworth: Penguin Books.

Gergely, A. (1999). *Culinaria Hungary*. Cologne: Konemann.

Getrich, C. M. (2008). Negotiating boundaries of social belonging: Second-generation Mexican youth and the immigrant rights protests of 2006. *American Behavioral Scientist, 52*(4), 533–556.

Gibson, J. (2005). Reflections on Australia's response to asylum seekers: A diary from six weeks as a counsellor with Curtin Detention Centre. *The International Journal of Narrative Therapy and Community Work*, 3 & 4, 23–28.

Gilman, S. (1998). *Love + marriage = death: And other essays in representing difference*. Stanford, CA: Stanford University Press.

Gonzales-Bachen, M. A. (2013, February). An application of ecological theory to ethnic identity formation among biethnic adolescents. *Family Relations, 62*, 92–108.

Gonzales-Baden, M. A., & Umaña-Taylor, A. J. (2011). Examining the role of physical appearance in Latino adolescents' ethnic identity. *Journal of Adolescence, 34*, 151–162.

Grassby, A. (1984). National identity: Cohesion or fragmentation? In D. J. Phillips & J. Houston (Eds.), *Australian multicultural society: Identity, communication and decision making*. Victoria: Dove Communications.

REFERENCES

Grassby, A. (1990). The homogenous society? A harmful myth. In M. Pagone & L. P. Rizzo (Eds.), *The first multicultural resource book*. Melbourne: International Press.

Greene, M. (2000) Foreword. In P. Willis, R. Smith, & E. Collins (Eds.), *Being, seeking, telling: Expressive approaches to adult educational research*. Flaxton, QLD: Post Pressed.

Grumet, M. (1995, Winter). Somewhere under the rainbow: The postmodern politics of art education. *Educational Theory, 45*(1), 35–42.

Gusdorf, G. (1956). The conditions and limits of autobiography. In J. Olney (Ed.), *Autobiography: Essays theoretical and critical*. Princeton, NJ: Princeton University Press.

Haaken, J. (1998). *Pillar of salt: Gender, memory and the perils of looking back*. New Brunswick, NJ: Vintage Books.

Hall, E.T. (1993). *An anthropology of everyday life: An autobiography*. New York, NY: Doubleday.

Hardgrave, G. (2002, May 9). The cultural divide: Central to our welcoming policies – the fair go. The *Australian* [Newspaper], p. 11.

Hart, D., Maloney, J., & Damon, W. (1987). The meaning and development of identity. In T. Honess & K. Yardley (Eds.), *Self and identity: Perspectives across the lifespan*. London, England: Routledge and Kegan Paul.

Hatoss, A. (2006). Community-level approaches in language planning: The case of the Hungarian in Australia. *Current Issues in Language Planning, 17*(2&3), 287–306.

Haywood, A., Honan, M., Miller, E., Nebesky, R., Oliver, J., Turner, R., ... Wilson, N. (2001). *Central Europe*. Melbourne: Lonely Planet.

Healey, J. (2000). *Issues in society: Multiculturalism* (Vol. 126). Sydney: Spinney Press.

Heilbrun, C. G. (1988). *Writing a woman's life*. New York, NY: Norton.

Herne, K., Travaglia, J., & Weiss, E. (Eds.). (1992). *Who do you think you are?* Sydney: Women's Redress Press.

Heywood, P. (2000). Bleeding on the page: Passion and process in writing research. In P. Willis, R. Smith, & E. Collins (Eds.), *Being, seeking, telling: Expressive approaches to adult educational research*. Flaxton, QLD: Post Pressed.

Hicks, G. (1977). Introduction: Problems in the study of Ethnicity. In G. Hicks & P. E. Leis (Eds.), *Ethnic encounters*. North Scitnate, MA: Duxbury Press.

Hirsch, T. L. & Lazar, A. (2011). Belonging here, not there: The case of attaining European passports by grandchildren of Holocaust survivors. *International Journal of Intercultural Relations, 35*, 387–394.

Horowitz, A. (1987). *Rousseau, nature and history*. Toronto: University of Toronto Press.

Hugo, G. (2004). Calling Australia home. In *Our Global Face: Inside the Australian Diaspora* (6th ed.). Meadowbrook, QLD: Griffith Review.

Hutnik, N. (1991). *Ethnic minority identity: A social psychological perspective*. Oxford: Clarendon.

Iles, T. (1992). (Ed.). *All sides of the subject*. New York, NY: Teachers College Press.

Izzard, J. (2011). The deceit of Immigration Nation. *Quadrant*, 28–33.

Jakubowicz, A. (2002, May 9). The cultural divide: Central to our welcoming policies – the fair go. The *Australian* [Newspaper], p. 12.

Jay, P. (1984). *Being in the text: Self representation from Wordsworth to Roland Barthes*. Ithaca, NY: Cornell University Press.

Jayamaran, R. (2005, September). Inclusion and exclusion: An analysis of the Australian immigration history and ethnic relations. *Culturescope: The Journal of the Society and Culture Association Inc. 77*, 26–36.

Jelinek, E. (1980). *Women's autobiography: Essays in criticism*. Bloomington, IN: Indiana University Press.

Johnson, B. (1996). Introduction. In M. Rhiel & D. Suchoff (Eds.), *The seductions of biography*. New York, NY: Routledge.

Johnston, R. (1976). The concept of the "marginal man": A refinement of the term. *Australia and New Zealand Journal of Sociology, 12*(2), 145–147.

Kambaskovic, D. (2013). Breaching the social contract: The migrant poet and the politics of being apolitical. *Southerly, 73*(1) 96–122.

Kane, J. (2012). *On being Australian: A view from south-east Queensland* (36th ed.). Melbourne, QLD: Griffith Review.

Kelly, P. (2002, May 4-5). The cultural divide: Diversity's test in face of unity. *The Weekend Australian* [Newspaper], p. 28.

Kiang, L., & Fuligni, A. J. (2009). Ethnic identity in context: Variations in ethnic exploration and belonging within parent, same-ethnic peer, and different-ethnic peer relationships. *Journal of Youth Adolescence, 38*, 732–743.

Kim, S. Y., & Chao, R. K. (2009). Heritage language fluency, ethnic identity, and school effort of immigrant Chinese and Mexican adolescents. *Cultural Diversity and Ethnic Minority Psychology, 15*(1), 27–37.

Kim, S. H.O., Ehrich, J., & Ficorelli, L. (2010). Perceptions of settlement well-being, language proficiency, and employment: An investigation of immigrant adult language learners in Australia. *International Journal of Intercultural Relations, 36*, 41–52.

Knowles, G., & Cole, A. (2008). *The handbook of the arts in qualitative research.* Los Angeles, CA: Sage.

Kuhn, A. (1995). *Family secrets: Acts of memory and imagination.* London, England: Verso Press.

Kunz, E. F. (1969). *Blood and gold: Hungarians in Australia.* Melbourne: Cheshire Publishing.

Kunz, E. F. (1985). *The Hungarians in Australia.* Melbourne: AE Press.

Lacan, J. (1975). *The language of the self: The function of languages in psychoanalysis.* New York, NY: Dell Publishing Company.

Lacan, J. (1981). *Speech and language in psychoanalysis.* Baltimore, MD: Johns Hopkins Press.

Laurie, V. (2002, May 8). The cultural divide: How do you teach children who've seen it all? *The Australian* [Newspaper], p. 13.

Leavy, P. (2009). *Method meets art: Arts-based research practice.* New York, NY: The Guilford Press.

Leggo, C. (2008). Astonishing silence: Knowing in poetry. In G. Knowles, S. Promislow, & A. Cole (Eds.), *The handbook of the arts in qualitative research.* Los Angeles, CA: Sage.

Lejeune, P. (1984). Women and autobiography at author's expense. In D. Stanton (Ed.), *The female autography.* Chicago, IL: University of Chicago Press.

Leung, L. (1992). Who do you think you are? Who do you think you are? In K. Herne, J. Travaglia, & J. Weiss (Eds.), *Who do you think you are?* Sydney: Women's Redress Press.

Lewis, R., & Gurry, T. (2001). *Australia 2030: Investigating the facts of immigration: An educational interactive multicultural resource kit.* Malvern, Victoria: Ryebuck Media, Department of Immigration and Multicultural Affairs.

Lionnet, F. (1989). *Autobiographical voices: Race, gender, self portraiture.* Ithaca, NY: Cornell University Press.

Loh, M. (1980). *With courage in their cases: The experience of 35 Italian migrant workers and their families.* Melbourne: F.I.L.E.F [Federazione Italiana Lavatori e Famiglia].

MacIntyre, A. (1981). *After virtue: A study in moral theory.* London, England: Duckworth.

Mackay, H. (1998, June 5). Why Hanson appeals to our darker nature. *The Age* [Newspaper], p. 13

Magris, C. (1997). *Danube.* London, England: The Harvill Press.

Mahar, A. L., Cobigo, V., & Stuart, H. (2013). Conceptualizing belonging. *Disability, 12*, 1026–1032.

Marchetta, M. (2002, May 8). The cultural divide: Schoolyard opens window on tolerance and dignity. *The Australian* [Newspaper], p. 12.

Marcus, L. (1994). *Autobiographical discourses: Theory, criticism, practice.* Manchester: Manchester University Press.

Mathews, G. (2000). *Global culture/individual Identity: Searching for home in the cultural supermarket.* London: Routledge.

McNicoll, P. (2000, November 6). *Participatory action research with women who had breast cancer.* University of British Columbia seminar. Curriculum Studies, Vancouver, BC.

McNiff, S. (1998). *Art based research.* London, England: Jessica Kingsley Publishers.

Megalogenis, G. (2002, May 4–5). The cultural divide: Ticket to hipdom comes at a price. *The Weekend Australian* [Newspaper], p. 20.

Middlebrook, D. W. (1996). Telling secrets. In M. Rhiel & D. Suchoff (Eds.), *The seductions of biography.* New York, NY: Routledge.

Mitchell, W. J. T. (1981). *On narrative.* Chicago, IL: University of Chicago Press.

REFERENCES

Nash, M. (1996). The core elements of ethnicity. In J. Hutchinson & A. D. Smith (Eds.), *Ethnicity*. Oxford: Oxford University Press.

Neilsen, L., Cole, A., & Knowles, G. K. (2001). *The art of writing inquiry*. Halifax, Nova Scotia, Canada: Backalong Books.

Nelson, K. (2003). Self and social functions: Individual autobiographical memory and collective narrative. *Memory, 11*(2),125–136.

Neville, B. (2000). Some Gebserian and Keganesque reflections on academic writing. In P. Willis, R. Smith, & E. Collins (Eds.), *Being, seeking, telling: Expressive approaches to adult educational research*. Flaxton, QLD: Post Pressed.

Nilsen, A. (1992). Using life histories in sociology. In T. Iles (Ed.), *All sides of the subject: Women and biography*. New York, NY: Teachers College Press.

O'Donoghue, D. (2009). Are we asking the wrong questions in arts-based research? *Studies in Art Education, 50*(4), 352–368.

Office for the High Commission for Human Rights [OHCHR] (2014). United Nations human rights. Geneva: Author. Retrieved June 6, 2014 from http://www.ohchr.org/EN/Pages/WelcomePage.aspx#

Offord, B. (2002). Mapping the rainbow region: Fields of belonging and sites of confluence. *Transformations, 2*, 1–17. Retrieved June 19, 2014 from http://www.cqu.edu.au/transformations

Örkény, I. (1995). *One minute stories* (J. Sollosy, Trans.). Sydney: Brandl & Schlesinger.

Osei-Kofi, N. (2013). The emancipatory potential of arts-based research. *Equity & Excellence in Education, 46*(1), 135–149.

Pagone, M., & Rizzo, L. P. (Eds.). (1990). *The first multicultural resource book*. Melbourne: International Press.

Palincsar, A. S. (2005). Social constructivist perspectives on teaching and learning. In H. Daniels (Ed.), *An introduction to Vygotsky*. Abingdon, OX: Routledge.

Papas, M. (2012). *My sweet canary: On being second-generation* (36th ed.). Melbourne, QLD: Griffith Review.

Phillips, D. J., & Houston, J. (Eds.). (1984). *Australian multicultural society: Identity, communication and decision making*. Victoria: Dove Communications.

Piantanida, M., Garman, N., & McMahon, P. (2000). Crafting an arts-based research thesis: Issues of tradition and solipsisim. In P. Willis, R. Smith, & E. Collins (Eds.), *Being, seeking, telling: Expressive approaches to adult educational research*. Flaxton, QLD: Post Pressed.

Pirani, A. (1992). Sources and silences. In T. Iles (Ed.), *All sides of the subject: Women and biography*. New York, NY: Teachers College Press.

Powell, S. (2002, May 7). The cultural divide: World events threaten national consensus. *The Australian* [Newspaper], p. 15.

Radhakrishnan, R. (1996). *Diasporic meditation: Between home and location*. Minneapolis, MN: University of Minnesota Press.

Rhiel, M., & Suchoff, D. (Eds.). (1996). *The seductions of biography*. New York, NY: Routledge.

Riemer, A. (1992). *Inside outside: Life between two worlds*. Sydney: Collins Angus and Robertson.

Riemer, A. (1993). *Hapsburg café*. Sydney: Angus and Robertson.

Riemer, A. (1994). Introduction. In I. Örkény (Ed.), *One minute stories* (J. Sollosy, Trans.). Sydney: Brandl & Schlesinger.

Rintoul, S. (2002, May 6). The cultural divide: Emerging from the shadows to face new crisis of whiteness. *The Australian* [Newspaper], p. 8.

Roach, N. (2002, May 9). The cultural divide: National pride goes out to sea. *The Australian* [Newspaper], p. 13.

Robinson, K. (2010). Changing education paradigms. *TED talks* [video]. Retrieved September 20, 2011 from http://www.ted.com/talks/ken_robinson_changing_education_paradigms

Rooney, R., Nesdale, D., Kane, R., Hattie, J., & Goonewardere, R. (2010). The development of the Universal Ethnic Identity Scale (UEIS) for use in an Australian context. *Australian Psychologist, 47*, 238–248.

Rose, P. (1996). *Confessions of a burned out biographer*. In M. Rhiel & D. Suchoff (Eds.), *The seductions biography*. New York, NY: Routledge.

Roth, W. M. (2005). *Auto/biography and auto/ethnography: Praxis of research method*. Rotterdam, The Netherlands: Sense Publications.

Rothwell, N. (2002, May 4-5). The cultural divide: Invitation to the great society. *The Weekend Australian* [newspaper], 30.

Rousell, D., Cutter-Mackenzie, A., & Cutcher, A. (2014, December). *'We Are No Longer Ourselves': Unravelling the harmonics of the collaborative voice in educational research*. Australian Association for Research in Education – New Zealand Association for Research in Education [AARE-NZARE] Annual Conference, Brisbane.

Rushdie, S. (1988). *The satanic verses*. New York, NY: Viking.

Rushdie, S. (1991). *Imaginary homelands: Essays and criticisms*. London, England: Granta Books, Rutgers University Press.

Sala, E., Dandy, J., & Rapley, M. (2009). Real Italians and wogs': The discursive construction of Italian identity among first generation Italian immigrants in Western Australia. *Journal of Community & Applied Social Psychology, 20*, 110–124.

Samuel, M. (2003). Autobiographical research in teacher education: Memories as method and model. In K. Lewin, M. Samuel, & Y. Sayed (Eds.), *Changing patterns of teacher education in South Africa: Policy, practice and prospects*. Sandown: Heinemann.

Sarbin, T. R. (1986). *Educational narrative psychology: The storied nature of human conduct*. New York, NY: Praeger.

Sasaki, B. (1996). Introduction. In M. Rhiel & D. Suchoff (Eds.), *The seductions of biography*. New York, NY: Routledge.

Saunders, M. (2002, May 8). Minister's stance on refugee intake 'a con'. *The Australian* [Newspaper], p. 2.

Schultz, J. (2004). Coming and going in the global village. In *Our global face: Inside the Australian diaspora* (36th ed.). Melbourne, QLD: Griffith Review.

Sharma, R. (2012). The relationship between loneliness, ethnic identity, and dimensions of membership across first, second, and third generation Americans. *Colonial Academic Alliance Undergraduate Research Journal, 3*, Article 9.

Siegesmund, R. (2014). The N of 1 in arts-based research: Reliability and validity. *International Journal of Education & the Arts, 15*(SI 2.5). Retrieved from http://www.ijea.org/v15si2/

Sinner, A., Leggo, C., Irwin, R. L., Gouzouasis, P., & Grauer, K. (2006). Arts-Based educational research dissertations: Reviewing the practices of new scholars. *Canadian Journal of Education, 29*(4), 1223–1270.

Skrznecki, P. (2004). Two wives in Krakow and a house in Treptow. In *Our global face: Inside the Australian diaspora* (6th ed.). Melbourne, QLD: Griffith Review.

Slugoski, B. R., & Ginsburg, G. P. (1989). Ego identity and explanatory speech. In J. Shotter & K. J. Gergen (Eds.), *Texts of identity*. London, England: Sage.

Smolicz, J. J. (1984). Ethnic identity in Australia: Cohesive or divisive? In D. J. Phillips & J. Houston (Eds.), *Australian multicultural society: Identity, communication and decision making*. Victoria: Dove Communications.

Springgay, S., Irwin, R. L., & Kind, S. W. (2005). A/r/tography as living inquiry through art and text. *Qualitative inquiry, 11*(6), 897–912.

Stanley, L. (1992). Process in feminist biography and feminist epistemology. In T. Iles (Ed.), *All sides of the subject: Women and biography*. New York, NY: Teachers College Press.

Steele, P (1989). *The autobiographical passion: Studies of the self on show*. Carlton, Victoria: Melbourne University Press.

Steinem, G. (1983). *Ruth's song (Because she could not sing it). Outrageous acts and everyday Rebellions*. New York: Holt, Rinehart and Winston.

Steketee, M. (2002, May 7). The cultural divide: Money rules migration policy, with fewer here to settle down. *The Australian* [Newspaper], p. 14.

REFERENCES

Stroink, M. L., & Lalonde, R. N. (2009). Bicultural identity conflict in second-generation Asian Canadians. *The Journal of Social Psychology*, *148*(2), 44–65.

Stuart, M. (1992). Making the choices: Writing about Marguerite Carr-Harris. In T. Iles (Ed.), *All sides of the subject: Women and biography*. New York, NY: Teachers College Press.

Sullivan, G. (2006). Research acts in art practice. *Studies in Art Education*, *48*(1), 19–35.

Tan, A. (1995). The hundred secret senses. New York, NY: G.P. Putnam's sons.

Teleky R. (1997). *Hungarian Rhapsodies: Essays on ethnicity, identity and culture*. Seattle, WA: University of Washington Press.

The Age. (1998, July 4). *Editorial* [Newspaper], p. 9.

Trezise, B. (2011). Discursive belonging: Surviving narrative in migrant oral history. *Cultural Studies Review*, *17*(2), 271–299.

Tsang, W. K. (2004). Teachers' personal practical knowledge and interactive decisions. *Language Teaching Research*, *8*(2), 163–198.

Tsiolkas, C. (2013, September). Strangers at the gate: Making sense of Australia's fear of asylum seekers. *The Monthly*, 22–31.

Varga, S. (1994). *Heddy and me*. Victoria: Penguin.

Varga, S. (2004). The gift of tongues. In *Our global face: Inside the Australian diaspora* (6th ed.). Melbourne, Qld: Griffith Review.

Varga, S. (2009). Dark times. In *Participation society* (24th ed.). Melobourne, QLD: Griffith Review.

Walton, G. M. Cohen, G. L. Cwir, D., & Spencer, S. J. (2012). Mere belonging: The power of social connections. *Journal of Personality and Social Psychology*, *102*(3), 513–532.

Waterhouse, P. (2000). Life as research: Reflections on poetry, postpositivist inquiry and professional practice. In P. Willis, R. Smith, & E. Collins (Eds.), *Being, seeking, telling: Expressive approaches to adult educational research*. Flaxton, QLD: Post Pressed.

Weinreich, P. (2009). 'Enculturation', not 'acculturation': Conceptualising and assessing identity processes in migrant communities. *International Journal of Intercultural Relations*, *33*, 124–139.

Whitlam, G. (2002). *In his own words* [documentary, 84 mins]. Produced by Andrew Williams and Robert Frances. Ronin Films.

Yip, T., Douglas, S., & Shelton, J. N. (2013). Daily intragroup contact in diverse settings: Implications for Asian adolescents' ethnic identity. *Child Development*, *84*(4), 1425–1441.

Yuval-Davis, N. (1993). *Women, ethnicity and empowerment* (Working paper series # 151). The Hague: Institute of social studies.

Zevallos, Z. (2008). 'It's like we're their culture': Second-generation migrant women discuss Australian culture. *People and Place*, *13*(2), 41–49.

ABOUT THE AUTHOR

Alexandra Cutcher is an academic in the School of Education, Southern Cross University, Australia. She comes to her teaching and research as a second-generation migrant woman for whom the Arts were an escape from marginalization and alienation. As a practicing artist she knows well from her own experiences of difference how powerful the Visual Arts can be as a vehicle for transformation, education, inspiration and relief. As a high school Creative Arts Head Teacher for almost thirty years, her experience has informed her practice and made her hyperaware of others who do not feel or look or act as if they belong. In her teaching, it has made Alexandra responsive to and appreciative of uniqueness and it has caused her to consciously and subconsciously cater for individual student need, utilizing curriculum and behaviour modification programs to that end. This hyperaware state has been of great benefit to Alexandra's teaching and to the learning of her students. She brings this powerful experience to her work in Teacher Education and as such has been recognized for her expertise through perfect student feedback scores and a national teaching award.

Alexandra's foundational experiences also informed her award-winning doctoral work which specifically examined migrant identity and belonging through the lens of arts-based research. Alexandra's current research and teaching interests focus on what the Visual Arts can be and do: educationally, expressively, as research method, as language, as catharsis, as reflective instrument and as documented form. To this end, the provision of high quality Visual Arts education for students of all ages is a professional priority. These understandings inform Alexandra's teaching and her spirited advocacy for Arts education.

CPSIA information can be obtained at www.ICGtesting.com
Printed in the USA
BVOW05s1415290415

398279BV00014B/518/P